A CENTURY OF
LONDON TAXIS

Other titles in the Crowood AutoClassic Series

A CENTURY OF
LONDON TAXIS

BILL MUNRO

THE CROWOOD PRESS

First published in 2005 by
The Crowood Press Ltd
Ramsbury, Marlborough
Wiltshire SN8 2HR

www.crowood.com

British Library Cataloguing-in-Publication Data
A catalogue record for this book is available from the British Library.

ISBN 1 86126 762 2

Typeset by Florence Production Ltd, Stoodleigh, Devon EX16 9PN

Printed and bound in Great Britain by CPI, Bath

Contents

Acknowledgements

All historians owe a debt to those who researched their chosen subject before they themselves did and the author is no exception. Following on from Anthony Armstrong's *Taxi*, published in 1930, two authoritative books on the subject of London cabs were Nick Georgano's *A History of the London Taxicab* (David & Charles, 1972) and Philip Warren and Malcolm Linskey's *Taxicabs: a Photographic History* (Almark, 1976); these later works set benchmarks in the historians' knowledge of the subject. Philip Warren's *The History of the London Cab Trade* (Taxi Trade Promotions, 1995) is a book on the politics of the trade rather than its vehicles but it has proved valuable in the writing of this one. Malcolm Bobbitt's *Taxi, the Story of the 'London' Cab* (Veloce, 1998) contained useful information on Citroën cabs, while *75 Years: The History of the London General Cab Company*, provided valuable information about that organization and the trade in general. John R. Hume and Michael S. Moss's *Beardmore – A History of a Scottish Industrial Giant* (Heinemann, 1976) and Ken Hurst's *William Beardmore:'Transport Is the Thing'* (National Museums of Scotland, 2004) have given fascinating insights into the background of the Beardmore story. All these books provided an invaluable starting point for my research. Furthermore, many documents stored in the National Archive (formerly the Public Record Office) have become available since these books were published.

There are also many individuals who have made contributions, large and small, to the content of this book and the author is extremely grateful for their help.

They are, from the car clubs: Robin Barraclough, Malcolm Jeal, Bryan K. Goodman and Perry Zavitz of the Society of Automotive Historians; Philip Hall of the Rolls-Royce Enthusiasts Club; Ian Cooper, John Freeston, Alan Hallpike, Murray Jackson, Peter Kimberley, Clive Loveless, Bob McPhail, James Strugnell, Ray Tomkinson, Keith White and Eddie Zetlin of the London Vintage Taxi Association; John Gray of the Sunbeam-Talbot-Darracq Register; and Irving Lomon of the Asquith Association.

The helpful independent enthusiasts were: Alan Broughton; Graham Hill; Melvyn Hiscock; Peter and Kevin Machin; Ian MacLean; Norman Painting; Chris Pearce; Derek Pearce; Nic Portway, Mike Reid, Owen Woodliffe; and R.J. Wyatt.

And from the cab trade and industry, past and present: Peter Bentley of the Public Carriage Office; Peter Da Costa of KPM (UK) Plc; Geoff Chater and Bob Parsons of CMAK (UK) Ltd; Steven Ferris of Metrocab (UK) Ltd; David Day and Stephen Tillyer, formerly of Metro Sales and Service; the late Ken Jaeger of Beardmore; Mal Smith of Vintage Taxi Spares Ltd; Roger Ward and the late Geoff Trotter, MBE from the London General Cab Company; Jamie Borwick, Peter James, Grant Lockhart, Bill Lucas, Ed Osmond, Andrew Overton, Jevon Thorpe, Barry Widdowson and the late Peter Wildgoose from LTI, Mann & Overton and Carbodies.

Photographic credits

Jamie Borwick, Geoff Chater and Bob Parsons of CMAK (UK) Ltd, Jon Day of the National Motor Museum, Bryan Goodman, Peter James, The Jewish Museum, Bethnal Green, Tim Loake of the BMIHT, The National Archive, Norman Painting, Derek Pearce, Stuart Pessok of Taxi Newspaper, The Public Carriage Office, David Riley of Chris Hodge Commercial Ltd, Mal Smith of Vintage Taxi Spares and Stephen Tillyer.

Introduction

The London taxicab is unique because its design is governed by a set of regulations called the Conditions of Fitness. These lay down, among other requirements, the body dimensions and layout and the need for a tight 25ft (7.62m) turning circle. They are written and enforced by the Public Carriage Office, once run by the Metropolitan Police but now under the jurisdiction of Transport for London.

The story of London's cabs is the story of two distinct groups, dynasties if you will. Most successful has been the group begun by J.J. Mann and Tom Overton, and run by the Overton family. Mann & Overton was eventually subsumed by the amalgamation of its very suppliers, Carbodies Ltd of Coventry, who had acquired the rights to the Austin cab that they had made for decades and eventually became London Taxis International. The other group was more diverse; it began around 1909 when Francis M. Luther took a financial interest in the W. & G. du Cros's fleet of Napier cabs. When supplies of the Napier ran out in 1914, Luther persuaded William Beardmore to build taxicabs and eventually took over the business himself. In the 1960s the cause was taken up by Metro-Cammell-Weymann, who had built the last Beardmore cabs and went on to design their own, the Metrocab.

But where does this 'century' of taxicabs begin and end? There is no doubt that the first horseless cab to operate in London was the Bersey Electric of 1897. However, I have not counted 1897 for two reasons: first, the Bersey was electric and I have decided that this book should be essentially about cabs powered by internal combustion engines; secondly, there was a gap between the demise of the Bersey and the date when The London Express Motor Service Ltd put a Prunel cab on test in 1903. However, the Prunel was not licensed until 1904 and it was in 1905 that the first successful commercial operations began. So the beginning might be 1903, 1904 or 1905. At the other end of the timescale, the result of an enquiry into the Conditions of Fitness were due in 2005, although after continual delays it had yet to be announced at the time of going to press. Thus this story covers a somewhat 'flexible' century and no apology is made for that.

Prologue

In May 1904 an inspecting officer at the Public Carriage Office in New Scotland Yard stencilled a mark on the back of a hansom cab. It bore the initials of the Commissioner of Police and the number of persons that the cab was licensed to carry. But this hansom was different from the 'gondolas of London' that the inspector and his predecessors had been passing for the past fifty years, for it was a motor cab. Since the previous December, The London Express Motor Service Ltd had been running trials of this vehicle, a French-built Prunel, and another identical to it. Now they had been approved for use by the strictest and most respected cab licensing authority that the world would ever see.

The Prunels were not London's first horseless cabs. In 1897 the Electrical Cab Company Ltd put a fleet of eighteen electrically-powered cabs on the streets of London. They were named Berseys, after the company's general manager and the cab's designer, the electrical engineer Walter C. Bersey. Cabs like the Bersey, or indeed any mechanically-propelled vehicles available for public or private hire might have appeared on London's streets earlier than 1897. There was the technology: in 1896 a petrol-powered Benz cab was plying for hire in Stuttgart and Paris and electric cabs had operated in Paris and Chicago. What had prevented the progress of the motor cab in Britain was what had also hampered automobile development in general: the Locomotives Act of 1865, the so-called 'Red Flag Act'. This reduced the maximum speed of a mechanically-propelled carriage to 2mph and demanded that it be preceded by a man on foot, carrying a red flag to warn of its approach.

In 1896 the Act was repealed, and from 14 November 1896 motor cars, and that expression had yet to come into use, could be driven on public roads without the absurd encumbrance of the man with the red flag. Members of the Royal Automobile Club celebrated the event by organizing a drive from London to Brighton. This event is still commemorated annually by the Emancipation Run, held on the first Sunday in November.

For all the freedom that the repeal of the Red Flag Act gave, the motor car was a very expensive machine and the public were extremely sceptical about it. Victorian Britain depended overwhelmingly on the horse for road transport and there was a huge infrastructure supporting it: breeders, dealers, carriage makers, farriers and many more who believed that their livelihoods would vanish if the motor car were a success. But there was one way of proving the motor vehicle's worth and ensuring a return on the investment needed to build it – that was to put it to work, and there was one sure way of giving the public a chance to experience travelling in a motor car and have them pay for the privilege into the bargain – build a motor cab.

The backers of the Electrical Cab Company Ltd, who were to operate the Bersey, were some of the most influential people in the field of road transport. They included H.R. Paterson, of the carriers Carter

Paterson, the Hon. Reginald Brougham, after whose immediate forbear the brougham style of carriage was named, J.H. Mace, a director of Harry Lawson's British Daimler Company, the coachbuilder H.J. Mulliner and the Hon. Evelyn Ellis, one of the men responsible for the repeal of the Red Flag Act.

There had been the question of which form of motive power they should use: petrol, steam or electricity, but, for reliability, electricity was the best option. Starting was instant, there was no engine to preheat and crank over, no boiler to stoke. An electric vehicle needed only a driver to throw a switch and the cab was in motion as promptly as if he had picked up the reins and given a command to his horse.

Although the Cab Drivers' Union was said to have welcomed these yellow and black broughams, the cab masters, the people who owned London's cab fleets, were reluctant to invest in machinery that was entirely new and untried. Thankfully, the cabs found approval from the Commissioner of Police, Edward Bradford, who was responsible for cab licensing. However, a second type of vehicle that replaced the original in 1898 proved unreliable and dangerous when one ran out of control outside Hyde Park Gate. They were removed from service in 1899 and the company ceased to trade. Electric cabs in Paris and in New York were also a failure. The Western world would have to wait for technology to catch up with ambition.

1   1903–07 In the Beginning

Britain, at the beginning of the twentieth century, was recovering from both the tragedy of the Boer War and the loss of Queen Victoria. The new king, Edward VII, had revolutionized high society when he befriended industrialists, men in trade and actresses, as well as, and sometimes in preference to, the nobility. The moral tone of the country, many more staid members of society would declare, was declining rapidly. Certainly Britain had

become an industrialized nation and the new century would reap the harvest, both bitter and sweet, sown in the Old Queen's reign.

It was into this changing world that Henry Vernon Remnant, the managing director of The London Express Motor Service Ltd, placed the first motor cab on the streets of London. In doing so, he began an inevitable revolution, the effects of which have lasted a full century. The London Express Motor

The hansom cab was perhaps the king of London streets in the latter half of the nineteenth century. The Prime Minister Benjamin Disraeli described them as 'The Gondolas of London'. (LVTA Archives)

Service was formed in January 1902; in Britain, the tide was turning in favour of the motor car and even in these early days there was a body of experience from which a fledgling motor cab company might draw. One of the world's first petrol-powered motor cabs was a Daimler, which ran in Stuttgart, and electric cabs ran in Paris at the same time as the Bersey was humming its way along the streets of London. French and German cars could be bought in Britain in these early years and there were British cars too: Daimler, Humber and Lanchester were all in business before the old century had expired. But the French had accepted the motor car far more readily than the British and it was because of this that London Express turned to France for a suitable vehicle. They found it in the Prunel, a Paris-built vehicle with a proprietary 2-cylinder Aster engine. By the end of 1903 London Express submitted a Prunel fitted with a hansom body by Henry Whitlock & Co., of Holland Gate, west London, to the Public Carriage Office (PCO) at New Scotland Yard for inspection. They were not prepared to license it immediately, but under pressure placed on the Police Commissioner by the prominent men on Express's board, they put it on test.

The choice of the body was limited by the 'Conditions of Fitness', the regulations that governed the design and construction of London's horse cabs, to either a two-wheeled hansom or a four-wheeled brougham or landaulet type, known as a 'growler'. The Prunel would be a two-seater. No matter: London cab riders were well used to hansoms, which outnumbered the growler by almost two to one and had been a popular choice for the previous seventy years. What was different with the Prunel was that the driver sat in front of the passengers instead of above and behind them. And why not? It was where the car's controls were placed and, being a four-wheeled vehicle, it did not require the driver to be placed at the rear as a counterbalance, as was demanded by the immensely front-heavy, horse-drawn hansom.

The inspecting officers of the PCO were serving policemen who had been transferred there. They knew about the welfare of horses, they understood carriage construction and were trained in the Conditions of Fitness and London's cab Acts, but in 1903 they had had

The Prunel, London's first petrol-powered cab, was a compact, chain-driven vehicle. For an Edwardian lady, access to the vehicle would have been rather more difficult than climbing into a Hansom. (Jamie Borwick)

neither experience with motor cabs nor any need of formal qualifications in motor engineering. However, once the Prunel had completed its tests, they formally licensed it and a second example in May 1904. Apparently these, a third hansom and another with a landaulet body ran well, 'giving the greatest satisfaction to both the public and the Vendor Company' in both cab and private hire work. But by October 1904 Express had withdrawn its Prunels and, for a short time, horse cabmen had the streets to themselves once more.

In February 1905 Chief Inspector Arthur Bassom, the officer in charge of the PCO, wrote a memorandum to his new chief at Scotland Yard, Commissioner Henry. He requested that he and Sub-divisional Inspector Beckley be trained in motor mechanics and driving to cope with 'the great increase in motor vehicles being presented'. He did not want to be 'at the mercy of every person who professes knowledge'. Henry approved and that spring, Bassom and Beckley attended a twelve-week evening course at one of the polytechnics that were offering tuition. On completion of it they passed on their knowledge to their staff.

Other Pioneers

During 1905 there were many more motor cabs put forward by aspiring proprietors. These vehicles included a 14/16hp Straker & MacConnell and a German Dixi hansom. The Lloyd and Plaister hansom had a 2-cylinder, underfloor engine and a roof that extended over the driver. This cab, built by Lewis Lloyd in partnership with W.E. Plaister, was renamed the Simplex, but it was short-lived. The partners experienced trouble gaining PCO approval for this already obsolete vehicle, but when it was finally licensed at the end of 1905 the cabs were put to work with the Motor Hansom Company. Some, if not all were rebodied as landaulets.

The Rational

If Vernon Remnant planned to be the first company to run a fleet of motor cabs on a commercial basis, he was beaten to it. That honour went to London Motor Cab Company of Manor Street, Chelsea, who put six Rational cabs to work in May 1905. The Rational also had the privilege of being the first British-built, petrol-powered cab to be licensed. It was designed and made by Heatly-Gresham Engineering at Bassingbourne, Cambridgeshire. The firm's owners, Harry Heatly and Frank Gresham, were members of the Royal Automobile Club. Heatly, in fact, was a founder member.

The Rational had a water-cooled, twin-cylinder engine slung horizontally under the driver's seat, driving through a two-speed,

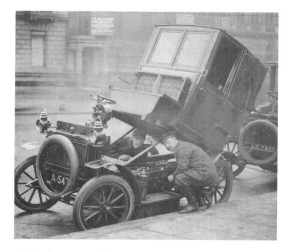

A Simplex. Originally this cab mounted a hansom cab body, with a roof that extended over the driver. The lifting body gave access to the underfloor engine. This picture must have been taken before July 1907 since the cab has no meter. It is possible that a vehicle as primitive as this did not last much longer than that date. Certainly it was approved in late 1905, before the Conditions of Fitness were written and it may have been subsequently barred because it did not comply. (Chris Hodge Trucks)

Rational cabs ranking in the Strand. Thanks to the design of its body, it was nicknamed 'the pillar box cab'. One of these, C360, undertook a journey from Northumberland Avenue, off Trafalgar Square, to Brighton. The trouble-free journey took 3 1/2hrs. Purley was reached in 90min, a time that would be hard to beat during today's daytime traffic. (LVTA Archive)

epicyclic transmission and a single chain. Its fully enclosed body was built by a Hertfordshire coachbuilder and was similar to a design fitted as early as 1903 on to a 6hp Wolseley chassis. An improvement over the open-fronted hansom, it had the look of a proper modern motor carriage, not a hybrid. David Hamdorff's book, *Seventeen Taxis?* tells the Rational story. A study of the vehicles illustrated in this book suggests that no more than the original six were licensed as London cabs as the others were fitted with private coachwork or had a wheelbase too long or too short for cab work. Heatly-Gresham Engineering soon moved to larger premises in Letchworth, just twelve miles from Luton, but it is not likely that motor vehicle production continued at the new factory.

Metropolitan Motor Cab and Carriage Company

The economics of running the Prunels had been carefully assessed by the chartered accountants William E. Pearse and the venture promised to be viable. Under the chairman-ship of the Earl of Ranfurly, a former governor general of New Zealand, the Metropolitan Motor Cab and Carriage Company was formed to take over the assets of the Express. Remnant would be the managing director. The share prospectus of May 1905 carried a picture of a Prunel, with the caption 'London's New Hansom Cab', and stated that Metropolitan's aim was to put sixty motor cabs on the streets within six months. Instead of Prunels, Metropolitan bought Manchester-built Heralds from S.R. Bailey & Lambert, Herald's London representatives. Twenty were already on order, with the rest to be delivered within three months of the date that the company began trading.

The Vauxhall Hansom– Metropolitan's Folly

The new Heralds were not delivered when Metropolitan had anticipated. One can only speculate why, but a possible reason was that Metropolitan were unable to raise enough capital. Even at this time, the threat of war was in the air and investors on the Stock Exchange were looking for safe, quick returns, not for untried, medium-term investments such as motor cab companies. However, in August 1905 Metropolitan ordered five 12/14hp Vauxhalls, reportedly at the instigation of Lord Ranfurly. The 12/14 car, with a 2400cc, 3-cylinder sidevalve engine and a three-speed gearbox, mounted in a flitch-plated, wooden chassis, was produced from 1904 at Vauxhall's original South London factory but it had been deleted from the catalogue by the end of 1905. Vauxhall were moving to new premises in Luton, Bedfordshire, and the 12/14s may well have been remained stock. Certainly the price suggests this; they were originally offered, with an open two-seat body, for £375. Vauxhall invoiced Metropolitan for £339 per vehicle, each to be fitted with a hansom cab body by Forder, one of the most popular and respected of hansom cab makers, with roof racks for luggage at £2.10s extra.

Metropolitan took delivery of their Vauxhalls, after one had been displayed at the Olympia Motor Exhibition, in November 1905. They were a failure. It was not the fault of the base vehicle but of the placing of the driver above and behind the passengers, which was done, not through some whim or tradition, but of necessity. The wheelbase was short, and placing him in front would make access for the passengers difficult.

It was reported at the time that the Vauxhall was popular with cabmen, but this is extremely doubtful. Every control was remotely operated, the linkage must have given a very vague feel and the seating arrangement must have unnerved the passengers. The hirer of a horse-drawn hansom knew that the horse would have more sense than to run into any danger, and he could at least see the effect of the cabman's taking up the reins. With the Vauxhall, he could see no signs and word would have quickly spread of such an unpleasant experience. A potential cab passenger has to this day the right to choose any cab from a rank that he or she takes a fancy to, and, if riding in a Vauxhall was now considered an unpleasant

The Vauxhall hansom. It can clearly be seen that the wheelbase would not be long enough to allow the driver to sit between the engine and the cab body. (Jamie Borwick)

This Vauxhall hansom was probably the only example to be fitted with a driver's seat over the engine. This vehicle was used, according to legend, to collect the wages for the Vauxhall works in Luton. (Guy Marriott)

experience, then the Vauxhall driver might well have found himself shunned.

Surviving records suggest that only three Vauxhalls were delivered: three engine numbers were recorded against the five chassis numbers. A second version with the driver seated over the engine was built but it is possible that cabmen simply refused to drive the cabs. The company withdrew them by March 1906 as fifteen of the promised Heralds fitted with hansom bodies had been delivered, while further examples would be fitted with landaulet bodies.

Enter Ford

Henry Ford founded the Ford Motor Company in the USA in 1903. British sales of the first Ford, the Model A, were handled by Percival Perry's Central Motor Car Company Ltd, in London's Covent Garden. In his *Brief History of Ford in Britain*, Perry says that it was subject to a popular prejudice that regarded American cars as cheap and crude. Ford's second model, the 4-cylinder, 20hp Model B, was exhibited at the Agricultural Hall in Islington in March 1905. Perry felt that cab work would convince the sceptical British public that Ford cars were worth buying, and by October the Automobile Cab Company of Chester Gate, London NW1 had announced its intention to put a fleet of Model Bs on to London's streets. The Ford had a two-speed, epicyclic gearbox and its ease of use would attract, according to Perry, a considerable number of horse cabmen. Initially three chassis were ordered, fitted with landaulet bodies and put to work by the end of the year. So that the public would easily recognize them as cabs as distinct from the growing number of privately-owned landaulets, the Automobile Cab Company intended to paint them white. However, surviving photographs do not show any finished in this way.

The Automobile Cab Company then announced that they had ordered 200 Fords at £360 each. In the event, Ford delivered fewer than twenty. At a shareholders' meeting in February 1906 the Automobile Cab Company's chairman Sir James T. Ritchie announced that the company had received less than one-quarter of its subscription target of £100,000. Ritchie also announced that Ford were changing their production methods and were unwilling to complete the order. New regulations, the Conditions of Fitness, were about to be announced by the PCO and the Fords would not comply with them. Ford was about to build a new factory, the Piquette Avenue plant in Detroit, where they planned a great increase in production and they may well have refused to build an especially adapted Model B for what would be, in comparison to their potential market, such a small order. The Automobile Cab Company considered legal action, but when they threatened Henry Ford, his reply was 'Fire away!'

Percival Perry would play a key role in establishing Ford as a major manufacturer in Britain, but in over a hundred years of Ford's history, the Model B was the only car that was ever licensed as a cab in London.

The Conditions of Fitness

Conditions of Fitness governing the design and construction of London's horse cabs had been in place for three and a half centuries. Armed with some knowledge of vehicle mechanics, Chief Inspector Bassom was moved to regulate the small but growing number of motor cabs. Already in existence was the Motor Car Act of 1903, which had introduced vehicle and driver licensing and following this in 1904 was the Motor Cars (Use and Construction) Act. For the first time brakes, lights, tyres and steering as well as the behaviour of drivers were regulated. Bassom felt that with regard to using motor cars to convey the general public for commercial gain, and in safety, the new laws did not go far enough.

Bassom accepted, quite properly, that first and foremost any motor cab had to comply with existing regulations, that is, the 1904 Act and the Locomotive Acts of 1896 and 1898, the Motor Car Act of 1903 and the Motor Cars (Use and Construction) Act. Over and above these, the PCO demanded that, when the car (this was at the time a common expression for all sizes and types of motor vehicle) was presented for inspection, it should have had no alteration made to it since it was previously inspected. And if any were made, then the PCO would, if necessary, employ an expert to advise on them.

The Conditions of Fitness placed safety above all; they demanded that liquid fuel tanks be made of a suitable material of sufficient strength and sited so that there should be no overflow on to woodwork where it might catch fire. Electrical wiring was to be sufficiently insulated. Neither of these points was addressed in the 1904 Use and Construction Act.

Two types of body were permitted: a hansom or, alternatively, a landaulet or brougham. The dimensions for the interior were quite specific, requiring, for instance, a distance between the seat cushion and the roof of 40in (102cm). Thus a gentleman could maintain the propriety of wearing his top hat while riding in a cab (this is still possible in today's cabs).

The first Herald, pictured at New Scotland Yard with Carriage Office personnel. The man second from the right may well be Chief Inspector Bassom. Unfortunately, no other contemporary photograph exists that would confirm his identification. (TfL/PCO)

The front road springs were to be fixed not less than 32in (81cm) apart from outside to outside and the minimum wheel track was to be 4ft 4in (1.3m). The turning circle was to be just 25ft (7.62m) and there was a reason for it: traffic congestion in London had always been bad, so anything that might cause a delay was to be avoided; where a street had shops, cabs were allowed to rank only in the centre of the road. If, when hired, a motor cab were required to travel in the opposite direction from the one in which it was facing, a three-point turn, with the primitive steering and transmissions of the day, would have taken far too long. Self-starters then were non-existent and, if the driver stalled the motor, restarting it by hand would have held the traffic up for several minutes. If a cab were capable of a U-turn then such incidents might be avoided. To emphasize how strongly the authorities felt about the possible disruption caused by three-point turns, a move to ban them within a 3-mile radius of Charing Cross was put forward, although not implemented.

There was a minimum ground clearance, as far back as the low point of the back axle, of 10in (25cm). This was to ensure that, if anyone were unfortunate enough to be hit by a motor cab, he would not be further harmed if the vehicle drove over him before coming to a stop. There would also be a maximum length of 14ft (4.3m). Last of all was a paragraph that would establish the PCO's complete authority in the matter of motor cab design. It stated: '*Note*: Though the above conditions may have been complied with, yet, if there be anything in the construction, form, or general appearance which, in the opinion of the commissioner, renders the carriage unfit for public use, it will not be licensed.'

The motoring press welcomed the principle behind the regulations, but the editor of *Motor Traction* was opposed to the tight turning circle. On reading an advanced copy dated 23 March 1906, he wrote to Commissioner Henry to say so, suggesting a 'more generous minimum' of 30 or 35ft (9.2 or 10.7m). Henry backed Bassom and stood firm on the 25ft rule. It is apparent from the motoring press of the previous year that the PCO had considered an even tighter, 21ft (6.4m) turning circle, so the established one was almost a relaxation.

Whatever their reception, the new Conditions of Fitness were timely. Between 1896 and 1905 more than thirty firms making motor cars had established themselves in Britain, but the numbers of vehicles they produced were still small. Between 1906 and 1907 the number of makers nearly doubled. To prosper, the makers had to build cars that were powerful and capacious enough but affordable to a greater number of people. They began to build cars to a standard type with the engine in front and the driver seated immediately behind it and to one side, with a wheel for him to steer. Most importantly for the cab trade, models with engines of around 2 litres capacity were beginning to appear, which was the optimum size for cab work. Now Londoners would see whether the motor cab was viable.

A New Cab for the Automobile Cab Company

In place of the Fords, Percival Perry supplied the Automobile Cab Company with thirty French Sorexes, powered by 2-cylinder, 10/12hp Gnôme engines. These cabs, built to meet the new Conditions of Fitness and fitted with landaulet bodies were paraded on Victoria Embankment on Saturday, 27 October 1906. Still aware of the need for the public to identify their vehicles as cabs, the company painted a letter 'A', for 'Automobile', on the glass of the lamps. But there would be other 'French Connections' that would have a great influence on the London cab trade.

Mann & Overton's

John Thomas Overton was a young man who, at the end of the nineteenth century, was living on his family's farm in Sutton, Surrey. Tom, as he was known, was more interested in motor cars than in farming and so in 1898 he went to the best place he knew to find out about them, which was Paris. There he met a Mancunian, John James Mann, who was buying and sending French and German cars to sell at his Motor Car Agency in London's Mortimer Street. They joined forces to form Mann & Overton's, to sell German Daimler, Hotchkiss and Georges-Richard cars from the Victoria Garage in Lower Belgrave Street, Pimlico. Tom's brother Will soon joined them.

As well as his interest in Mann & Overton's, Mann became the works manager of the Manchester car firm of Marshall and he drove one of their cars in the 1900 1,000-mile trial. He was happy to leave the running of Mann & Overton's to the Overtons, but Mann and the Overton brothers knew full well cab work would be an excellent way of testing and promoting motor cars. What they wanted was the right vehicle; for them, it was the 12hp Richard-Brasier, which they introduced to London in 1906. The Richard-Brasier came from the Paris factory owned originally by brothers Georges and Maxime Richard, but that was not the name of the first car to be made there, that was the Georges-Richard, which, from 1901, was designed by Henri Brasier. In 1904 Georges Richard left the company to set up on his own and subsequent models made in the factory were sold as Richard-Brasier.

J.T. 'Tom' Overton (left) and J.J. Mann. (Author's collection)

The Town Motor Carriage Competition

Between 15 and 17 October 1906 the Automobile Club held a Competition for Town Motor Carriages at the Wolseley Tool and Motor Company's garage in Waterloo, South London. Mann & Overton's entered two 12hp Richard-Brasiers in class A for vehicles costing up to £600. They were fitted with limousine bodies by Alfred Belvalette and Bagley & Ellis. Another Richard-Brasier was entered by one of Mann & Overton's customers, the City and Suburban Motor Cab Company. This had a cab body by the French company La Carrosserie Industrielle. All three put up a respectable showing, with the City and Suburban cab winning a silver medal for a Public Service Vehicle.

Also entered was a 16hp Argyll cab, driven all the way from its factory north of Glasgow. Since 1900 Argyll had been building cars with a reputation for solidity and reliability. The 1905 Argyll cab was a heavy, close-coupled vehicle with the driver placed above the engine. It was designed to replace the four-wheeled growler whose domain, because of its capacity for carrying luggage, was the railway station. Despite some intense promotion, the Argyll cab was not adopted in London since its 30ft turning circle did not comply with the Conditions of Fitness.

It was a sign of the times that the highest placed vehicle in class A was an American Oppermann Electric, with a hansom cab body by Cleaver Brothers. Pitted against internal combustion-engined vehicles, its success was virtually a foregone conclusion since the judging criteria included smooth starting, absence of fumes and silence in running. However, the Oppermann was not licensed for use as a cab in London and the company went out of business the following year.

Union Interest

Few investors seemed to be willing to risk their money in the motor cab, and the major horse cab masters were opposed to their introduction, fearing that the enormous investment required would not yield the return they were then enjoying. However, the London Cab Drivers Trade Union realized that motors were the future and in January 1905 set up driving and mechanical knowledge classes for their members. Writing in their official publication, the South London area secretary Will Wright, asked what would happen if, 'a company decides to place a fleet of 400 motor cabs on the streets and we don't get our men [that is, Union members] on them?'

'The General'

Wright knew something of which the public at large were unaware: among the spectators of the Town Motor Carriages Competition may well have been the Hon. Davidson Dalziel, MP and Edward Cohen, directors of the General Motor Cab Company Ltd, a company formed by using a considerable amount of capital from the Paris-based *Compagnie Generale des Voitures*. If so, they were taking time off from a massive project of their own, which had been under way since May of that year. Less than six weeks before the competition, the General Motor Cab Company's contractors had begun clearing a site occupied by old houses and overgrown with trees and grass, at the junction of Brixton Road and Camberwell New Road. Using a structure of steel joists covered in red and yellow brick, they were erecting a new, purpose-built cab garage.

These premises, built on three levels, were the largest of their kind anywhere in the world. There were offices to the side, fronting on to Brixton Road and running along Camberwell New Road, overlooking Kennington Park.

Ramps led from either side of the forecourt to a high level access road with entrances to the body shop, chassis shop and motor repair shop. Here would be serviced the fleet of 500 cabs that were on order from Renault in Paris. The General had originally ordered Charron cabs but the maker could not produce a satisfactory vehicle. Instead, the cabs would be 500 2-cylinder AG Renaults, a later version of the single-cylinder models that had been run by the General's Parisian sister company *La Compagnie Française des Automobiles de Place*. The first of London's Renaults, part of the biggest single order yet placed for motor cars, arrived in October 1906, long before the building was completed. They were put to work immediately, not for public hire, because they had yet to be licensed, but for private hire work at 7s.6d (37.5p) an hour. This work served to advertise the General's name in advance of the grand opening on 21 March 1907. The following day the first cabs, painted bright red with yellow wheels, set out for public hire.

Although the London Cab Drivers Trade Union wanted their members to drive motors, they were totally opposed to the rate that General were proposing to charge their drivers. Other motor cab companies were paying their drivers a set wage of around 5s. (25p) a day plus 2s. (10p) in the pound commission. The General were to fit their cabs with meters and pay their drivers a percentage of the meter reading. The Union claimed that this would result in a reduction in earnings. The General's manager Edward Cohen was intent on driving a wedge between his company and the Union by claiming that the Union were anti-motor and anti-taximeter. In an attempt to exclude those members who had learned to drive motors, Cohen set up a driving school for the cabmen who were not members.

The Unic 10/12

In October 1904 Georges Richard left the company he had founded with his brother Maxime to set up on his own. Financed by

A 12hp Renault, one of the 500 ordered by the General Cab company in 1906. (Jamie Borwick)

21

'The home of the Motor Cab', was the caption to this illustration, printed in a book published in 1909 to celebrate the founding of the London General Motor Cab Co. The buildings exist to this day, although the solid pillars and arches at the vehicle entrance were replaced by railings. (G.W. Trotter)

Baron Dr Henri de Rothschild, he planned a single model, which he would call the Unic. Two years later a new factory was built on the Baron's land at Puteaux in north-west Paris. An economical and very serviceable vehicle, the Unic was soon adopted by Parisian taxicab fleets. It attracted the attention of Mann & Overton's and they successfully negotiated for an agency. The City and Suburban Motor Cab Company bought four 10/12hp 2-cylinder Unics to add to their Richard-Brasiers, and another twenty-five the following year. The National Cab Company of Hammersmith bought 250, which they painted bright red. In the capacity of what we would now call fleet manager, the National were to hire the services of a young man who would later make his mark with high performance luxury cars – W.O. Bentley. In his book, *W.O.: An Autobiography* (Hutchinson, 1958) Bentley acknowledged the important lessons he learned about running motor vehicles in his time with National.

The assets of City and Suburban Cab Company were taken over in early 1907 by The United Motor Cab Company of Walham Green, Fulham, west London. Already on the

City and Suburban's board were some of the directors of the General Cab company's French associates. Between 1907 and 1908 City and Suburban bought 224 10/12 Unic cabs, with Christopher Dodson landaulet bodies from Mann & Overton's, considerably boosting the number of Unics on the street.

The Hurmid: a Late Attempt by an Independent

Although the big names were already a powerful force, they did not stop the small makers from trying to enter the trade. After splitting up with Lewis A. Lloyd (maker of the Simplex) in 1900, George Hurst began making a small number of 12hp, 2-cylinder and 24hp, 4-cylinder cars. They were described by *Car Illustrated* as being of poor finish. Hurst was joined in 1906 by R.E. Middleton and they produced a 40hp, 6-cylinder car in addition to Hurst's previous models, all of which were sold under the portmanteau name of Hurmid. The 12hp 2-cylinder was approved as a cab and examples survived in service as late as 1910, three years longer than the company that made it.

Conflict over the Conditions of Fitness

The motor industry was disturbed by another aspect of the General's operations. Henry Sturmey, the founder of *Autocar* magazine and one of the original members of the British Motor Syndicate, examined the Renault's chassis and found that the width between the side members was 26in (66cm), not the 32 (81cm) required by the Conditions of Fitness. Sturmey and many others interested in the motor cab trade were outraged; as a member of the Society of Motor Manufacturers and Traders, he spoke from a position of authority when he stated that the Conditions of Fitness were too great an obstacle for motor manufacturers to overcome. The reason the PCO gave for allowing the Renaults to be passed was that the vehicles were experimental and that, 'in the interests of the public, they should be given a trial'. It is possible, however, that as the General began building their premises in May 1906, the PCO may have approved the Renault before the Conditions of Fitness came into effect.

The Rover Cab

The General's initiative was the spur the British motor industry needed to consider the cab market. In the summer of 1907 the Coventry company of Rover launched the Rover Motor Cab Company. Much was made of the fact that the Rover enterprise was entirely British. Indeed, the General's chairman, Davidson Dalziel, MP, had been criticized for his involvement with a French company. (We must remember that the Entente Cordiale, the agreement formulated to end centuries of war and discord between England and France had been signed only three years before.) Rover's promotional material declared that 500 cabs would be put into service, not only in London, but also in Liverpool, Manchester, Glasgow and other major British cities. This was somewhat optimistic since their weekly production rarely reached twenty, but no doubt they hoped that the cab company would generate an increase in production. Their cab was based on the 10/12 chassis, with a monobloc, 4-cylinder engine. It had a transverse front spring, a

The Unic 10/12 was introduced by Mann & Overton's in 1906 and carried a body by Christopher Dodson of Hampstead. Dodson advertised in Mann & Overton's annually published Motor Atlas, *purporting to specialize in 'Landaulet bodies for Unic chassis'. (Chris Hodge Trucks)*

23

feature that would soon be banned from London cabs because the PCO believed it to be an unstable arrangement. Landaulet and closed bodies were offered, the latter being promoted as the Station Cab, with a luggage rack fitted to the roof. Space for a passenger was provided beside the driver and the company would fit all cabs with taximeters. The cabs would be sold to other proprietors through the Rover Cab Agency of Victoria Street, at the very reasonable price of £350 or £375 complete with meter. This would be the only cab to be licensed in London that carried Rover's name.

A New Cab Act

The General's operations had upset the Union and the motor industry and now they were to test the PCO. The General proposed to fit taximeters to their London cabs; these were intended to take away the biggest source of complaints that the PCO received from the public about cabmen, that of overcharging. However, the London Cab Acts, written when all cabs were horse-drawn and without meters, allowed for a hirer to take a cab on a time basis. This practice was permissible for motor cabs, but the virtue of a motor was that it was, unlike the horse, tireless. Thus motor cabs were popular for long journeys when they were hired at an hourly rate. However, the advent of a taximeter created a number of anomalies. There exists a letter written to the PCO from a passenger complaining that, although he had hired a cab on a time basis, the cabman had attempted to charge him the fare shown on the meter, which exceeded the hourly rate. There was no clear guidance in the statutes as to how the PCO should adjudicate.

The Taxameter Syndicate

The name 'taxi' is said to come from a German nobleman, Baron von Thurn und Taxis, who set up a mail delivery service in the eighteenth century. So that his customers knew how much to pay for the delivery, he designed a device that recorded the distance travelled by the coach. This was the forerunner of the modern taximeter and, when such a device was installed on a cab, the vehicle became a 'taxicab'. Frederick Simms was the first Englishman to acquire the British rights to Gottlieb Daimler's patents and became, in 1898, the chairman of the Taxameter Syndicate Ltd. He wrote to the Metropolitan Police Commissioner Edward Bradford at Scotland Yard, asking him to examine a new 'Taxameter' – the spelling used by the machine's German maker – that his syndicate planned to introduce for London's cabs. This machine calculated the fare by measuring distance travelled, by connection to a road wheel, and by time (by clockwork) when the cab was stationary. When hired, the cabman would set the meter in operation by lowering a red flag. Simms claimed that this machine would remove all the arguments that arose over cab fares. He also put forward the idea of a 'sixpenny fare' for short distances in place of the one shilling (1s., 5p) charge for the first mile that might attract businessmen away from the buses, the underground and the trains and thus generate more work for cabmen. The Commissioner was interested in Simms's proposal but Chief Inspector Dormer of the PCO pointed out what he called two 'fatal flaws' in the proposal: first, it was the responsibility of the cabman to set the meter in motion. If he chose not to, there was no law compelling him to do so. Secondly, if there were a dispute over the fare charged the distance recorded by the Taxameter would not be accepted as evidence in a court of law. Only the distance prescribed by the Commissioner in the authorized 'fare book', which set out the legal fares chargeable by cabmen, would be admissible. Nevertheless, Commissioner Bradford allowed Simms to try out his device, provided that the machines were set to run at the legal tariff and not at Simms's own 'sixpenny' fare. The experiment was a failure; few cab masters were willing to invest in the machine, cabmen refused to take out cabs so fitted and the Union supported their members. Within six months of its introduction, the Taxameter was gone.

The second problem was one of apparent fraud. At first, the PCO made no record of which taximeters were fitted to which cabs. In fact, the number of cabs that the London General claimed to have fitted with meters was much higher than that recorded at the PCO. The General appeared to be acting in this way because the law did not say it could not: there were no specific regulations applicable to either the fitting of taximeters or to specify what tariff they should show.

A simple means of recording meter numbers against cab plate numbers cured the numbers problem and, on 1 July 1907, the fitting of taximeters became mandatory for motor cabs in London. The world now had a new word: taxicab.

The General's Renaults were licensed to carry two passengers. They were also fitted with a third seat beside the driver and there were cases of two of the General's cab drivers being prosecuted for carrying more than the permissible number of passengers. This prompted the General's solicitor to write to Superintendent Bassom in August 1907, suggesting that their cabs should be licensed for four persons, with a third squeezed on the inside seat and a fourth carried beside the driver. Bassom disagreed; he considered that the Renaults were neither spacious enough nor powerful enough and that the small flap beside the driver was 'not suitable for a seat but might be useful for ladies' shopping or to put small parcels on'.

Bassom's objections were based on safety considerations; he felt that a passenger could distract the driver's attention if seated beside him and he was also well aware of a type of

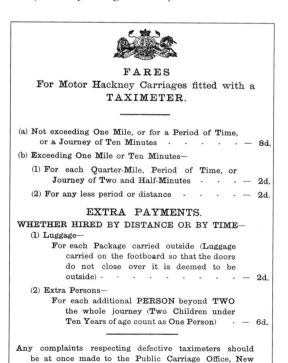

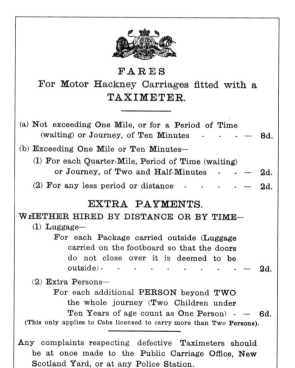

The first fare tables for taximeters: left, for two-seater cabs and right for four-seaters.

person who occasionally took cabs. In somewhat picturesque language, he wrote,

> Further, it must be remembered that cabs are not like private motors where the owner knows the class of person he has beside the driver, but public carriages are frequently used by persons who are more hilarious than wise and one can easily imagine a party of students, young men about town or others leaving a place of entertainment, getting beside the driver and interfering with the mechanism . . . so as to be a source of danger to themselves and others using the roads.

Very quickly new fare tables were printed, one for two-seater cabs and one for four-seaters, stating on the table for two-seaters that the extra charge of 2d. for each additional person above two would apply to four-seater cabs only. Fares for taximeter cabs were different from those for hansom cabs and motor cabs without meters. The rate for hansom cabs was 1s. (5p) for the first mile plus 6d. for every subsequent mile and waiting time at 2s.6d. (12.5p) for the first hour and 8d. for every subsequent quarter-hour. The rate for a taxicab was 8d. flagfall for the first mile (referred to as the hiring charge or 'flagfall') or 10min and 2d. (0.7p) for each quarter-mile or 2 1/2min. This would create problems in the immediate future, as cab companies, struggling to turn a profit on their considerable investment, were powerless to raise extra revenue from metered cab work. Only with private hire would companies be able to charge their own rates and this work was seasonal, unpredictable and subject to strong competition.

These matters were already under the scrutiny of Parliament. The London Cab and Stage Carriage Act 1907 came into force on 1 February 1908. The installation of taxi-meters had been mandatory on all motor cabs since 1 July of the previous year. The new Act added the proviso that meters were to be of a type approved by the Commissioner of Police and sealed by both the PCO and the National Physical Laboratory to ensure accuracy and the prevention of fraud. Also under the Act, it would be illegal for a motor cabman to carry a passenger on the driver's seat (still called a 'box' in accordance with horse-drawn vehicle parlance) and compelled him to take a fare if the distance was under 6 miles or of one hour's duration. Vehicle licences were set at £2 per annum.

A further part of the Act dealt with the abolition of the privilege system at London's railway stations. This had been introduced in 1839, when an agreement was made for a cab master to guarantee twelve cabs to the London & Birmingham Railway Company's terminus at Euston. Other railway companies soon adopted this practice. Despite the fact that the cabmen had to pay, at first, 1s. a day to the railway company, it engendered a lot of ill-feeling from cabmen not included in the agreement. Because of the nature of the work, cabs used on privilege ranks were growlers, with capacity to carry the large amounts of luggage that the hansoms could not. With the privilege system abolished in central London (some suburban ranks were allowed to carry on) station work became available to the motor cab and larger, four-seat vehicles were seen on the terminus forecourts.

With this Act, the stipulation of the Conditions of Fitness of a 25ft turning circle and a partition between the driver and passengers, the criteria for the London cab were set, not just for the immediate future but for the rest of the century and beyond.

2 1908–18 Turbulent Peace and Devastating War

The Edwardian era became known as '*la belle époque*', 'the beautiful time', a time of increased prosperity and advancement in the arts. It was also a period of political unrest. With the death in 1910 of Edward VII, 'the Peacemaker', domestic troubles came to a head amid an economic depression. As a service industry, the London cab trade suffered, as well as experiencing upheavals of its own. When war broke out, the trade was in a far more vulnerable position than any that first ventured into it may have thought.

By the end of 1907 there were 723 motor cabs on the streets out of a total fleet of 10,512. Of these, 500 were the General's Renaults, and it was the General's operations, coupled with the improvements in motor car design that spurred initially reluctant investors to risk their money in the cab trade. In 1908 the PCO granted type approval to more than a dozen makes of motor cab, increasing the total number on the road to 2,805, with much of the growth at the expense of the hansom. By the end of 1908 there were eighteen types of cab in service, with 2,480 cabs run by just six owners. Most of the makes were French, in particular Renault, George-Richard and Unic, but the Italian FIAT also had a substantial presence. Other French makes were Panhard, de Dion, Darracq and Vinot. The remaining 325 cabs were run by 169 proprietors, indicating either small fleets of a dozen or so cabs or owner-drivers. The British makes to challenge the French dominance in any number were Napier and Belsize, though not one British maker was producing cabs by the outbreak of war.

W & G du Cros

The most successful British cab of the later pre-war years was the Napier, run by W & G du Cros. The du Cros family feature prominently in the early years of British motoring history. Harvey du Cros made his fortune in the late nineteenth century by investing in and becoming chairman of the Dunlop Rubber Co. Ltd. He established contacts with Darracq in France, acquired British concessions for Panhard and Mercedes, and invested in, among other motor companies, Austin and Napier. However, his health began to deteriorate and in 1908 two of his six sons, William and George took over some of his workload by forming W & G du Cros. This company, based in Acton, west London, was engaged in a number of activities, including the running of a substantial fleet of cabs.

W & G preferred to call their vehicles 'hiring landaulets', since, in addition to the cabs, there was a large private hire fleet, composed in part of vehicles other than those type-approved by Scotland Yard. Five hundred 15hp, 4-cylinder Panhards were ordered through Harvey du Cros's agency. Between 500 and 600 of the fleet's cabs, however, came from W & G's London neighbour, Napier. The first were 12hp, 2-cylinder cabs but the remainder were 15hp, 4-cylinder models. At its peak, the fleet numbered over 1,000 cabs. Napier had already established itself as a quality make and had been made famous by the successful racing exploits of S.F. Edge. W & G also ran a small number of Unic 10/12s. With the adoption of four-seat cabs

The du Cros brothers: William (left) and George (right). (John Gray)

A Panhard of the W & G fleet. Note the company logo on the door and on the lapel of the cabman's coat; see also the lamp carried within the 'Stepney' spare wheel. This picture is actually a postcard, produced for W & G. The message on the back is written by one of W & G's drivers Fred Walker. Walker describes the Panhard as 'the smartest on the road'. (Bryan Goodman)

by the trade, the more powerful 15hp, 4-cylinder Napiers were added to the fleet. It is understood that the managing director of the Austro-Daimler concession for England, Francis M. Luther, assisted with the finance. In addition, Luther ran his own cab fleet, the Coupé Cab Company. He ran 150 10hp 2-cylinder Napiers, which were serviced by W & G, as well as a substantial number of private hire vehicles.

The centre gangway of W & G's garage in Acton, with a mixture of Panhards and Napiers. This picture is another of the series of postcards produced by W & G. (Bryan Goodman)

A 15hp Napier, depicted on another of W & G's postcards, in the same location as the Panhard. The bodies of the cabs are identical in every respect, being built by W & G. The pagoda-top oil lamps are identical too, as are the tail lights carried beside the spare wheel. Just visible is the sharp, inward curve of the chassis to accommodate the turning circle. The Napier was perhaps the finest Edwardian London cab. (Bryan Goodman)

Napiers of the Coupé Cab Co. lined up for a maker's publicity photograph. (Jamie Borwick)

Bodies for W & G's cabs were built in-house and were painted in their own livery of dark green with yellow bonnets and a yellow panel below the door window, bearing the W & G logo. The same logo was also mounted on the front of the radiator, leading many people to believe that W & G actually made the cabs themselves. To make the case that the Napiers were a British stand against the French dominance, a Union flag was painted on the doors. No such confusion arose over the Coupé Company's Napiers; although these were also painted green and yellow there was no W & G logo on the radiator and the name 'Napier' appeared on the yellow door panel.

The Best of the Rest

Few of the literally dozens of other makes, both British and foreign, that were licensed lasted for very long. We shall speculate on the reasons why the companies that ran them foundered a little later on, but the following is a summary of some of these makes.

Adams

The epicyclic gearbox seemed an ideal feature for London's traffic and one make that used it exclusively was Adams, produced by the Manufacturing Company of Bedfordshire. Entering the cab market in 1911, the company used the advertising slogan, 'Pedals to push – that's all' because its three-speed transmission was foot-operated. They were offered on 10/12hp, 2- and 12/14hp, 4-cylinder chassis. The company was renamed Adams-Hewitt and went on to make larger cars until the outbreak of war, but no more cabs were made after 1911.

Argyll

In contrast to its original 16hp cab, the model that Argyll introduced for London in 1908 was entirely conventional, with a 12/14hp, four in unit with the gearbox. It carried a yellow livery, which prompted cab drivers to christen it 'the mustard pot'. It was built from the outset as a four-seater, with two extra seats designed to fold down from the front of the carriage interior so that the occupants sat facing the rear seat passengers. It is believed that it was the first cab to have these rear-facing, folding, 'cricket' seats. In 1910, Argyll built a second, equally conventional, 15hp cab.

Austin

Austin, whose name became the biggest in the trade, made a modest debut in London in

This Ballot cab of 1909, probably belonging to the Express Motor Cab Co., is fitted with a Brulo taximeter. (Derek Pearce)

The Manchester-built Belsize was advertised as 'The All-British Cab'. (Jamie Borwick)

A 15hp Argyll cab, the last model from this maker to be licensed in London, pictured in Fleet Street. (LVTA Archives)

1909. Herbert Austin had made a centre-drive, 15hp limousine that could be used for cab work but it was never licensed in London. The first Austin cabs to be licensed by Scotland Yard were also 15hp models of a conventional design. Ten of these were run by Urban Taxicabs Ltd of west Kensington. In 1910 nine examples were introduced by Taxis de Luxe of Hammersmith. In the early years, motor cabs were not particularly well appointed, but the Austins of Taxis de Luxe lived up to their name, having much more luxurious trim.

Ballot

A hundred Ballot cabs, powered by 4-cylinder, 10/12hp engines, were operated by the Express Motor Cab Company, an affiliate of the French Express de Paris, while the Quick Motor Cab Company operated a number which were painted white. Before the Great War, Ballot concentrated on commercial vehicles and engine manufacture, with the taxicab their most important vehicle. They ventured into sports car manufacture during the 1920s.

Belsize

Belsize was a Manchester company. Originally called Marshall, the firm's new name saw it through until its demise in the early years of the Great War. Standing firm against the French invasion, the Belsize was sold as 'the All British Cab'. Its 4-cylinder, 14/16hp was a tough and reliable unit.

Darracq

Darracq supplied 450 vehicles in 1908 to several London proprietors, including London United, who ran 250, London and Provincial, who had 100, and the Stanhope Motor Cab Company, who operated a single example. The original model was a 4-cylinder, 18hp model, but it was too large. It had gone by 1911, replaced by a more acceptable 2-cylinder, four-seater.

De Dion

The De Dion-Bouton Company operated 2-cylinder, 10hp cabs of their own make from 1908. These were replaced in 1909 by a more popular, single-cylinder model.

The extension to the roofline of this 2-cylinder Darracq suggests that the cab may have been in service since at least 1907, when it would have been built without cover for the driver. One might surmise that that, due to his age, the standing figure is a horse cabman; it would be unlikely that he would trouble to learn to drive a motor at his age. Old boys like him would eke out their days on horse cabs into the 1920s. (LVTA Archives)

FIAT

One of the biggest foreign makes represented was the Italian FIAT. The FIAT Motor Cab Co. began in 1908 with a modest thirty-seven 12/15hp, 4-cylinder Tipo 1 cabs, operated from Lupus Street, Pimlico. This number grew to 400, following their move to St Pancras Road, King's Cross.

Electromobile

The Electromobile was the last attempt by an electric vehicle manufacturer to enter the London cab trade. Based in Lambeth, the British Electromobile Company ordered fifty chassis from Greenwood & Batley, a machine tool manufacturer from Leeds, in October 1908. They were fitted with bodies by the Gloucester Carriage and Wagon Company. Operated by the Electric Taxicab Company, they were heavy, bulky four-seaters but with a substantial luggage carrying capacity and a range of 45 miles (72km). These were to work the main London railway termini and oust the horse-drawn growlers, but just twenty out of a promised 500 were delivered.

The increased power of petrol cabs, which enabled them to carry four-seat bodies and luggage, plus their unlimited range, meant the end of electric cabs.

Gamage-Bell

Cab masters and cab dealers were able to manufacture if they had sufficient financial backing. One such organization was Gamage-Bell. Gamage's was a famous department store in London's Holborn. In partnership with Horace Bell, who had worked for the General Cab Company, they ran 15hp Napiers with high quality coachwork of their own construction and also ordered chassis from BSA in Birmingham.

Hillman-Coatelen

The Coventry company of Hillman was a late-comer into the trade. The Frenchman Louis Coatelen became one of William Hillman's sons-in-law. The first cars he designed for Hillman, named Hillman-Coatelen, were big, but a more modest 12/15hp model followed and formed the basis of a cab which, in 1911,

Performing the job for which it was intended, the Greenwood and Batley Electromobile, photographed outside Euston Station Arch. (Chris Hodge Trucks)

was the last new make to be type-approved before the Great War. Few were built because its arrival coincided with the beginnings of the trade's decline.

Humber

At the time one of the biggest makers in the country, Humber made their debut in the London cab trade in 1908. Their de Luxe model, a short-wheelbase vehicle with its engine placed underneath the driver, did not operate in London, but the conventional 10hp model, designed by Louis Coatelen and built in the Beeston factory near Nottingham, was approved. Humber's Beeston-built vehicles were better appointed and better made than the Coventry-built vehicles and the cab was no exception. The Humber Cab Company ran a fleet of forty-seven in London and another thirty-two were owner-driven. It proved reliable and economical and Humber hoped for an expansion in these numbers, but 1908 was a very bad trading year for them and they closed the Beeston factory, concentrating car production in Coventry. After 1909 they made no more cabs for London.

Lotis

Henry Sturmey founded *Automobile* magazine but in 1906 he left to write for the rival publication *Motor*. He also contributed to *Motor Traction* and quite likely influenced the editor's opinion of the 25ft turning circle. Sturmey was a car maker too, building the American Duryea under licence in Coventry under his own name until 1904. Sturmey's opposition to the turning circle was no doubt the result of his desire to enter the motor cab business. In 1908 he introduced a vehicle of his own design and manufacture, the Lotis. To achieve the turning circle, the wheelbase was a very short 4ft 10in (1.5m) and its 10/12hp, 1357cc,

V-twin Riley engine, mated to a two-speed epicyclic gearbox was under the driver's feet. In both the cab and the private limousine form the Lotis continued in production until 1912. It was the first cab to have a purpose-built luggage space beside the driver.

Vinot

The 14/16hp Vinot was first operated by a suburban proprietor, Oates Brothers of Wimbledon, in 1909 and proved to be a reliable cab. It is most likely that it was actually a Gladiator cab that had been specially built for London. Another French company, Vinot et Deguingand, took over Gladiator in 1908 and continued to make Gladiator cars with Vinot badges. It was most likely that Vinot et Deguingand continued manufacture of the Gladiator cab, fitted with a Vinot radiator and badge in order to regain some of the investment money.

Wolseley-Siddeley

Wolseley-Siddeley cars were made in Birmingham by the Wolseley Tool and Motor Car Company and named after the general manager J.D. Siddeley. In 1907, a 2-cylinder, 8/10hp was introduced, featuring an especially-built, dropped chassis to give passengers easier access. The London General ordered 250, fitted with two-seat bodies. The cab had a reputation of being difficult to drive and cabmen used to say that it 'needed humouring', and

The Wolseley-Siddeley of 1908, built by Wolseley at their massive Adderley Park, Birmingham factory. (Norman Painting)

35

when four-seat cabs became more common, cabmen refused to take it out. In 1908 it was replaced by a 4-cylinder, 12hp model, of which London United ordered 250. After 1913 they were gradually withdrawn from service.

Farewell to a Pioneer

By 1908 the Herald, the Vauxhall, the Simplex, the Sorex and the Ford were all gone. The remarkable exception was the London Motor Cab Company's Rationals. This company had done some important pioneering work, establishing, with little fanfare and even less controversy, a reliable motor cab presence. It is to Heatly-Gresham Engineering's credit that these early vehicles lasted to as late as October 1909, but their lack of sophistication caught up with them and they were replaced in the fleet by French Brouhots. Brouhot cabs had been introduced in Paris in 1907. The company had been in existence since 1898, but from 1911 they abandoned cars and taxicabs and concentrated on building agricultural machinery.

A New Taxation System

Until 1910, cars over one ton in weight had been subject to a £2.17s. (£2.85) annual tax, payable to the Inland Revenue in addition to the road fund licence. Hackney cabs were exempt from the weight tax if they were licensed for the whole year. However, during the London Season, which lasted from May to July, many proprietors let their cabs out on private hire, handing in the hackney plate for the duration. An allowance of 7s.6d. (37.5p) per annum was made against the tax if a cab was licensed for part of the year. The London Motor Cab Proprietors Association wrote to the Home Secretary, Winston Churchill complaining that some cabs were under 1 ton in weight and not subject, while others were over; but, since cabs needed to be stronger for

public hire, they would generally exceed 1 ton. As they already paid a 15s. (75p) annual licence fee to Scotland Yard for each vehicle, regardless of how many months of the year the vehicle carried its plate, the proprietors felt hard done by in having to pay any surcharge.

But it was the Chancellor, David Lloyd George, who settled the matter. The Finance (1909–10) Act stipulated that all cars would pay an annual Road Fund Licence, based on a sliding scale according to a formula devised by the Royal Automobile Club. Besides being one of a number of incessant assaults upon the motorists' pocket by successive governments, the formula had the effect of standardizing the ratings that manufacturers gave to their models. Until then, makers had used a figure that, with the inefficiency of engines at the time, was close to their actual brake horsepower figure. The 2 guinea fee (£2.10p), now superfluous, was scrapped. But the Commissioner of Police made one order that would prove extremely unpopular with cabmen: from 1910 he banned the fitting of full windscreens on cabs —he maintained that a cabman's visibility in London 'pea souper' fogs would be limited by a glass screen.

The Decline of the Horse Cab

Between 1909 and 1911 the number of horse cabs halved, while the number of motor cabs more than doubled. Horses were sold off and horse cabs burned. At the outbreak of war, just 232 hansom cabs survived and their virtual extinction was marked by the presentation of one to the London Museum in 1914. The growler lingered on, favoured by elderly ladies who mistrusted both motors and hansoms, and its luggage capacity meant that it would continue to serve railway stations for a while longer. However, the introduction of more powerful four-seater motor cabs consigned the growler to the scrap yard. A handful of

The 'Also Rans'

Makers and proprietors both large and small went to the wall after 1911. Much of attrition in numbers can be blamed on the strikes, the slump in work and above all, the Home Secretary's refusal to raise fares to a level that allowed economic survival. Here is what we know for certain about those that were lost, both to the cab trade and to the motoring world.

Cottereau (France) Cottereau as a company declined and ceased manufacture in 1910; their cabs were recognizable by their circular radiator.

Charron (France) Some 2-cylinder, 8/10hp Charrons were included in the fleet of the General Cab Co. in 1908.

Adler (Germany) Adler as a company was in existence between 1900 to 1939; the 12hp cab introduced very early, probably in 1907; Adler were represented in England by the coachbuilders Morgan and Co.

Albion The Albion cab was made by the Albion Motor Car Company, Scotstown, Glasgow; Albion ceased to make cars from 1915, concentrating on commercial vehicles.

DPL Made by Dawfield and Philips in 1907, this very compact cab had a 2-cylinder, horizontal engine and a 20ft (6m) turning circle and was probably constructed from proprietary automotive parts.

Leader Made by Charles Binks & Co. of Apsey, Nottinghamshire, between 1905 and 1910 the Leader had a 14/16hp four cylinder engine; it is unlikely that any more than a handful of these cabs saw service in London.

Marlborough The Marlborough had a 15.9hp Malicet et Blin proprietary engine; it was made between 1905 and 1910 by T.B. André, who took over the British concession for *Malicet et Blin*.

Marple The coachbuilder Stephen A. Marples built the body of the Marples cab in 1907 for the London Improved Cab Co.; it probably used a proprietary chassis, fitted with a 2-cylinder, 12hp engine.

Masco All that is known of the Mascot is that it had a Forman engine and was built in 1907.

Star Star was a manufacturer of some importance in the early years of motoring, continuing in production up to the mid 1930s; originally the 12hp, 4-cylinder model was adopted for cab work but the 2-cylinder, 9hp proved more popular, but the make's importance was not reflected by its continued presence in the cab trade and no record of its use is found beyond 1910.

Thames The Thames Shipbuilding and Engineering Co., of London built a 2-cylinder, 12hp cab in 1908 for the Motor Cab Syndicate of Cannon Street; Thames abandoned car manufacture in 1910 to concentrate on commercial vehicles.

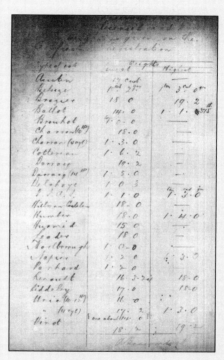

A remarkable document: a list of cabs licensed in 1909, written by Chief Inspector Bassom in reply to a query regarding the tax imposed on cars over 1 ton in weight. Listed are: Austin, Belsize, Brazier (sic) Ballot, Brouhot, Charron (10hp), Charron (4-cylinder), Cottereau, Darracq, Darracq (14hp), Delahaye, FIAT, Hillman-Coatelen, Humber, Hurmid, Leader, Marlborough, Napier, Panhard, Renault, Siddeley, Unic (10/12hp), Unic (4-cylinder), Vinot. Notable by their absence, in some instances only two or three years aftere their introduction, are: Adams, Adler, Argyll, DFP, De Dion, Electromobile, Ford, Herald, Lotis, Marples, Mascot, Prunel, Pullcar, Rational, Rover, Simplex, Sorex, Star, Thames and Vauxhall. (National Archive)

horse cabs survived after the Great War, the last disappearing as late as 1948, but, seven years after the first Prunel was licensed, the motor cab had reached its pre-war zenith, with almost 8,000 on the streets. It would be another half-century before that number was exceeded.

Opposition to the Turning Circle

In 1911 Henry Sturmey attended a meeting of the Royal Automobile Club to hear J.S. Critchley read his paper on 'The Evolution of the Motor Cab'. Critchley was a noted automobile engineer and a founder member of both the RAC and the Society of Motor Manufacturers and Traders (SMM&T). Following the reading, Sturmey told the audience that the combination of the 25ft turning circle and the width between the chassis rails had been causing great difficulties for manufacturers. He claimed that many of his colleagues in the SMM&T agreed with him. But whatever the level of opposition to the regulation, Scotland Yard were not about to change it.

Disputes over Extras

1911 saw the London motor cab trade's first major industrial dispute. When more than two people were carried in a taxicab, the cabman could charge 6d. (2.5p) per person in addition to the fare. These 'extras' became a source of dispute when four-seater cabs came into service. The first motor cab masters had calculated their running costs on the horse cab tariff and its 1s. (5p) hiring charge. When the 8d. taximeter was introduced, they experienced a shortfall in turnover. This they intended to make up by claiming the extras, since there was no statute to say to whom they belonged. The cabmen had other ideas, and the dispute came to a head in October 1911 when the National Cab Company dismissed a driver who refused

to hand over the extras he had collected. The London Cab Drivers Trade Union (LCDTU) called a strike and by 3 November some 15,000 drivers, mechanics and cab washers were out. A committee of enquiry was set up to review the situation, but the Home Secretary, Winston Churchill, refused to allow a fare increase, despite the fact that London fares were noticeably cheaper than those in most provincial British towns and cities.

Provincial fares were set by local authorities. *The Times* claimed that the government would not raise London fares because 'cabs were the buses of the Parliamentarians'. Eventually on 12 March 1912 a court of arbitration awarded cabmen the extras. The cabmen were also given a set 25 per cent commission on the metered fare and a set price for petrol at 8d./gal, subject to review should it go up in price by more than 12 per cent per annum. (Excise duty had already been imposed on petrol in 1909, but not for commercial users.) The London Motor Cab Proprietors Association were placed in a difficult position: thanks to the inadequate tariff, cab masters were now deprived of the income generated by the extras; the drivers were, of course, delighted but their satisfaction would be short-lived.

Another cause for dissatisfaction among cabmen and cab masters was that there were, by 1910, too many cabs for the work available. Not only were the total numbers higher than in 1903 but motor cabs could do a job more quickly than a horse cab and, in consequence, were ranking up for longer – as much as three hours. Because the Home Secretary refused to increase fares, cab masters promoted private hire business, for which they could set their own rates.

Mann & Overton's and a New Unic

The year 1910 saw some significant changes for Mann & Overton's. In March they vacated

Unic 12/16s in an unidentified cab yard. Edwardian cabmen took great pride in their appearance and the smartness of their cars. (Bryan Goodman)

Victoria Garage and moved to premises at 15 Commercial Road (now Ebury Bridge Road), Pimlico, which they had been converting from stables for the previous two years. In May they took out a formal agreement with Unic Automobiles Ltd, the importers, to sell a new 4-cylinder, 12/16hp cab chassis that was specially designed to meet the Conditions of Fitness. This chassis, which was also sold in France, had a drop in the centre of the side members to allow the body floor to be lower, thus giving the passengers easier access. The importance of Mann & Overton's deal with Unic was highly significant: here was a cab specifically commissioned and designed to meet the Conditions of Fitness.

In December Mann & Overton's acquired showrooms and offices at 10 Lower Grosvenor Place, allowing space at Commercial Road for coachbuilding. Taxicabs would now be Mann & Overton's core business. But J.J. Mann did not live to see this large expansion; he had not attended a board meeting for some time as his health had been deteriorating and in 1908, at the age of 36, he died, leaving the business in

the hands of Tom and Will Overton. The 12/16 would prove solid and reliable and Unic became the most numerous make of London cab, with 2,500 of both models in use by 1911.

Two Big Fleets Merge

The United Motor Cab Company in Walham Green, west London and the General had been cooperating with each other, but in the autumn of 1908 they merged to form the London General Cab Company. One of the main investors in 'the General' was Associated Newspapers Ltd, which held an interest for the whole of the company's life. United ran 224 10/12hp Unics and 250 Darracqs. For a while the two companies continued to run independently, but the Brixton concern bought Unics as well as the ninety-four Darracqs that they had acquired to replace the Renaults, which had been converted into four-seaters but were underpowered for the job. Besides buying in 1908 some 2-cylinder, 8/10hp Charrons, the General bought the new 4-seater, 12/16hp Unics.

Advertisements on Cabs – a Firm Rebuttal

As always, cab proprietors looked for ways of gaining extra revenue and advertising, not permitted on cabs, was one way in which they hoped to make an extra shilling or two. Rex Woods, a solicitor representing a hansom cab proprietor, wrote to Scotland Yard in May 1910, asking for permission to place an advertisement on the back of the splashboard, just below the fare table. He pointed out that it would be of a discreet size, just one-foot square and tasteful. Woods was over-optimistic; trade vehicles have never been permitted to drive through Royal Parks and so the idea of either horse or motor cabs carrying advertisements on the outside, as a trade vehicle might, was out of the question. Chief Inspector Bassom considered his office to be not only the arbiter of public safety but of taste as well and refused the request. Advertisements on London cabs had been banned since 1886. Bassom said in his reply, 'It is always held that the hirer of a hackney carriage (cab) has the exclusive use for the time being of the vehicle therefore he should not be forced to have a vehicle placarded with advertisements . . . until the cab becomes both inside and out nothing but a medium for advertising. The only safe method is to prohibit entirely.'

The Great Petrol Strike

With fares, and thus income, strictly controlled by the government, the control of expenditure by cab proprietors was critical for survival. Not surprisingly, it was one of those expenditures, the price of fuel, that triggered the longest running and most acrimonious industrial actions in the history of the London cab trade, and, along with the dispute over extras, heralded the decline of the big fleets. When the price of petrol rose by 70 per cent to 1s.1d. (5.4p) a gallon, the LMCPA decided that drivers would have to pay the full cost. This was a substantial slice out of their income and the Union threw down the gauntlet. Alfred Smith, the Union's President, declared that, while the Union was happy to abide by the court of arbitration's decision, 'the men cannot bear the huge increase demanded by the LMCPA . . . I warn the masters that the time is coming when it will not be a fight to reduce petrol prices but a fight for free petrol'.

The Times reasoned that, if the cab trade were not to be allowed a concession on fuel costs such as the oil companies gave the bus companies, then a sensible way to resolve the dispute would be to increase fares. But the paper considered that a fare increase would be highly unlikely. Talks between the Union and the LMCPA on 30 December 1912 broke down. The cab masters stood firm and the Union called a strike. It was during this action that the Union underwent a change, taking on a new name, the London and Provincial Licensed Vehicle Workers Union. The strike took place at a time of economic downturn and when the number of cabs, both motor and horse, had peaked and was then declining. Much of the shake-out was within the ranks of the smaller motor cab companies, but the number of hansom cabs was dropping quickly under the inevitable march of modernization. The financial insecurity of the cab masters would be their undoing as the Union held firm. By the end of January the London Improved Cab Company gave in and agreed to charge their drivers 8d. (about 3.5p) a gallon. W & G du Cros accepted the same offer in mid March and by 23 March the LMCPA agreed that their members would charge drivers the same amount. But the real winners were the bus, tram and underground train operators whose cheap fares and regular service retained the passengers they had won during the cabmen's strike. The cab masters lost an estimated £1 million and the Union paid out strike pay amounting to £40,000.

The cab masters demanded a fare increase, but Churchill turned them down. Both cab masters and cabmen suffered. W & G Du Cros cut back on their fleet of cabs, re-bodying 100 cabs to light vans, hiring them out to organizations such as W.H. Smith and the Post Office and converting a section of the Acton works into a parcel depot. Their new company, W & G Express Carriers, became a successful business. The General fared badly, having run up debts of over a £0.5 million against assets of £1.3 million in 1911, and had faced the fuel strike in a weakened position. Nevertheless, the company stuck with its core business. FIAT, the British Motor Cab Company and the London Improved Cab Company closed down. In the short term, cabmen found themselves with no cabs to drive. One of their options was to buy cabs of their own, but PCO regulations put such men in a difficult position. Because the controls on vehicles at this time differed greatly from one make to another, a cabman had to take a driving test for every individual vehicle type that he wanted to drive; unless he took the time to pass a new driving test on a different cab, he would have to buy the cab he had driven from the garage from which he once rented it. To make ends meet, the owner-driver, driving the cab himself with no 'double' partner, was working a seventy-hour week.

The increase in the number of owner-drivers was Mann & Overton's big opportunity and they took it. Close to 4,000 Unic cabs, both 12 and 16hp, left the factory between 1906 and 1913. It was a joint success. By 1914 there was only one company making vehicles for the London cab trade, Unic, and there was only one company selling Unics – Mann & Overton's. If the beginning of 1908 saw vehicle design established for the rest of the century, then the events of 1913–14 set the way that the business of running and selling cabs would be.

World War

In August 1914 many people in Britain believed that the war with Germany would be over by Christmas. For the first few weeks, life in Britain continued much as it had before the declaration. At first, private individuals offered their vehicles to the War Office and a significant number of lorries were accepted, often remaining for some weeks in their original owners' colours. But the war continued as opposing forces dug themselves in for a prolonged fight. In 1915 Lloyd George revealed the frightening shortage of ammunition, caused by the inability of the War Office to understand the scale of the war and to mobilize Britain's industry. He called upon the Asquith government, of which he was Finance Minister, to increase the production of arms. In May 1915 Asquith made Lloyd George Minister of Munitions.

The Origins of the Beardmore

As the war escalated, imports of goods from France ceased. With France fighting for her very existence as a free nation, every part of her industry was dedicated to that effort. Mann & Overton's found themselves with nothing to sell since Unic's Puteaux factory was turned over to the manufacture of munitions. If finding new French vehicles was out of the question, keeping the existing cabs, French or English, on the road during wartime was most difficult. Napier had ceased making the 15hp chassis in 1914, and the impossibility of finding a cab manufacturer, British or French, prompted Francis Luther of the Coupé Cab Company to find someone to make a cab for him.

Luther had held the Austro-Daimler concession for England. He had returned from a visit to Austria in 1913 with the rights to an Austro-Daimler aero engine and sought a British manufacturer for it. He was eventually put in touch with William Beardmore and Co. Ltd, the largest industrial complex in Scotland. Beardmore himself was the chairman and major shareholder in the Scottish car maker Arrol-Johnston, which in 1911 had relocated to a superb new factory at Heathhall, Dumfries. There was spare capacity in its factory to make the aero engine and William Beardmore entered into an agreement to do so. It would, after a protracted development, appear as the 120hp and the 150hp Beardmore engine.

With these connections established, Luther and his business partner George Allsworth approached Beardmore's with the proposition to build a cab for London. Arrol-Johnston's Underwood Works in Paisley lay idle and it was here in August 1915 that the new cab would be built and Superintendent Bassom of Scotland Yard was pleased to advise on its design. But the escalation of the war meant that Beardmore's contribution to the war effort, a major one that already included building over dozen warships for the Royal Navy and the construction of field guns, increased and the Underwood Works were converted to shell production. Work on the taxicab ceased.

The Effects of War on the Cab Trade

The call for troops in 1915 took a great number of Britain's young men, including more than 10,000 cabmen from across the country, keen to fight for King and Country. When conscription was introduced in February 1916 more cabmen still were taken out of the trade. Vast numbers of the young men who went to fight never returned. Many cabs, no longer having drivers, were laid up or sometimes used as free transport for wounded or convalescent servicemen.

W & G du Cros's cab operations, already reduced after 1913, were further affected by the war. In July 1914 they appointed their works manager William Turpin to the board. The works were turned over to munitions production, making 1.5 million shells. For this work, Turpin was awarded the OBE.

In August 1917 the shortage of cabs prompted *Punch* to print the comment, 'The Home Secretary [H.H. Asquith] has determined to put a stop to the practice of whistling for taxicabs in London. It is suggested that he would confer a still greater boon on his fellow-townsmen if he would provide a few more taxis for them not to whistle for.'

The introduction of petrol rationing made life even more difficult for the trade, as cabs were allowed just 1 1/2gal (6.8ltr) per day for singled cabs, that is, those with just one driver, and 2gal (9ltr) for doubled cabs. A number of well-to-do young women became volunteer nurses and a tradition grew at this time for London cabmen to carry them, if in uniform, without accepting any fare. The number of servicemen on leave created some work, although fuel rationing made it hard to cover it. Women who worked in munitions, nicknamed 'canaries' because of the colour the picric acid in explosives turned their skin, began earning considerable amounts of money and they too used cabs when they could be found. For the first time, the PCO allowed women to take the Knowledge of London, but all failed. Inflation made life harder for the cabman who, unable to cover the work either because of petrol rationing or his cab's being laid up because it could not be repaired, was faced with rising food prices. In 1917, the words of the LCDTU's President Alfred Smith, came true: after a six-week strike, cabmen would have their petrol provided free. A second strike in the same year resulted in the abolition of charges to railway stations. But still the Home Secretary refused to increase fares, and by the time of the Armistice London's cab fleet had dropped to 3,821.

3 1919–28 The Seeds of Change

It was the Prime Minister David Lloyd George who promised that Britain would be 'a land fit for heroes to live in'. It was to this promise that the armed forces came home, from the mud of Flanders, the sand and flies of the Middle East and from the open seas. And for a time, Britain's economy promised much. If £7 million a day could be found to fight the war, then a prosperous peace was a certainty. But that war had brought Britain to her knees financially and within three years the dream had turned into a nightmare. In 1921 the economy collapsed and millions were thrown out of work. Ex-servicemen, no longer heroes now that they were without their uniforms, made up the dole queues and the lines at soup kitchens to took to selling matches on street corners. The limbless and the blind were forced to beg.

Cabmen who had signed up for the duration at least had the prospect of employment on return, but the war had decimated London's cab fleet. Both motor cabs and cab horses had been commandeered by the Army and by 1918 the numbers of cabs licensed had dropped from 8,651 to barely 5,000. Cabmen demobbed after the war who were expecting to find cabs to work were bitterly disap-

Edwardian cabs were still prevalent after The Great War. This picture of one of the General's old Renaults was taken at Egham, Surrey in the early 1920s. (Author's collection)

pointed, especially when they discovered that some cab masters sought to make money out of the cabmen in their time of need by selling off reconditioned, pre-war cabs at highly inflated prices. Cab unions had complained that there were some 500 to 600 cabs lying idle because they did not comply with the 10in (25cm) ground clearance demanded by the Conditions of Fitness. It is possible that some of these were the Renaults that had caused such controversy back in 1906. Certainly the numbers were coincidental, but although a demand by the unions that the 10in ground clearance be relaxed was met by the PCO, the cabs were not offered immediately for sale. Ford offered a prototype, two-seat cab based on the Model T; it would have been a cheap cab to buy, but Scotland Yard turned it down. The reason for this is not on record, but the Ford had transverse-leaf front suspension, which had already been banned for cabs by the PCO. One must wonder how different the future of the trade might have been if the Ford cab been passed.

Through the Depression of the 1920s, car companies would concentrate on trying to survive in the potentially far bigger and much more lucrative private and commercial markets. There must have been some anticipation among interested manufacturers that the Conditions of Fitness would be amended to keep pace with the advance in car design, but Bassom would not budge. There would be no change to his firm rules on ground clearance and turning circle. Whatever makes might have been presented for approval, Bassom knew that there was one make from a solid and highly regarded company that had invested heavily and given the utmost commitment to the development of a new cab – Beardmore.

The Beardmore Appears

The cab that had begun development in 1915 at Arrol-Johnston's was now made ready for production under the Beardmore name, and it was made known that the cab was the first to

Antiquated as it may look compared with cars of the 1920, this 12/16 Unic would still be no more than ten years old by 1920 and little different from the post-war model that Mann & Overton's were to sell. (Bryan Goodman)

be developed in conjunction with Scotland Yard. It received type approval in September 1919 and was announced at the London Commercial Motor Exhibition that year. Its arrival was not before time.

The Beardmore's introductory price of £795 highlighted the extreme inflation brought about as a result of the war. It was quickly brought down to £675, but even this was about twice the price of a suburban house. In 1914 the Unic 12/16hp had cost £405. The Beardmore was heavily built and, because of the Conditions of Fitness, somewhat old-fashioned looking, but its quality and modern technical specification were claimed to be justification for its higher than average cost. Beardmore's advertising slogan was 'For Comfort and Speed, It's All You Need'.

Its pressed steel chassis (Beardmore were pioneers in this field) had a dropped section adjacent to the passenger doors to allow for easy access and the front of the frame was steeply stepped in to allow for the tight lock. Its monobloc, five-bearing, sidevalve engine was the work of G.W.A. Brown, who had

joined Arrol-Johnston from Humber's Beeston factory when it closed in 1908.

The engine had a detachable head for easy decarbonizing and a water pump. The four-speed gate change gearbox was separate from the engine to make the replacement of the leather cone clutch a simple job, and the foot brake operated on the transmission. Each engine was run in at the works on coal gas by the use of a special carburettor, then the completed chassis were road-tested before the bodies were fitted. Beardmore owners could be sure of the cab's reliability and serviceability from day one.

There was a choice of two body styles: the full- or the three-quarter landaulette, built in-house, of ash. All the body parts were built on jigs and sold as separate sections to allow quick replacement with minimal fitting after an accident. The cab was sold from Beardmore's own dealership in Great Portland Street, London and serviced at their depot in Hendon, north London. A fleet of 2,000 went into service with Francis Luther's Coupé Cab Company and these numbers helped it

When it was built, the MkI Beardmore received sixteen coats of paint and varnish and was finished in the standard coach green. It was a short vehicle, with a wheelbase of just 8ft 7in (2.6m) to comply with the maximum permissible length of 14ft (4.3m). (Vintage Taxi Spares)

Beardmore Mk1 Technical Specifications			
Engine	4-cylinder water cooled sidevalve, monobloc cylinders, detachable head, separate alloy crank case and sump, five-bearing crank	**Transmission**	four-speed manual, separate from engine, right-hand gate change
		Clutch	cone
		Brakes	footbrake on transmission, handbrake on rear wheels
Capacity	2388cc		
Bore and stroke	80mm × 120mm (3.15in × 4.7in)	**Front suspension**	half-elliptical
Wheelbase	8ft 4in (2.54m)	**Rear suspension**	three-quarter elliptical
Track	4ft 6in (1.4m)	**Body (PCO specification)**	option of full- or three-quarter landaulet

to become the most numerous cab model in the capital. Despite its high initial cost, it was a cab much respected by mushers, who christened it 'the Rolls-Royce of cabs' and by 1923 the total number of cabs had risen, thanks largely to the Beardmore's introduction, to 7,283.

Other Makes

There were others who entered, or re-entered the market, some hopeful of relaxed Conditions of Fitness. One re-entry was FIAT, who presented the model IT cab at the 1920 Commercial Motor Show. It was built on the 1912 Tipo Zero chassis, with an 1847cc sidevalve engine. This was replaced in Italy by more modern vehicles, none of which complied with the Conditions of Fitness, but Fiat, nor apparently anyone else, were prepared to adapt them and FIAT cabs soon disappeared from London. Also at Olympia in 1920 were Associated Motors Ltd, who exhibited their AML. This was a cab of their own manufacture, having a proprietary French Chapuis Dornier engine of 2297cc. Like the Beardmore, it had a dropped frame but it did not materialize.

The S.K.A.M. and the Kingsway

In March 1921 a completely new cab, the S.K.A.M., was announced. It was produced by Skam Motors of Uxbridge Road, west London. One must comment on what would be, today, an unfortunate choice of name, but a prototype received approval and covered 7,000 working miles (11,300km). The engine was a proprietary 4-cylinder, sidevalve Dorman of 2613cc, rated at 16hp, with a constant mesh, four-speed Dux gearbox. Separate from the engine, it was designed and built by the British Transmission Co. Ltd of Portsmouth Street, off Kingsway, London, and of a similar design to that of the Whippet light tank. The chassis was of pressed steel with, as *Commercial Motor* put it, 'none of those sharp bends that weaken the average taxicab frame'. Cantilever rear springing was chosen to give a comfortable ride and to eliminate any rear overhang to prevent street urchins cadging a ride by hanging on the back. There was only one grease point on the cab, on the fan bearing; all the suspension bushes were oilless graphite and bronze. The bare chassis was to be made available, but a three-quarter landaulette body was offered, the hood of which was designed to fold down without projecting behind the cab.

It was over a year, in November 1922, before the new cab was heard of again. It would now be called the Kingsway and the British Transmission Company would be responsible for it. The body had been updated with a full height radiator, level with a scuttle. The name S.K.A.M. seemed to have disap-

Associated Motors Ltd produced the AML cab, one of several makes that never went into production. (Chris Hodge Commercials)

Some cabs were designed with London in mind, but never ran in the capital. Such a vehicle was Wolseley; this was introduced in 1923 and was powered by a 4-cylinder, 14hp side-valve engine. Some were sold to the provinces. (Norman Painting)

peared without trace. So would the cab: priced at £720, just as the economy had slumped, this was not surprising.

Mann & Overton and the 'Gate' Unic

As soon as they could, Unic resumed production of an updated version of their pre-war cab. Apart from a gate-change gearbox and a modern radiator, it was the same Edwardian cab that Mann & Overton's had commissioned in 1910, but owing to the McKenna Duties that were levied on luxury imported goods, it was very expensive. Mann & Overton's had moved from Pimlico to new premises in Battersea Bridge Road, and with the move they ended body manufacture. It is possible that they did not have sufficient space or felt that they should no longer be in this side of the business. It is also possible that the body and its manufacturing rights were sold to Dyer & Holton of Effra Road, at the southern end of Brixton. Certainly the body of the post-war Unic was similar to that of the pre-war cab. An arrangement of this nature would keep Mann & Overton's supplied and would allow others to use the body.

Mepward

The Mepward, made by Mepstead and Hayward of Pentonville, north London, was introduced in 1920, just before the collapse of the post-war boom in the economy. Only twelve were believed to have been made and it was, by most accounts, a very poor cab. It was powered by a 2178cc, 4-cylinder, side-valve engine, possibly a Dorman, and its all-wood body made it slow and heavy to drive. The company that ran the cabs foundered. Hayward disappeared from view under, legend has it, shameful circumstances, but Ernest Mepstead continued in the motor business and we shall encounter his name later.

Citroën

In 1923 London car dealer Maxwell Monson introduced the Citroën cab from his premises in Brook Green, Hammersmith. Citroën was a new make to its native France. Like William Beardmore, André Citroën made artillery shells during the Great War. When peace came, his factory at the Quai de Javel, Paris, was turned over to the manufacture of cars. But, unlike the Beardmore, he made a cheap

47

car, claiming, to much ridicule, that he would make one hundred a day. By 1923 he was making more than double that number. From the start, Citroën exported his cars and his Type A tourer sold in Britain for £395. The Type A was even cheaper in France, where it was adopted in 1921 as a taxicab.

It was a modified 11.4 Type B chassis that Monson introduced as a cab to London in 1923. At £540 it was substantially more expensive than the private car, but that was because of its chassis modifications. Its 8ft 1 7/8in (2.49m) wheelbase was shorter than the car's and the steering was adapted by placing the drop arm inside the chassis instead of outside, setting the drag link at an oblique angle to the frame. The suspension was the same as the car's, with quarter-elliptical springs, two leading at the front and trailing doubles at the rear. Included in the price were electric headlamps, the first to be offered on a London cab. At 1453cc, its 4-cylinder, side-valve engine was noticeably smaller than its competitors' and this undoubtedly helped its fuel consumption. The gearbox was a three-speed manual crash box, with a single dry-plate clutch and a heavy-duty rear axle. The disc wheels were much bigger than those on the standard Citroën. Besides being required for the specially approved taxi tyres, they also helped to create the regulation 10in (25.4cm) ground clearance.

The body came from Brixton coach-builders Dyer & Holton. Although Monson sold cabs on hire purchase to mushers and provided driver training and 'wangle' (i.e. driving test) cabs, it was the London General Cab Company that were the biggest fleet purchasers. Their old pre-war Unics and Renaults were well overdue for replacement and the £625 price of the 'gate' Unic was much more than the General were prepared to pay. The Citroën cab provided the ideal solution, and by 1928 the General had acquired 220 examples.

W & G Try Again

W & G were still running pre-war Panhards and Napiers and were in a difficult financial position. Their Acton premises were acquired in 1920 by A. Darracq & Co. (1905) Ltd, who used half the building space to make bodies for Talbot and Darracq chassis. Much of the business conducted there was on behalf of the consortium of Sunbeam, Talbot and Darracq, collectively known as STD. The cab business was transferred to a subsidiary company, Turpin Engineering Co. Ltd, and the STD connection would bring some hope for the new cabs that the W & G organization badly needed. An announcement in *Commercial Motor*, 22 August 1922, said,

The expensive and antiquated 12/16 Unic was only distinguishable from the pre-war model by the Vee-shaped radiator and the steel-panelled body. (Vintage Taxi Spares)

Solid Michelin disc wheels distinguished the Citroën 11.4. As well as having a small engine, its wheelbase was also short. (Jamie Borwick)

The Citroën 11.4 came with electric lights, despite the fact that the PCO frowned on all lamps that might dazzle other road users. Nevertheless, all were fitted with oil sidelights to save the battery. (Malcolm Bobbit)

The W & G cab reappears: The W & G taxicab is again to be placed on the market. The chassis of the new model has been designed by Mr L. Coatalen. The chassis only, or the complete vehicle, will be sold as customers may require, whilst the price will be competitive.

Louis Coatalen was Sunbeam's chief designer and he had produced some memorable cars. He had already become acquainted with the PCO when he was employed by his future father-in-law William Hillman to design the Hillman-Coatalen cab. The chassis of the cab, made in Paris, was a Talbot-Darracq Model DC, with a 1597cc, 4-cylinder engine. W & G or one of their associates was to supply the body if required. However, it did not go beyond the preliminary stages.

The Yellow Cab

A better and cheaper option, W & G decided, was to buy American, from a man whose name would become a legend in the car rental world, John Hertz. Hertz went into the taxicab business in Chicago in 1910, running cars that the dealers he worked for had acquired as trade-ins but could not sell on. After spending some time studying the London cab trade, Hertz built his first cabs in 1915. He called them Yellow Cabs, using them in his own fleet and selling them to others across the USA and Canada. After the war he established an assembly plant in Orillia, Ontario, a small town, 55 miles (89km) north of Toronto, to serve the Canadian market and to avoid McKenna duties when selling to prospective customers in the British Empire.

The London version of the Yellow Cab was introduced at the 1923 Commercial Motor Exhibition at Olympia. It was a specially adapted version of the American cab, most likely the '03' model, fitted with a 2.25-litre, Continental 4-cylinder, sidevalve engine and a Brown-Lipe three-speed manual gearbox. There was some controversy over it, not least because of an advertisement that appeared in *Steering Wheel* stating that Yellow Cab were

Citroën 11.4 Technical Specifications

Engine	4-cylinder, water-cooled, side-valve, monobloc cylinders, detachable head, three-bearing crank	**Transmission**	three-speed manual, centre change
		Brakes	handbrake on transmission, foot-brake on rear wheels
Capacity	1453cc		
Bore and stroke	68mm × 100mm (2.7in × 3.9in)	**Front suspension**	leading quarter-elliptical springs
Wheelbase	8ft 1 7/8in (2.49m)	**Rear suspension**	trailing quarter-elliptical springs

The Canadian-built Yellow Cab was operated and sold by the W & G subsidiary Turpin Engineering. Shown here are the first nine cabs of the total of 100 built. (National Motor Museum)

'manufacturers and operators' and the cab masters feared a big American invasion. Yellow Cab certainly operated cabs in America but the British subsidiary, The Yellow Cab Manufacturing Company of England Ltd, had no intention of doing the same in Britain, preferring to sell to cab masters and mushers alike. The advertised price was £590, complete with body, or £100 down and the rest paid over five years, although the first examples shipped over were complete vehicles.

W & G's subsidiary Turpin Engineering bought 120 Yellow Cab chassis in early 1924 and fitted them with bodies not unlike their American counterparts, although the London cabs were on a 99in (2.5m) wheelbase compared to the American's 109in (2.8m). Turpin would not only be a proprietor, but an agent, selling the cab to mushers, who ran small fleets under contract. Hertz had also gone into truck and bus manufacture and this operation attracted the attention of the American giant General Motors. In 1925 they bought Hertz's manufacturing business, including the cabs. Shortly after, the delivery of Yellow Cabs to London ceased.

The Death of Arthur Bassom

Despite the fact that car design had moved on considerably since the Conditions of Fitness were introduced in 1906, the PCO made no attempt to update the rules in the immediate post-war years. In 1924 Superintendent Bassom died while still a serving police officer. He was not replaced immediately, and where there might have been changes to the Conditions of Fitness to take into account progress in the design and development of the motor car, there would now be none. Consequently, any interested parties who had expected a change soon turned their backs on London.

The Beardmore Super

Despite the depressed economic climate and the troubles that were besetting Beardmore's,

demand for the MkI cab was steady, but it was now looking almost as antiquated as the survivors of the pre-war years. It was time for a replacement and in the spring of 1925 it arrived. It was simply called the MkII 'Super' and was based on the chassis of a new 30cwt truck, introduced in 1923 by the works manager of the Underwood factory in Paisley, B. Angus Shaw.

The side members of the 9ft (2.74m) wheelbase chassis were of the new 'double drop' design, obviating the dip in the chassis by the passenger doors. There was a more modern radiator, and the antique ribbed body was replaced by an up to date, steel panelled, three-quarter landaulet, finished in a choice of colours: green, maroon or blue. The same 4-cylinder, sidevalve engine and the separate four-speed gate-change gearbox were carried over, but the brakes were new. Although still two-wheel, both the hand and the foot brake

In 1923 the MKI Beardmore's body was modified slightly, with its straight-topped, front wings replaced by the more rounded ones fitted to the light van that shared the cab's chassis. The full landaulette body was dropped, leaving just the three-quarter type available. Although electric lighting was available, most cab proprietors preferred oil lamps. (Vintage Taxi Spares)

operated on the rear drums, with two separate sets of shoes. Sankey pressed steel artillery-type replaced the wooden artillery wheels of the MkI and once more Brolt electric lighting was offered as an optional extra. Again the dead hand of the PCO affected the specification as 'dazzling' headlights were not permitted.

Beardmore also made a high quality, if expensive, 12hp car, but it was a poor seller. The Anniesland factory that made it was closed and a new 14/40 car for the private hire market was built at Paisley. Although Paisley also was losing money, the taxicab business was a vital one to preserve. After all, Beardmore was the only British-owned cab maker. In 1925 the Treasury guaranteed a £350,000 loan from the Trade Facilities Act Advisory Committee, on the condition that the Underwood works were run as a separate entity from other parts of the Beardmore organization. The managing director Francis Luther and his fellow director

The MkII Beardmore used a totally new chassis, radiator and body while retaining the original engine; also new were the steel artillery wheels. (Vintage Taxi Spares)

Beardmore MkII Technical Specifications

Engine	4-cylinder, water-cooled sidevalve, monobloc cylinders, detachable head, separate alloy crank case and sump, five-bearing crank	**Transmission**	four-speed manual, separate from engine, right-hand gate change
		Clutch	cone
		Brakes	footbrake and handbrake on rear wheels
Capacity	2388cc		
Bore and stroke	80mm × 120mm (3.15in × 4.7in)	**Suspension**	half-elliptical springs on front and rear
Wheelbase	9ft 0in (2.74m)	**Body (PCO**	three-quarter landaulet, finished
Track	4ft 7in (1.40m)	**specification)**	in green, blue or red

George Allsworth, along with John Gird-wood, Beardmore's company secretary, formed Beardmore Taxicabs Ltd to sell cabs and Beardmore (Paisley) Ltd to finance sales. The new organization then leased the Underwood works from William Beardmore & Co., enabling them to make the Super with some degree of financial security.

William Watson and the Hayes Cab

William Watson's name occurs many times in the motoring history of first half of the twentieth century. He won the 1908 Isle of Man Tourist Trophy race and he was a close friend of William Morris, establishing, in his native Liverpool, one of the first Morris dealerships. In 1925 he entered the London cab trade with an American/British hybrid, the Hayes. The chassis was built by the Hayes Co., a substantial wheel and motor component manufacturer in Ontario, to avoid paying the McKenna Duties. The cab featured a Continental engine of 2.5 litres. At £425 it was the cheapest on the market and, by contemporary accounts, a very good cab. However, it disappeared in 1928, most probably because Hayes merged with Kelsey and concentrated on wheel manufacture.

The 'Jixi'

If Bassom's death had created a hiatus in the progress of the motor cab in London, then a much greater danger was the proposed introduction of two-seat cabs. These, which were planned to operate at a lower tariff, were the idea of Sir William Joynson-Hicks, the Home Secretary in the Conservative government of Stanley Baldwin, elected in November 1924. 'Jix', as he was known, was reputed to be an unpopular and self-opinionated man and had been company solicitor to the London General Omnibus Company when his father Henry Hicks had been chairman. With this background and his new position as supremo of the Metropolitan Police and thus head of the PCO (and at the time responsible for London's buses as well as taxicabs), Jix thought to revolutionize London's public transport. He started by setting up a committee to investigate the possibilities of a two-seater cab to operate at a lower fare.

Jix imposed the plan upon London against great opposition from the trade. Similar vehicles – they would be called 'Jixis' in London – had appeared in the provinces, following unsuccessful attempts to use motorcycle combination taxicabs. A parliamentary committee was set up in July 1925 to investigate the matter and the cab trade's Joint Trade Committee (JTC) made strong representations to it. Already, the JTC said, cabs were ranking for hours on end; they had been demanding cabs that were cheaper to buy and to run but that they should be four-seat vehicles, not two-seaters and run on a higher tariff. Cabmen and cab masters had invested in expensive four-seat cabs and their investment would be lost

*Despite there being several makers interested in producing 2-seater cabs, little photographic evidence survives of any offerings. This picture of a Berliet is a rare exception. (*Taxi *newspaper)*

if the Jixi were to become numerous. The committee were doubtful of the practicality of having different cabs with different fare structures and working alongside each other on the same rank, but this gave the JTC only slight cause for hope.

The paradox was that both the trade and the public had made their choice between two-

---

Beardmore's Industrial Empire

The Beardmore heavy engineering concern was Scotland's largest. The Parkhead Forge, the centrepiece of the whole business, dated from 1836. In 1877 William Beardmore inherited joint control of it with his Uncle Isaac when his father died, and, on Isaac's retirement, took complete control. A growth in warship building prompted Beardmore to start making armour plate and a site at Dalmuir was bought to build battleships. Beardmore part-financed Ernest Shackleton's Antarctic expedition in 1908 and the Beardmore Glacier on that continent was named in his honour. For his efforts in the field of shipbuilding, Beardmore was created a baronet in 1914.

Beardmore, along with many other companies, turned to arms manufacture in the Great War. In 1915, to make artillery shells, Beardmore's purchased Arrol-Johnston's Underwood Works at Paisley, the Victoria Ironworks at Airdrie and Lidgerwood's Speedwell Works at Coatbridge, where they also built aero engines. Contracts were given to armament manufacturers by the government, but there was a price to pay for the war profits – all factories that were specially acquired for the arms business had to be turned over to peacetime manufacture. Sir William Beardmore saw the field of transport as a new and exciting one, he invested in everything from merchant ships and marine engines and from aero engines to airships – huge Beardmore aero engines were to power the ill-fated R34 airship on its record-breaking flight over the Atlantic – to aircraft and railway locomotives, cars, trucks, buses, motorcycles and, of course, taxicabs.

For his contribution to the war effort was given the title Lord Invernairn in 1921. But, although he was a very good engineer, he had no formal training in business management. When almost none of his post-war products sold enough to show a profit, his preferred method of borrowing and reinvesting to get himself out of trouble failed. Interest rates were the highest in living memory and Beardmore could not service his debts. When in 1929 the financial situation reached crisis point, the government called in the Bank of England. The Bank's Governor, Montague Norman, asked for Invernairn's resignation. Speaking of his business abilities, Norman described him as 'a brilliant amateur'. Invernairn retired and took no further part in the running of his business empire. He lived out his days at his country home, Flichity House, near Loch Ness, where, in 1936, he died, aged 79.

Sir William Beardmore, later Lord Invernairn (Author's collection)

---

and four-seat cabs almost two decades previously, when motor vehicle chassis became powerful enough to carry four-seat cab bodies. But in August 1925 the committee reported in favour of two-seat cabs and a two-tier tariff. Jix warned the JTC that lower fares would be imposed if the two-seater cab were not accepted and the JTC had to concede. Specific Conditions of Fitness were prepared for the new cabs, which allowed a lower ground clearance of 8in (20cm), a narrower track of 48in (1.22m) and required smaller wheels and tyres. A smaller passenger compartment was specified but the driver's compartment was the same as for four-seaters. Fares were set at 9d. (3.75p) flagfall and 9d. per mile thereafter and was to come into force on 1 May 1927.

One voice had spoken wholly in favour of two-seat cabs, that of R.W. Owen, who was a director of White, Holmes & Co., previously known as the National Cab Company (1922) Ltd. This was hardly surprising. White, Holmes & Co. had already built a two-seat cab, the KRC. It took its name from its designers Kingston, Richardson and Crutchley, who were making a light sports car under the same name. The cab was presented to the PCO a full month before the committee reported its findings and it was put on test as soon as the report, which found in favour of the 'Jixi' was published.

Other makes came forward. One was the Trojan, whose popular if crude, two-stroke car formed the base. From France came a 12hp Berliet, which gained approval in March 1927. Berliet planned to make 200 but failed to do so. There was an entrant expected from Beardmore, but that too did not appear. Nor, after all the publicity, did the KRC. White, Holmes & Co. claimed that the General Strike had affected the motor industry, rendering them unable to manufacture the cab in quantity.

Now the cab trade, having endured the 1926 General Strike on top of an economic depression, suffered another blow. In April 1927 Jix changed his mind and rescinded the Order that would have brought in two-seat cabs. He also announced a new lower tariff, even lower than that set for the Jixi. On top of this, the trade were dismayed to discover that he had not actually banned two-seat cabs, he allowed them, but by default required that they comply with the Conditions of Fitness for four-seat cabs and run on the same tariff. Cab trade representatives withdrew their support for the lower tariff, claiming a complete breach of faith. After much argument it was agreed that the new fares would be tried for an experimental period, but the trade knew the effect would be dire. Inflation had risen by 55 per cent since the end of the war. The price of cabs had doubled, but fares had risen only once, in 1920 by 17 per cent. Cab masters and cabmen were facing bankruptcy and, within a month, the JTC asked Jix to reconsider his decision. He held firm. The cab trade were told to make the best of what they had been given.

No More Citroëns

The Citroën cab was cheap – £325 by 1926 – but it was now in limited supply. The chassis was made in Paris but the car on which it was based was nearing the end of its production life. To get around the McKenna duties when selling in Britain, Citroën had built a new factory at Slough, which started building the latest model, the steel-bodied 13/30 in late 1926. A special seven-passenger model was to be introduced and it would be used in Paris as a cab. It was offered to British provincial cab operators but Citroën was either not able or not willing to provide a modified version of the 13/30 chassis for the London trade.

The Conditions of Fitness Under Review

It may have been a point of honour that Superintendent Bassom, having encouraged Beardmore to develop their first cab, was loath to pull the rug from under them by letting more modern designs in until they had recouped their investment. The same might be said about Mann & Overton's and the 'Gate' Unic. But whatever Bassom's reasoning, the Conditions of Fitness had remained unchanged during the last years of his life.

The simplest and most effective way of keeping passenger numbers and profits up and fares at an economical level was to provide cheaper, four-seat cabs. This was the message delivered to the Home Secretary Sir William Joynson-Hicks, by a rather insidious source, British fascist Sir Oswald Moseley of the Unionist Party, who had sided with the cab trade (or at least with its non-Jewish membership); 'Jix' agreed with his Fascist ally and on 5 July 1927 wrote to the Commissioner of Police, Sir William Horwood, saying, 'At the present tariff an owner driver was quite unable to meet the large instalments as they became due on his cab.' Sir William replied, 'I fancy you will find that the inflated cost of our present taxicab is maintained by the ring of manufacturers, who keep the cost up for their own financial gain, and who, when attacked, use "the requirements of Scotland Yard" as an excuse.' However, some things were considered sacred at all levels and he went on, 'One of the things I shall direct Supt Claro (the new head at the PCO) to press for is the retention of the present "lock" of the taxicab.'

Joynson-Hicks set up a technical committee under Capt Douglas Hacking, MP, the Parliamentary Secretary of State at the Home Office, to 'consider how far the present cost of motor cabs in London is affected by these conditions or other circumstances, and to advise whether any alteration in these condi-

tions is desirable'. Besides Hacking, the committee was composed of Superintendent Claro of the PCO, and three engineers, E.S. Perrin, BSc, AM Inst CE, of the Ministry of Transport, H.C. Clarke, AMI Mech.E and G.W. Watson, MI Mech.E, MIAE. Claro's duties with the committee were in addition to the work he undoubtedly had to do when, in the same year, the PCO moved from Scotland Yard to a new building in Lambeth Road.

The Committee's initial findings were a damning indictment of both the lack of care given to the trade by the government and of Jix's capricious adventure with two-seater cabs; the episode of the Jixis caused anyone who may have been interested in building a cab for London to shy away. Jix should have been in touch with what was happening on London's streets and in the rest of the country instead of driving the cab trade up a blind alley. In 1927 there were four makes available, but the situation was worse than this suggests. The Beardmore MkII was readily available but expensive; Unic had stockpiled a quantity of chassis for about a year's sales after production ended in 1926, but these guaranteed only a limited supply and the cab was highly expensive; the Hayes was listed but almost unobtainable; and the Citroën was in limited supply, although chassis had been stockpiled.

But by far the biggest factor for the committee to take into account was that car design had outrun the Conditions of Fitness and the market was too small to interest most big makers in Britain in making a specialist vehicle. The answer to the problem seemed to be to bring back the big boys, who had reduced car prices by a considerable amount due to improved production methods. But how could they achieve it? The committee contacted the Society of Motor Manufacturers and Traders to ask them to find whether any manufacturers were interested. Three companies responded, but only Miles Thomas of Morris and Ted Grinham of Humber attended, their

New Cabs Licensed in London during the Early 1920s

Year	Number
1920	211
1921	506
1922	793
1923	973
1924	959
1925	287
1926	383

In 1927 there were approximately 8,000 cabs licensed in London. The figures show how dramatically the numbers increased in the early 1920s when the Beardmore Mk1 and the Citroën were introduced. They also show how those numbers fell, as a result of both the depressed state of the economy and the deep uncertainty surrounding the 'Jixi' fiasco.

presence indicating a real interest. Humber had introduced the excellent 14/40 but it cost £575. Grinham was not, it seems, committed to the idea, reckoning that they could not make a cab for under £600, a serious blow to the PCO's aspirations of seeing cheaper cabs. Morris had a new Oxford that sold for £240 in saloon form. Thomas reckoned that they might be able to produce a cab on a production chassis that sold for around £335. But both Thomas and Grinham agreed that the ground clearance, the turning circle and the fuel-tank location were the main obstacles to their producing a suitable vehicle for the London market.

The committee finally agreed to lower the ground clearance to 7in (18cm) and allowed the relocation of the fuel tank to a position under the bonnet. A rear location would not be permitted. The committee were split over the issue of the turning circle and the final report declared this, as minority reports by Claro (who went on record as saying that 'the mobility of the cab was its greatest asset') and Clark opposed the change. Advertising on the inside of cabs was also allowed. The new Conditions of Fitness would take effect from 30 April 1928.

4 1929–39 Mann & Overton Supreme

Britain came out of the depression of the 1920s in poor shape. The 1930s brought some improvement, albeit patchy. The cab trade would see a revival of its fortunes and also see Mann & Overton's take an unassailable market lead with a marque that had already been licensed for cab work: Austin. But while the old Conditions of Fitness were still in force, two new cabs were being prepared.

The first was the Morris-Commercial G-Type from the giant Nuffield Organization, but it was not the result of a decision made within Nuffield, but the suggestion of George Kenning, a Morris dealer and proprietor of the International Cab Company of Leeds. Kenning proposed that the unsuccessful

Morris Empire Oxford would make a good taxi. William Morris had seen what he had considered to be potential markets in the British Empire and his truck company, Morris-Commercial, designed the Empire Oxford, based on a shortened 30cwt (1,524kg) van chassis. Unfortunately, it was too expensive in the face of competition from cheap American makes, which were built in Canada to avoid paying the punitive McKenna Duties.

The cab took its 'International' name from Kenning's cab company. Produced alongside GPO vehicles at the giant Morris-Commercial plant at Soho, Birmingham, the first 840 were converted from unsold Empire Oxfords, using narrower axles to meet the

A 1929 Morris G-Type International in its original form, with its driver, 'French' Smithy. This cab was operated out of the Devonian Garage in Carthew Road, Hammersmith. Along with most others it was later fitted with headlights front bumpers and four-wheel brakes. (LVTA Archive)

A Morris-Commercial G-Type with a two-seater 'Cape' body. This body, pictured with its sliding doors held open, was designed in 1929 by a South African W. Gowan. Because of its reduced seating capacity and the complication of its doors, it was not popular. In 1933 twenty Austins were fitted with similar bodies. (Bryan Goodman)

PCO's maximum specified track. The engine was the 30cwt truck's 2.5-litre sidevalve and an overhead worm drive rear axle helped to achieve the 10in (25cm) ground clearance. Originally, the cab was sold without headlights, but later a full lighting system was fitted. The rear brakes were fitted with two sets of shoes, but later models were fitted with four-wheel brakes when the new Conditions of Fitness came into force.

The cab appeared in January 1929. The only body was a three-quarter landaulet, finished in brown and built in-house at Morris Bodies in Cowley. A further 860 cabs were built, making a total of 1,700. George Kenning was the first dealer to sell the cab, but soon London sales were transferred to William Watson, who, shortly after acquiring the dealership, moved from Eccleston Place, Victoria into new

premises on Grosvenor Road, close to Chelsea Bridge. The price of the cab in the capital was a highly competitive £377.10s. or £465 on hire purchase, with a £50 deposit and 50s. (£2.50) per week for four years. Very shortly after, the cash price was raised to £395.

A New Citroën

The second new cab was a Citroën and it came from the London General. The 11.4hp Citroëns that the General had bought during the 1920s were ageing. The Paris factory had ceased to make its base model and the General was not prepared to pay the cost of the MkII Beardmore or the Unic. To meet the requirement for a new cab, the General had their chief engineer P. Geldard design their own cabs with a longer wheelbase chassis. To this

When the London General built their own Citroën cabs they first tried stretching the bodies from the original 11.4hp models to fit. As can be seen from this picture, the result was, to say the least, inelegant. (Vintage Taxi Spares)

The London General Cab Co.'s 13hp Citroën. Its disc wheels carried the new 30in × 5in balloon tyres as opposed to the 11.4 Citroën's tall and skinny 815 × 105 tyres. (Vintage Taxi Spares)

he fitted the suspension and axles, radiator and bonnet from the old 11.4hp cabs, the 1.6-litre sidevalve engine from the new Citroën C4 and 18in disc wheels. The old Citroën body was tried on the new chassis but it made an ungainly, top-heavy vehicle and so it was cut down, fitted with a fixed head and covered in fabric. The remainder of the old bodies were put into storage.

The Beardmore Hyper

Besides cabs, Beardmore made a high-quality but expensive 12hp passenger car. It had sold poorly and the Anniesland factory that made it closed in 1926. However, it was from this car chassis that Beardmore developed a chassis they could use to build a cab to meet the new regulations. It was possibly the chassis that

The Beardmore Hyper was a much more compact cab than the MkII. It came complete with electric lights; it was also the first London cab to be fitted with four-wheel brakes. The PCO had earlier not allowed them because they believed that they would encourage fast driving and jolt passengers. (Bryan Goodman)

they had intended for their 'Jixi', though no records exist to establish this. When Anniesland closed, a new 14/40 car began production at Paisley, based on the 12hp car chassis. This was updated a year later as the 16/40, aimed squarely at the private hire market. Beardmore's brochure for the new cab, the MkIII, stated, 'The impression that . . . any reasonably good motor chassis . . . is suitable for a taxicab . . . is very far from being the case.' However, close comparison of the MkIII's 9ft (2.7m) wheelbase chassis with an illustration of that of the 16/40 indicates that it was a shorter version.

The more compact MkIII was christened the Hyper. The engine was a new, cast iron, 4-cylinder sidevalve unit, unique to the cab. It had a detachable head, its cylinder block was integral with the crankcase and it had an elec-

tric self-starter. At 1954cc it was smaller than the old engine, but it was more powerful and returned a fuel consumption of over 26mpg (10.9ltr/100km). Much of the improvement was due to good inlet port design, which also increased the time between decoking. It is possible that it was a smaller bore, cast iron version of the 16/40 engine, but insufficient information exists to confirm this. Fuel consumption was further improved by reducing the cab's weight to 25cwt (1,270kg). The MkII's separate, four-speed, gate-change gearbox was carried over so that the clutch, now a single-plate Ferodo, could be changed easily. This cab was the first to be licensed in London with four-wheel brakes and earned the nickname of the 'Farthing Cab', possibly because it was so economical to run, the farthing (1/4d.) then being the smallest coin of the realm.

United Motors Ltd and the Unic KF1

Mann & Overton's continued to hold the concession to sell Unic commercial vehicles and cars after the Great War, but in 1922 this was lost to United Motors Ltd of north-west London. The managing director of this company was Ernest Mepstead, late of the ill-fated Mepward concern. Since production of the Unic cab chassis had ceased in 1926 and Unic had ceased to supply Mann & Overton's, so Mepstead was free to talk to them about cabs. In the 1920s Unic made the 11cv Type L, with a 1993cc sidevalve engine. Mepstead decided that this would make a good base for a cab and so he formed a new company, Unic Motors (1928) Ltd, to build it. He would call the cab the KF1. Imported chassis were modified to meet the Conditions of Fitness and fitted with bodies by Jones and Goode and Cooper and, later Gardner Motors of Willesden. The engine, however, was unreliable and sales of the cab were poor, probably fewer than a hundred in four years of production. Sales were not helped by the cab's price of £575, 'fully equipped', according to a letter sent by United Motors to the Motor Cab Owner-Drivers' Gazette. Mepstead's own Fulham Garage at 296/298 Wandsworth Bridge Road ran more than seventy, the bulk of the production run. Although few survived the Second World War, the last was taken out of service in the early 1950s.

Major Changes Ahead

Although the amendments to the Conditions of Fitness had achieved the results the PCO had wanted, it is significant that the Morris-Commercial, the new Citroën and the KF1 were the result of dealer and proprietor initiatives rather than those of manufacturers. In 1929 898 Morris-Commercial, Citroën and Beardmore cabs were newly licensed in the

capital, close to the thousand a year figure that the PCO thought necessary to maintain a desired 11,000-strong fleet. The change in the Conditions of Fitness had begun to bring about the desired changes, but no one could have predicted what was to come next.

The Austin 12/4

With sales of the expensive 12/16hp Unic brought almost to a standstill by competition from the Morris-Commercial and the Beardmore Hyper, 1929 would be a crucial year for Mann & Overton's. Tom Overton had become involved in another family business and his brother Will had taken over control of the firm with their cousin Herbert Nicholls. But Will Overton was not to sit, like Poor Jenny, a-weeping over his predicament, for he had the solution in-house, in their Manchester dealership. Here, they were supplying the Austin 12/4 for cab work.

By the end of the 1920s Austin was the second largest car maker in Britain. The Austin 20 had been advertised as 'Austin's American Car'. Herbert Austin had run a Hudson through the Great War and for the 20, adopted the way it had been engineered for production with what Laurence Pomeroy of *Autocar* called a 'fewness of parts'. But, like the Empire Oxford, the 20 was too big for Britain and too costly for the Empire market against cheap, rugged American makes. It continued in British production but a new, scaled-down version, the 12/4, was one of the two cars that saved Austin from collapse in the early 1920s (the other, of course, being the legendary Seven).

Manchester and other provincial towns and cities could use the Austin 12/4 in its standard form because the licensing of hackney cabs in the provinces was, and still is, governed by different regulations from those in London: the Town Police Clauses Act 1847. This is a type of legislation known as 'enabling regulations', which allow but do not compel local police commissioners to license cabs in their area. This power now rests with local authorities, but the Act gives firm rules for the licensing and behaviour of drivers and also gives the authorities freedom to choose which type of vehicle to license.

Now that London's Conditions of Fitness had been changed, Will Overton turned his thoughts to having the Austin 12/4 adapted to meet them. The chief designer at Austin, Mr Harfield, was a friend of Overton and he confirmed that the steering could be modified to meet the turning circle requirement and that brake rods could be substituted for the original cables. But first Overton had to get Sir Herbert Austin to agree to the idea and so he went to Longbridge. Austin had a significant number of London dealers and, possibly believing that Overton was chasing yet another car dealership, kept him waiting all day. It was only as Austin was leaving that Overton confronted him, saying that he was not there on a fool's errand, he wanted to order 500 specially adapted cab chassis. Austin recognized Overton's sincerity and agreed to supply him. Austin would gain too. Austin cabs in London would provide excellent publicity for the company and gain an advantage over their big rival, Morris.

In late 1929 the PCO gave the Austin 12/4 cab chassis type approval and Mann & Overton's introduced it in 1930 from their premises on Battersea Bridge Road. The first vehicle was delivered on 7 June and it was equipped with Austin's new, ball-change, four-speed gearbox, which made the vehicle a little easier to drive. As Austin was supplying only the chassis, Mann & Overton's had to find some coachbuilders. The first 12/4 was fitted with a Dyer & Holton body, probably the same that as fitted to the Unic. Elkington, who were supplying bodies for the provincial 12/4, supplied some more and the Chelsea Carriage Co. were known to have provided

some too, but it was two coachbuilders, Strachan and Jones, whose bodies were to prove the most popular in the catalogue. Austin's model code for the cab chassis was HL. The cab trade, fond of nicknames, saw how tall it stood and christened it the 'High Lot'. A healthy 271 Austin cabs were sold in that half-year against annual sales of 535 for Beardmore, Morris-Commercial and KF1 combined.

The 'Chinese' Austin

Of those 271 Austins, 196 were sold to the London General Cab Company as bare chassis since the General considered that buying the Austin 12/4 was a much better option than building more Citroëns. They still had the bodies from the old 11.4hp Citroëns in storage and fitted them to the new Austin chassis. But the bodies were not a good fit and the General's drivers gave the odd-looking new cabs the nickname 'Chinese' Austins because they had seen how Chinese immigrants mixed Western culture with their own in ways curious to English eyes. The sale of more chassis to the General helped Mann & Overton's increase total sales to 400 in 1931. In contrast, a total of 243 Beardmore, Morris-Commercial and KF1 cabs were sold.

A New Morris-Commercial

The G-Type Morris-Commercial International was looking antiquated, and for 1932 Morris-Commercial introduced the new G2. It was based around the G-Type's chassis, but the G-Type's engine was now available only in a 17.9hp version since the truck for which it was used had been enlarged. This engine would be far too big for the cab and so the 14bhp engine from the Morris-Commercial light van was used. This was the Hotchkiss type, Morris's first major production engine and an even older design than the Austin 12.

A 'Chinese' Austin, photographed at the top of the ramp at the General's garage at 1–3 Brixton Road. Whereas the first Austin 12/4 cabs had the old type Austin radiator, the HLs and subsequent models up to the LL had the later 'ribbon' radiator as shown here. (Vintage Taxi Spares)

A Morris-Commercial G2 'Junior' with a factory-built three-quarter landaulet body. A full landaulet body could also be ordered and this, with the addition of a window in the driver's door and a full windscreen, would be fitted on the last Morris-Commercial cab, the six-cylinder G2SW. (LVTA Archive)

The body for the cab was new: it was, like the G-Type's, a composite of pressed steel panels on an ash frame. Because it was smaller than the old G-Type the cab trade nicknamed it the 'Junior'. Its availability would be limited because Morris-Commercial would soon move home to the old Wolseley plant at Adderley Park.

The Removal of Aged Cabs

Mann & Overton's were not immune to the economic depression that gripped Britain in the early 1930s: just 309 Austin cabs were sold in 1932 in comparison to 204 other types. However, 1933 was a pivotal year for Mann & Overton's. Now that there were three makers supplying up-to-date models, the Assistant Commissioner of Police, the London cab trade's supremo put out an official directive: to remove any cab over fifteen years old from the streets unless it was in exceptional condition, but even then there would be no guarantee of a licence for it. Added to this, Dunlop had been making 815 × 105 Taxicord tyres for the decreasing number of

Unics, Citroëns and older Beardmores, and with the arrival of more and more vehicles that used the smaller diameter, 30in × 5in, balloon tyres, would soon cease to make the old types. However, Dunlop supplied a conversion to adapt older cabs to take balloon tyres, enabling the older cabs that would still be under ten years old in 1933 to carry on working.

For Mann & Overton's and for Austin this could not have been better or more timely news. Cab masters were now obliged to replace their aged cabs and Mann & Overton's had a very saleable cab and little competition. Beardmore had yet to resume production after their move; the Unic KF1 had proved unreliable and would no longer be available and Morris-Commercial production was limited by a factory move. As a result, 834 of the latest model, the TT, with a new four-speed gearbox with constant-mesh synchro between third and top gear were sold against the others' combined sales of 128. But Austin's success was not due to the lack of competition alone, theirs was a good cab in its own right. The big fleet owners, the 'cab masters', liked it because Austin was a big, stable company, the cab was

A 1933 Austin 12/4 TT with a Goode and Cooper body. The TT had a new, four-speed gearbox with synchromesh between third and top gears. The trade gave this model the apt nickname of 'Twin Top'. This is a preserved example; note the later type of number plate with plastic letters and the American licence plate on the front bumper. (Vintage Taxi Spares)

reliable, the spares were readily available and, thanks to mass production, it was cheap. Most important of all, the cab was based on a private car chassis, which meant that Mann & Overton's orders could be fulfilled without interrupting car production. The price was significant too. Mann & Overton's could supply a 12/4 cab complete with body for £395, but by supplying bare Austin chassis fleet owners were able to build their own bodies or negotiate a rate with their choice of coachbuilder, which would reduce their capital outlay.

Beardmore Move Home

Although Beardmore's business empire had collapsed, Beardmore Taxicabs Ltd continued to make the Hyper at Paisley. Luther and Allsworth bought the whole taxicab business and in the process acquired Lord Invernairn's 50 per cent stake. Beardmore (Paisley) Ltd remained within the remnants of the Beardmore group and was reconstructed as a company making high-speed diesel engines for truck and marine applications. They continued to supply chassis and axles but not engines or gearboxes. In 1932 taxi production was moved to the Grove Park, Colindale in north London, premises that Luther had originally taken over when he acquired the Austro-Daimler concession before the war.

Beardmore had a new, MkIV model under development. For the engine and gearbox, Luther and Allsworth turned to William and Reginald Rootes. The Rootes brothers were originally car dealers from Maidstone in Kent. The continuing unreliability of their suppliers made them decide to go into manufacturing and in 1929 they bought the struggling Coventry company of Humber-Hillman, which also owned Commer commercial vehicles. At the end of the year they headhunted a new chief engineer from Sunbeam. He was Jack Irving, the man who had designed Sir Henry Segrave's land speed record cars, and in

1931 the Rootes brothers sent Irving to Beardmore as a consultant for the MkIV. Rootes's new Humber 12 had an excellent 1669cc, 4-cylinder, sidevalve engine. There was a larger, 1994cc version for a new Commer van, in unit with a four-speed crash gearbox, which Irving recommended for the cab. To accommodate the new power unit, the Hyper's 9ft (2.7m) wheelbase chassis was altered by replacing the ladder-type crosssections with a substantial X-brace. The front and the rear axle were carried over from the Hyper. The new model, named the Paramount, went on sale in 1934 with a body that was a modernized version of the Hyper's, with smart swage lines and domed wings. Three body styles were available: the full landaulet, the three-quarter landaulet and a fixed-head saloon in a two-door, four-light version for London and a four-door, six-light model for the provinces.

Whatever the MkIV's choice of body and specification, Beardmore, like Morris-Commercial had missed the boat, but with a cab selling for £435 they had little chance of making any inroads in any case; nor had they the production capacity. Irving had recommended that the price should be higher, but Luther and Allsworth, as directors of the sales company Beardmore Taxicabs Ltd, knew that the MkIV had to be priced as close as possible to the Austin and the Morris-Commercial.

Morris-Commercial at Adderley Park

Unlike Austin, whose principal production was private cars with commercial vehicles as a small sideline, Nuffield placed equal importance on cars and commercial vehicles. In 1932 Morris-Commercial moved from its original Soho, Birmingham factory to the old Wolseley plant at Adderley Park and had begun to make new, larger trucks that would

The first Hendon-built Beardmore, the MkIV Paramount, photographed beside a 1923 MkI. The road in which this picture was taken in Grove Park, Hendon, was near to Beardmore's works. Although his identity is virtually impossible to confirm, the man in the picture is most likely Francis Luther. (London Transport Museum)

sell profitably and in substantial numbers. At this time, the Nuffield Organization was experiencing its first ever downturn in business. Britain's economy was back in depression as a protracted result of the 1929 Wall Street crash, and Nuffield's market share was being dented by competition from Ford, Standard and the new Rootes Group. There was little spare cash for new projects and the new engines for the next generation of passenger cars were not yet ready. From 1933 all Morris cars of 14hp and over would be powered by 6-cylinder engines.

A new cab, the G2S, was introduced in late 1934 and would have a sidevalve, 6-cylinder engine of 1938cc derived from the 'Q' Type engine of the Oxford Six. It would be the first London cab to have a 6-cylinder engine. The body and chassis were otherwise identical to those of the G2 and the cab was nicknamed, not surprisingly the 'Junior Six'. Because the

Morris-Commercial plant was primarily geared up for truck production, cab production had to be slotted in wherever it could and orders suffered accordingly. Nor could supplies of the specially detuned engine, made at the car engine plant, be guaranteed since the far bigger car market had to be supplied first. After the success of the G-Type the restriction in the supply of cabs would be a bitter disappointment for William Watson.

A New Austin Chassis

From 1934 Austin ran down the production of the 12/4 passenger car, whose chassis the cab shared, finally ending it at the end of 1935. Demonstrating their commitment to the London cab trade, Austin designed a completely new cab chassis which, although continuing with the original engine, rod brakes and modified steering, had an underslung, worm drive, rear axle and a lower ground clearance than the 7in (18cm) demanded by the Conditions of Fitness. From 1934 this rule was to be eliminated and the change was almost certainly made to allow the new chassis to be type approved. The Home Office realized

that they had to compromise with what the motor industry was producing in order to balance the need to keep the cab trade as up to date as possible, while keeping faith with those who had invested in the trade and not bring in drastic changes. Certainly, the records show

---

Morris-Commercial Taxicabs: Technical Specification

International 'G' Type

Engine

Type	4-cylinder petrol, water-cooled, side-valve, monobloc 3-bearing crankshaft, cylinders, separate cylinder head
Treasury rating	15.9HP
Capacity	2,513cc
Bore and stroke	80mm × 125mm (3.1in × 4.9in)

Dimensions

Wheelbase	9ft (2.7m)
Track	4ft 8in (1.4m)
Overall length	12ft 8in (3.9m)

Running Gear

Transmission	four-speed manual, centre change
Brakes	mechanical operation, rear only, two sets of shoes acting on drums, one foot-operated, one hand-operated
Front axle	beam
Rear axle	overhead worm drive
Suspension	semi-elliptical leaf springs all round

G2
As for G-Type with the following changes:

Engine

Type	Morris-Commercial type CR, 4-cylinder petrol, water-cooled, sidevalve, monobloc cylinders, 3-bearing crankshaft, separate cylinder head
Treasury horsepower	13.9HP

Capacity	1802cc
Bore and stroke	75mm × 102mm (3in × 4in)

Dimensions

Wheelbase	9ft (2.7m)
Track	4ft 8in (1.4m)
Overall length	13ft 10in (4.2m)

Running Gear

Brakes	mechanical operation, foot-operated on all four wheels, handbrake on rear wheels
Rear axle	underslung worm drive

G2S
As for G2 with the following changes:

Engine

Type	6-cylinder petrol, water-cooled, side-valve, monobloc cylinders, 4-bearing crankshaft, separate cylinder head
Treasury horsepower	15HP
Capacity	1938cc
Bore and stroke	63.5mm × 102mm (2.5in × 4in)

G2SW
As for G2 with the following changes:

Engine

Type	6-cylinder petrol, water-cooled, overhead valve, monobloc cylinders, 4-bearing crankshaft, separate cylinder head
Treasury horsepower	14HP
Capacity	1818cc
Bore and stroke	61.5mm × 102mm (2.4in × 4in)

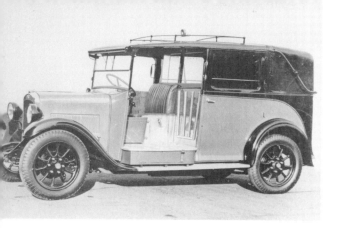

A Strachan bodied Austin 12/4. The Strachan body is distinguished by the rearward rake of the centre body pillar and the outward flare at the bottom of the doors. (Derek Pearce Collection)

The most common of all 1930s London cabs, the Austin 12/4 LL, lined up at the works of the coachbuilder Strachan, in Acton, west London. These cabs were destined for the London General who bought several hundred LLs with Strachan bodies and a plainer level of trim. (Derek Pearce Collection)

that the Home Office did not feel the need to have a full review with regard to these changes.

Austin's model code for the new cab was LL and, because it sat lower than the previous models, the trade nicknamed it the 'Low Loader', a slight variation of the description 'low loading' printed on the brochure produced for the cab. Sales of it were even better than those of the TT, with 1,111 sold in 1934. Beardmore and Morris-Commercial managed to sell just 302 cabs between them, a reflection of their situations. Mann & Overton's were riding high. Tom Overton's son Robert moved from another family business to join Mann & Overton's new finance company Mechanical Investments Ltd, and Robert's cousin David Southwell also joined the firm. That year the company went public and changed its name slightly to Mann & Overton; 1935 would be their best year yet, with 1,178 Austins sold.

A total of 337 Beardmores and Morris-Commercials were sold in 1935, but in fairness it must be said that this represents a quarter of the market and it is not unreasonable to assume that Morris-Commercial's share might have amounted to about one-

fifth. However, were a greater priority to have been given to cab production, Adderley Park might have gained a noticeably larger share.

The Beardmore MkV

In 1935 Beardmore introduced a MkV, named the Paramount Ace. The Paisley factory was soon to close and there would be no more of the old-type chassis made, so Rootes offered Beardmore the new 9ft 6in (2.9m) wheelbase Hillman 14 saloon chassis. This had Rootes's new 'Evenkeel' transverse leaf, independent front suspension, but the PCO had not allowed such a design since before the Great War and thus a beam axle and leaf springs from the Commer 15cwt van were fitted. The Commer engine was retained, but the crash gearbox was replaced by the four-speed, synchromesh gearbox from Rootes's large passenger cars. The MkV exceeded the 14ft (4.3m) maximum length previously allowed by the Conditions of Fitness. The Home Office conceded this amendment with the same attitude as they had the minimum ground clearance rule.

The Jones body as fitted to the Austin 12/4 LL, identified by the curls on the front of the roof rack. (Author's collection)

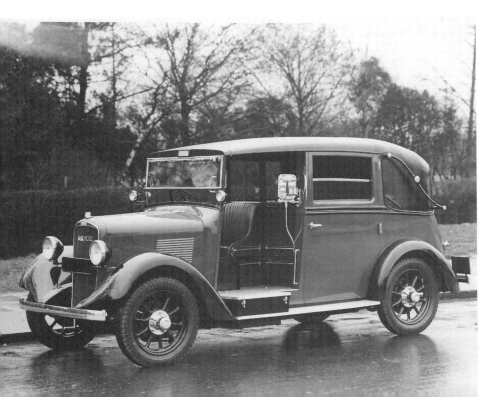

The MkV Beardmore Ace. The extra length of the Hillman 14 chassis meant that a bigger passenger door could be fitted; the back axle was moved to a position behind the rear seat instead of slightly in front, giving the passengers a more comfortable ride. A three-quarter landaulet body was also available. The MKVI would have a full-height, one-piece windscreen, the first ever to be fitted to a London Cab. (Vintage Taxi Spares)

Changes for Mann & Overton and Austin

The Austin LL remained current for 1936 and 1937, but with a lower than previous 875 and 659 models sold, respectively. From 1937 Austin cars were fitted with Girling hydraulic brakes, but the PCO would not allow them for cabs, still insisting on rod-operation. Although the British economy was once again in recession, Mann & Overton now regained the mantle that Beardmore had taken in the 1920s – that of supplier of the most prominent cab in London, but this time with Austin instead of Unic. Total sales of the Morris-Commercial and the Beardmore dropped, although they gained an improved market share in 1936, with 307 sold. In 1937 they both crashed, with a mere ninety-six combined.

In 1938 Ernest Mepstead sold his Fulham Garage at 296–8 Wandsworth Bridge Road to Mann & Overton. Austin brought out a revised model, the FL. It carried a grille shell, similar to that on the mid-1930s passenger cars, and coachbuilders made a 'streamlined' body to match it, but underneath, however, it was the same LL running gear. Only 213 of these were sold that year, principally for two reasons: in 1934 and 1935 the big fleets had invested in considerable numbers of Austin LLs which would not need replacing for a while, but, much worse, war was looming and the economy was again in recession. Cab masters had spent their available money and would hang on to the rest.

Preparations for war had made considerable demands on raw materials and non-military users found prices already escalating. In 1939 Mann & Overton advertised that their coachbuilders had 'large stocks of materials in hand', but that they were 'compelled to make the same additional charge this month of £8.15s. (£8.75) to cover extra costs'. August 1939 saw Mann & Overton deliver thirty-two

---

Austin 12/4 Taxicabs: Technical Specifications

Type 'HL'
Engine

Type	Austin 4-cylinder petrol, water-cooled, side-valve, monobloc cylinders, separate cylinder head, 5-bearing crankshaft
Capacity	1861cc
Bore and stroke	72mm × 114.5mm (2 13/16in × 4 1/2in)
Treasury rating	12.8HP
Power	27bhp @ 2,000rpm

Dimensions

Wheelbase	9ft 4in (2.8m)
Track	4ft 8in (1.4m)
Overall length	13ft 6in (4.1m)

Running Gear

Gearbox	four-speed manual
Brakes	mechanical operation, drums on all four wheels, handbrake on rear wheels
Front axle	beam
Rear axle	crown wheel and pinion
Wheels and tyres	30in × 5in Dunlop Taxicord tyres

Type 'TT'
As for 'TT' but with the following changes:

Gearbox	four-speed manual, synchromesh on 3rd and 4th brake

Type 'LL'

Overall length	13ft 10in (4.2m)

Running Gear

Rear axle	underslung worm
Differential ratio	5.12:1

new and eight reconditioned cabs, which was something of an achievement in the circumstances.

The Morris-Commercial G2SW

New for 1938 was the Morris-Commercial G2SW. Morris had discontinued the G2S's sidevalve 6 and replaced it in the cab with the 1818cc ohv 6 used in the Morris 14 Series III. The body was basically of the same composite construction landaulet as that of the G2S, but fitted with a window in the driver's door. The G2SW sold for £405, and possibly with this model Morris-Commercial could have gained a little ground on Austin and Beardmore, but

The last of the 12/4 series was the FL. It used the same design of radiator shell as late 1930s Austin private cars and was optimistically described as 'streamlined'. This body is the standard Jones landaulet. The steel artillery wheels were retained since they fitted the special Dunlop Taxicord tyres. (Author's collection)

The 'fishtail' body by Jones was an attractive option that was available on the LL and this, the FL 'Flash Lot' of 1938. Note that the driver's door has a window; there are trafficators and the flag on the meter is of a type that lights up when the cab is for hire – progress, indeed. (Author's collection)

in 1938 Beardmore and Morris-Commercial managed to sell only sixty-five cabs between them in London. Beardmore suffered from their small production facility and the cab's higher price, while at Adderley Park Morris-Commercial were still placing priority on high-profit, commercial and a growing number of military vehicles.

The Beardmore Paramount Ace

The last pre-war Beardmore was the MkVI Paramount Ace of 1938. The Beardmore earned the nickname of the 'Greengrocer's Barrow', since, it was said, 'all the best was in the front'. The MkVI carried on this tradition, taking advantage of the new regulations that allowed a driver's door window. The Ace also had an all-synchromesh gearbox, developed for the new 1939 Hillman Minx. Production was tiny and in January 1939 Beardmore Taxicabs Ltd, the sales company, was liquidated in preparation for a new liaison with the Nuffield Organization.

Private Hire Licensing and Cheaper Cabs

The first real challenge to the licensed cab trade came in 1938, when a type of private hire car, fitted with taximeters set at a lower

rate and called 'Streamliners', began operating in the suburbs. The instigation of a suburban taxi driver's licence in 1937 angered the private hire operators who felt that the suburbs were their domain. Many 'streamline' groups were opened, sometimes employing licensed cab drivers and paying them a set wage. The Joint Trade Committee asked the Home Secretary Sir Samuel Hoare to investigate, with the view to licensing private hire. He commissioned the Hindley Report; this was published in January 1939 and recommended the licensing of private hire.

The report was not acted upon and fuel rationing during the Second World War crippled the operations of the Streamliners. Part of the report looked the possibility of seeing cabs being replaced at more frequent intervals than ten years, which, it suggested, would be achieved by manufacturing vehicles to sell at a cheaper price. By saying that 'there would be no economy in using vehicles as lightly built as the ordinary, mass-produced private car of similar horsepower', the Commissioner was mindful of the hard work that a London cab did. But he was aware that cab riders would prefer to ride in up to date vehicles. As for price, an Austin 12 cab cost around £395 when the new Austin 12 private car sold for around £200. Building a slightly less robust cab to sell at around £300, and thus introduce

An illustration from an advertisement for the Morris 'Super Six' cab. Like the MkVI Beardmore and the Austin FL, the driver's door had full glass. (Stuart Pessok Collection)

73

a lower tariff, might, he felt, result in 'a permanent increase in hirings' and would be 'in the best interests of the trade'. The economic and political situation did not improve through 1939 and the debate over cheaper cabs was swamped by the more urgent demands of war.

Beardmore Taxicabs, 1929–38: Technical Specifications

MkIII Hyper

Engine

Type	Beardmore 4-cylinder petrol, water-cooled, side-valve, monobloc cylinders, separate cylinder head
Capacity	1954cc
Bore and stroke	72mm × 120mm (2.8in × 4.7in)
Treasury rating	12.8HP

Dimensions

Wheelbase	9ft (2.7m)
Track	4ft 7in (1.37m)

Running Gear

Gearbox	four-speed manual
Brakes	mechanical operation, drums on all four wheels, handbrake on rear wheels
Front axle	beam
Rear axle	fully floating, spiral bevel drive
Differential ratio	4.55:1
Suspension	semi-elliptical leaf springs all round
Steering	worm and sector
Wheels and tyres	steel artillery type, with 30in × 5in Dunlop Taxicord tyres
Electrical equipment	12v

MkIV Paramount

Engine

Type	Commer 4-cylinder petrol, water-cooled, side-valve, monobloc cylinders, separate cylinder head
Capacity	1944cc
Bore and stroke	75mm × 110mm (2.95in × 4.3in)
Power	51bhp @ 3,600rpm
Treasury horsepower	13.9HP

Dimensions

Wheelbase	9ft (2.75m)
Track	4ft 7in (1.4m)

Running Gear

Gearbox	four-speed manual
Brakes	mechanical operation, drums on all four wheels, handbrake on rear wheels
Front axle	beam
Rear axle	fully floating, spiral bevel drive
Differential ratio	5.5:1
Suspension	semi-elliptical leaf springs all round
Steering	worm and sector

MkV Ace

As for MkIV with the following changes:

Dimensions

Wheelbase	9ft 6in (2.9m)
Rear track	4ft 8in (1.42m)

Running Gear

Gearbox	four-speed manual, synchromesh on 3rd and top
Rear axle	fully floating, underslung worm drive
Differential ratio	5.4:1
Suspension	semi-elliptical leaf springs all round
Steering	worm and nut

MkVI Paramount Ace

As for MkIV with the following changes:

Gearbox	four-speed manual, synchromesh on all four forward gears

---

5   1939–45 Cabs in Wartime

The sheer scale of the Great War, in which every citizen became affected, was unexpected. But the lesson had been learned, and when war broke out again in 1939 the whole country was mentally, if not materially, ready. Rearmament had been under way since 1938, the Territorial Army had already been mobilized, when war broke out children were evacuated to the countryside and everyone carried a gas mask in preparation for German aerial gas attacks. In reality, little happened at first. The British Expeditionary Force (BEF) was sent to France to assist the French against a German invasion but stood by, waiting, in what was known as the 'Phoney War', as

Germany conquered Poland and Norway. Then, in the spring of 1940, the Germans crashed through Belgium, drove the BEF out of France and in July launched an aerial attack on southern England. With this attack, the Battle of Britain and the Blitz that followed, the war was brought to Britain's doorstep.

Beardmore and a New Nuffield Cab

In the first few months of the war, the cab trade, like the rest of the country, carried on as normal an existence as possible. Beardmore were building and selling new cabs for a short

The Oxford prototype, photographed at the Wolseley factory at Ward End, Birmingham after completing its trials with Beardmore Motors. Note the smaller 16in wheels. (Norman Painting)

The rear view of the Oxford prototype. At one point during the blitz, its driver Roy Perkins took the cab too close to a fire, which resulted in the paint blistering in the heat. (Norman Painting)

time, but ceased manufacture when supplies of Hillman chassis ran out. The Colindale works were turned over to the manufacture of aircraft components, gun parts and electronic gear for rockets. Their showroom at 112 Great Portland Street in London was demolished in the Blitz and business was transferred to 167–9 Great Portland Street, which had been the offices of Francis Luther's Austro-Daimler Concessionaires.

Beardmore were still interested in the cab trade and Luther negotiated with Nuffield to replace William Watson as the London agent for Morris-Commercial cabs. Before the outbreak of war, Nuffield had begun work on a new cab. Whereas the previous models had

come from, originally, Soho and then Adderley Park, the new vehicle would be a product of the Wolseley factory at Ward End, Birmingham. It had a new box-section, X-braced chassis, designed by Charles van Eugen, who had moved to the Nuffield Organization after joining Riley from Lea-Francis in 1938. To power the cab, the engineers in the Nuffield's Marine and Commercial Division built a unique derivation of the XP series engine used in the Morris 10 and the MG Midget. It had a capacity of 1.8 litres and a dry sump with an oil tank mounted below the cab's radiator. In 1940 the chassis was fitted with a conventional, coach-built landaulet body by Jones Brothers of

Paddington and painted dark blue. This prototype, registration no. EOM 844, was presented for approval on 15 July 1940. The PCO were reluctant to accept this body, since although it was a standard type, they had decided that, in future, cabs should resemble as much as was possible modern saloon cars, although, as they stated, there must be 'demarcation between car and cab'.

Based at Beardmore Motors' depot in Kentish Town, north London, the cab covered some 100,000 miles (160,000km) throughout the war at the hands of Roy Perkins, who had become, just after his twenty-first birthday in 1938, one of the youngest men to hold a cab licence. Perkins had been exempted from National Service on medical grounds as he had suffered an injury as a child that left him with a permanent limp. To enable Perkins to cover such a high mileage, Beardmore drew petrol from the rations of other cabs in their fleet. Perkins recorded every detail of every job he did and even such details as how many times he stopped at traffic lights. With the help of his wife Alice, he collated this information and presented it to Nuffield in the form of regular reports.

Cabs and Cabmen in the Auxiliary Fire Service

Before 1938 the government had followed a policy of appeasing the Fascist dictators in Europe and had made no formal preparations for war. Only individuals and private organizations had done so. One exception within government was A.L. Dixon, the assistant under-secretary of state with responsibility for the Police Division of the Home Office. He had recently been given responsibility for the new Fire Brigades Division. He knew of the *Blitzkrieg*, the lightning war that the Nazis had prosecuted in the Spanish Civil War and in particular he had recognized the damage that aerial bombardment had caused. In partial preparation for the possibility of similar action against British cities, he instigated the design of fire pumps, either for installation in boats and lorries or mounted on trailers, and by early 1939, 2,800 had been made and deployed.

In 1938 an Act of Parliament was passed that allowed the formation of the Auxiliary Fire Service (AFS). This enabled fire brigades throughout the country to enlist volunteer fire fighters and commandeer, where appropriate, suitable vehicles. The London Fire Brigade (LFB) knew that with only its peacetime strength it would not have the slightest chance of dealing with a major series of air raids. Before the trailer pumps had been distributed, it had been assumed that there would be enough lorries and large cars available for the AFS to commandeer to tow them. In the event, there were not. The Cab Trade Committee of the Transport and General Workers' Union had foreseen this and in 1938 wrote to Herbert Morrison, the former leader of the London County Council and now a prominent MP. They suggested that the AFS should recruit cabmen and their taxicabs. If the route to a blaze were blocked by bomb damage, the men would know the quickest way around, and the cabs could, it was thought, tow the pumps.

Morrison spoke to the head of the LFB, Sir Aylmer Firebrace, who liked the idea. He contacted departments of the government to see whether they already had any plans to commandeer cabs for their own use. They had not and so, immediately after the Act came into force, the LFB borrowed an Austin 12/4 Low Loader, BYV 35, from the London General and fitted it with a tow bar and bracket, designed to tow a trailer pump. Described as a 'sound engineering job', the tow bar was passed by the PCO in November 1938. In January the LFB began to requisition a significant number of cabs and the cabmen to drive them. All the cabs came from fleets so as not

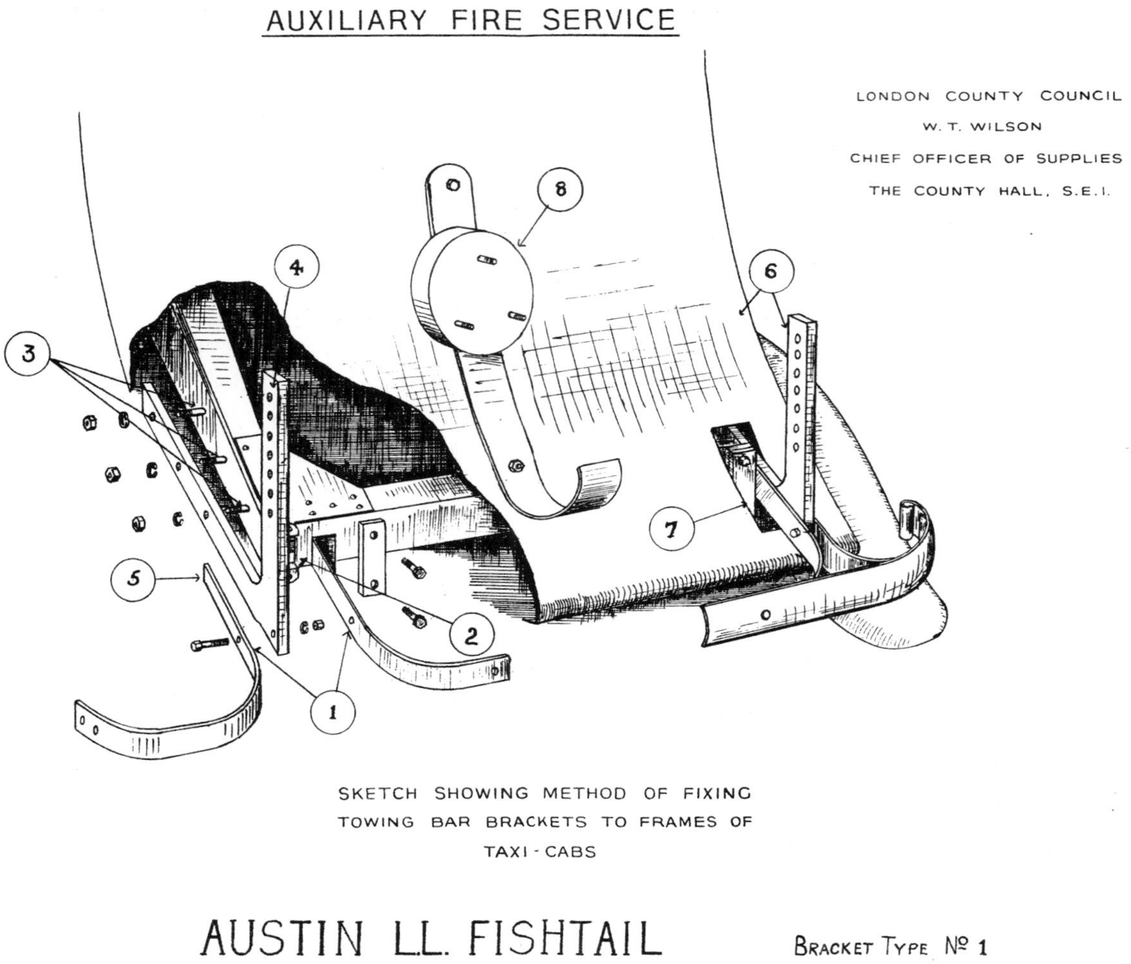

AUXILIARY FIRE SERVICE

LONDON COUNTY COUNCIL

W. T. WILSON

CHIEF OFFICER OF SUPPLIES

THE COUNTY HALL, S.E.I.

SKETCH SHOWING METHOD OF FIXING
TOWING BAR BRACKETS TO FRAMES OF
TAXI-CABS

AUSTIN LL. FISHTAIL BRACKET TYPE Nº 1

The towbar for the Austin LL with a Jones 'fishtail' body.

to compromise the livings of owner-drivers. The AFS offered cabmen a wage of £3 per week for 12hr shifts, which would ally the fears of those who knew of the difficulties faced by their older colleagues in the Great War.

At first, the scheme called for 2,000 cabs, which was a significant slice of the 10,000 or so that were then licensed. Towing brackets for different types of cab were designed and made, but it was decided that the AFS would use the Strachan-bodied Austin LL, the most common cab in London, to simplify the supply of towbars. The cabs' proprietors had to surrender the licence plates because the vehicles would not be suitable for hire.

When Britain declared war on Germany in September 1939 London's auxiliary firemen were told to report to their stations. They

*The five-man AFS crew of this Mk V Beardmore look very smart. The cab has yet to be painted in AFS livery and so this picture may well have been taken before 1940. It was possibly part of an AFS division stationed in Hendon, even attached to Beardmore's own factory. (*Taxi *newspaper)*

*An Austin LL, newly acquired by the AFS, with its trailer pump. (*Taxi *newspaper)*

were formed into crews of five and, with their cabs and trailers, were posted one to each of London's street fire alarms. For the first few weeks the crews were stationed on street corners, with no food nor shelter provided, but soon sub-stations were set up, often in whatever buildings could be requisitioned. Between ten and twenty cabs were housed in a sub-station, crewed by up to 30,000 auxiliary firemen and women. Some fire stations in London had more than 1,000 auxiliaries

attached to them. The proposed 12hr shifts were replaced by a three-watch system, with 24hr on and 48 off, and were paid £2.18s.5d (£2.92) per week. The cab owners were paid £1.17s.6d (£1.87) a week for the hire of the cabs.

Exercises were set up to train the crews, including one on Hampstead Heath. It was on an exercise like this that the AFB discovered that the Austin 12/4 was not powerful enough to tow the trailers. When the cabs failed to climb Haverstock Hill, the crews were ordered to get out and push! However, many AFS volunteers offered their own private cars for towing trailers, which the AFS accepted with alacrity, especially since most of the cars were large, including many American models and more powerful than cabs. In view of the severe petrol rationing, the owners were glad to see the cars put to good use rather than be laid up for the duration, if not for ever. The result was that most of the cabs that had been taken out of work were returned to their owners, leaving just over 294 with the AFS.

Despite the government's saying that they had no specific need for cabs in wartime, the AFS were not the only users. A revised total of 2,112 were earmarked for towing trailer pumps, fourteen were requisitioned by the LCC and some London boroughs as ambulances for the walking wounded and twelve for rescue and demolition work; sixty-four were designated for what was described as 'staff care'. In 1940 the remaining cabs were painted grey to match other AFS vehicles. On 7 September, the first night of the Blitz, the AFS went into action, employing nearly 1,000 appliances, including the cabs. They continued serving throughout the Blitz until its end in May 1941 and through the V1 and V2 rocket attacks of 1944 and 1945. While AFS volunteers were originally thought of as men who were trying to avoid conscription into the armed forces, their critics were quick to recognize the dangerous work they did. The Prime Minister Winston Churchill described them as 'the heroes with grubby faces'.

Mann & Overton Struggle On

At the outbreak of war, Mann & Overton were able to supply new cabs. Indeed, there were a significant number awaiting delivery. As the war progressed, delivery became more and more difficult due to the shortages of materials. Prices were gradually increased and

by March 1941 a new Austin cost £451. In late 1941 'government restrictions' curtailed manufacture. From then on, Mann & Overton increased the capability of their machine shop to make or recondition such spare parts as they could. They ventured, for the only time in their existence, into the fleet business, running their own cabs. In 1944 they bought two garages, Star Garage and Parsons Green Garage. An advertisement placed by Mann & Overton in *The Steering Wheel* in April 1945, just a month before VE Day, advised

THE OWNER-DRIVER AND M.C.O.D.A. GAZETTE.   AUGUST, 1941

POLICE NOTICE

Immobilisation of Cabs in the Event of Invasion

All cab owners should be ready, in the event of invasion, to immobilise their vehicles the moment the order is given. Failure to act promptly would give the enemy the chance to provide himself with transport.

It is important that cab owners should understand now what they and drivers in their employment have to do, and satisfy themselves that they can carry out the order at any time without delay.

In the event of owners being informed by the Police or through the Civil Defence Services that immobilisation of vehicles has been ordered in their area, they must take the following steps in regard to all their vehicles.

(1) (a) remove the distributor heads and leads, and

(2) (b) either empty the tanks or remove the carburettors and

(2) hide the parts removed well away from the vehicles.

If vehicles are required for Home Guard purposes, special instructions will be given.

Fuel tanks can be emptied through the drain plug if one is provided or, as an emergency measure, the tank can be punctured (e.g. by a large nail) at its lowest part. Care should be taken that fuel drained from tanks is not emptied where it will flow into drains ; otherwise a serious explosion may occur.

These things are the least that must be done. It will be all to the good if other readily removable parts of the mechanism are also taken well away from the vehicle.

Where no order has been issued but it is obvious that there is an immediate risk of the vehicle being seized by the enemy, the distributor head or magneto should be smashed with a spanner or hammer and tension leads removed.

Owners of garages and large fleets of vehicles in specified areas may be required to remove stocks of spare parts or parts taken from their vehicles and they should make provisional arrangements accordingly.

As vehicles may be on the road a long way from their garages when an order for immobilisation is given, owners should ensure that drivers are properly instructed as to the correct method of immobilising their vehicles.

16

In order to prevent any usable motor vehicle from falling into enemy hands, it was compulsory to immobilize it; cabmen failing to do so faced severe disciplinary action by the police.

of the expected supply of mechanical and body components for cabs of more than ten years old.

Wartime for Cabmen

The London cabman was as a much victim of the attention of the PCO in wartime as he was of the bombs of the Luftwaffe. The laws governing the blackout were strictly enforced, and rightly so, for the slightest glimpse of light from the ground would make a certain target for the enemy. To maintain a total blackout,

street lights were not turned on at lighting up time and motor vehicle lights had to be masked. Special headlight masks were made and it was compulsory for them to be fitted to all motor vehicles, taxicabs included, from 22 January 1940, but Joseph Lucas, the manufacturer, had neglected to obtain approval for them from the PCO for use on cabs. Thus, until the masks had been approved, cabmen had to suffer the ludicrous situation of having carriage officers order them to remove the headlight masks, rendering them liable to prosecution by the police.

Personal Testimonies

We have an insight into the lives of cabmen in wartime from the testimony of two brothers Jim and Jack Dowling. Jim, the older, became a cabman 1938, driving an Austin before buying a Morris-Commercial. Jack learnt to drive on his father's Beardmore, and recalls going with his father to pick it up when he bought it.

Dad had a Unic, which had wooden wheels that squeaked in hot weather. He sold the cab for thirty shillings (£1.50) and I went with him to pick up a new Paramount Beardmore from Holmes Road in Kentish Town. He wasn't too pleased about the extras it had, especially the red brake light, which he reckoned would run down the battery. As soon as I was seventeen I used to meet him in the West End. He allowed me to drive around Regent Street and Oxford Street with L-plates on the cab. I suppose it was illegal, but we got away with it. I passed the test with the examiner sitting on a box in the luggage space.

After the outbreak of war Jim got his call-up papers. He was married on the Saturday, but failed his medical on the Monday because he had contracted tuberculosis as a young man. This kept him out of military service, but not from the dangers of war. He remembers:

I went all through the war, driving night work, mostly. One night I was setting a naval officer down in Harley Street and the sirens went. I thought I'd better go home, so I crossed Putney Bridge, and, as I got near the milk bar near the corner of Putney Bridge Road, a bomb dropped and blew away the whole offside of the cab. The bomb had dropped on the dance hall there. A lot of people were killed, but a bus shelter protected me from the blast. I left the cab in the middle of the road and went over the bridge to Ball's Garage and phoned home. My father took me home. The next morning I went over to get the cab. It was piled up around with rubbish. We took it to Ball's garage and got it mended. I didn't go to work for about eight weeks after.

When the hostilities were almost over, Jim's luck turned sour. 'I had a Morris Six', he recalled,

I was coming down King's Road, Chelsea, on VE Day, and there's bonfires everywhere. Just before you got to Sydney Street, there was a cinema on the right. They'd pulled the hoarding down in front in the middle of the road and made a bonfire and there's me coming down the King's Road. I turned left to avoid it all and the cylinder head gasket went! I was sitting there suffering, watching it all, not working!

Petrol rationing was introduced on 16 September 1939. Posters urged people to consider the question, 'Is your journey really necessary?', but for the cabman, who would sometimes provide a far better service than public transport could offer, the initial limit of 2gal (9ltr) a day was punitive. It was barely enough for a one cabman, let alone a double team, and this, along with the short-lived fiasco of the headlight masks, drove cabmen to work days in a time when the blackout made their availability to provide safe transport at night all the more desirable. Ken Drummond, chairman of the Motor Cab Owner-Drivers' Association (MCODA), pushed for more, claiming with justification that petrol was the cabman's 'bread and butter'. In December 1940, just after the start of the Blitz, an extra 20gal (91ltr) of petrol per month were made available. This, at the request of the Secretary of Mines, was further increased by 30gal (136ltr) per month. Although far from generous, this would be a recognition of the valuable work performed by the cab trade throughout the war when public transport had been steadily reduced.

The difficulties of driving in near total darkness may be imagined, but these were compounded by the constantly changing hazards and road closures caused by bomb damage. A 20mph (32km/h) speed limit imposed for the duration was an important rule in maintaining safety, but it is to the cab trade's credit that the accident rate actually fell during the war.

Military Service for Cabmen

At the beginning of the war, conscription took a substantial number of young men in their twenties from all walks of life, including the cab trade. After the retreat from France, Britain and her Allies began rebuilding the armed forces. The call-up extended to men in their thirties and later to those in their forties.

Not only that, but cabmen who had other skills were transferred to industry and other occupations to help with the war effort, which, although vital in keeping the troops on the front line well supported, further depleted the numbers of working cabmen. These jobs were known as 'reserved occupations'.

Some of those men formed part of the Home Guard, the non-professional fighting unit originally formed in May 1940 as the Local Defence Volunteers, whose task was to act as a rear guard against a German invasion while the regular army formed a front line. Besides those in reserved occupations, Home Guard personnel consisted of men too old or too young for enlistment but who would nevertheless be fit enough to defend their country. Home Guard battalions were formed from all walks of life, including small communities, factories and trades. In the spring of 1941 a London Taxicab Battalion was formed, recruiting cabmen and others in the trade. The Home Guard London District Commanding Officer, Brig J. Whitehead wrote to the MCODA Gazette, saying:

In response to the many enquiries which have been made, I desire to confirm that the men enrolling in the 59th County of London (Taxi) Battalion, Home Guard, will be called upon *only* when an emergency arises for *the sole purpose of driving (or maintaining)* taxicabs according to the declaration made upon their Enrolment Forms.

There are no parades, guards or drills for the men of this Battalion, who will be required for work in connection with the local defence of an area where their particular knowledge will be invaluable in the circumstances which may prevail.

It is for this reason that an urgent appeal is now made to taxicab drivers throughout London to enrol in this Battalion for this particular work, in order that we may be fully prepared to meet the emergency when it arises.

Dad's Army? Cabs of the London (Taxi) Battalion on exercise with a detachment of the County of London Home Guard. (London Transport Museum)

There would be provision for payment of up to 10s. (50p) per day when called up for full time service as a compensation for loss of normal earnings. Proprietors who loaned their cabs to the Home Guard were paid 9d (3.75p) per mile for the use of the vehicle plus an extra petrol ration. Cabmen have always been notoriously difficult to organize, but despite a very shaky start the Taxi Battalion grew, according to one of its members, Simon Kogan, into 'an efficient body of men, disciplined and well trained'.

Increasingly Difficult Times

As the war progressed, the shortage of spare parts and the loss of vehicles to bomb damage became more acute and the ten-year life of a cab was extended by the PCO to minimize that loss. Shortage of tyres was also a problem with, at one point, cab proprietors having to obtain consent from a Carriage Officer to have a tyre retreaded. Fuel availability resulted in other road users calling on the cab trade to help them out. Some cases were from those in genuine need but others were from those all too happy to take advantage. There were stories of wealthy women sending cabs to collect their shopping instead of using their own cars and companies using cabs to make deliveries when they wanted to save their own petrol ration. The Motor Fuel (Cab Service) Order, 1942 would prevent private individuals from using cabs to make long journeys for which they would have used their private cars by restricting journeys made by cab to those

A Jones-bodied Austin LL of the London (Taxi) Battalion provides a base for other members of the County of London Home Guard to practise anti-aircraft fire. (London Transport Museum)

'within the area in which they are licensed to ply for hire plus a distance not exceeding five miles (8km) beyond the boundary of the area'.

When the war ended in August 1945, many members of the public expressed their gratitude. One writer to *The Times* said,

When handing out awards for gallantry is finally made, I hope the London taxi driver will not be forgotten. Invariably cheerful, invariably when wanted, night or day, he will take you anywhere and appears to have no thought at all for his personal safety. Post offices close down, banks cease

to function but after the crash of the bombs comes the starting up again of the taxi's engine.

The columnist Oliver Stewart of *The Tatler* wrote, 'I think that most Londoners will join me in paying tribute to the taxi men. At many times they are the only above-ground transport that keeps at it.' But however hard the trade had struggled and whatever accolades its members received, London's cab fleet had suffered as much damage as it had in the Great War. It would take at least as long to rebuild as it had in the 1920s.

6   1946–55 Diesel and Steel

As 1945 began, Britain and her allies were sure that it was not a matter of whether the war would be won, but when. The British motor industry was already gearing up to produce the models that it had stopped making at the outbreak of war and planning to make the new models that it had begun designing in the war years. For once, the cab trade would be ahead of the industry in introducing new models, not because it chose to, but because it had to. All the pre-war models were out of production. But when they went into service, those new cabs would be too expensive in the austere economy of the post-war years and the cab trade would endure hardship once more.

The Oxford Cab

By mid 1945 Nuffield were happy with the way the Oxford had performed in its protracted test and decided that they wanted to put it into production. The Home Office had been considering a review of the Conditions of Fitness, so Jack Hellberg of the Marine and Industrial Division, wrote to them, asking whether they were going to do so, as any changes might severely compromise the new cab. He was told that the regulations would stay the same, so, by a very great effort, Nuffield's engineers, under the guidance of their chief experimental engineer Charles

At the end of World War II, the Taxicab Fleet Operators' Federation commissioned this body on an Austin FL chassis to illustrate the kind of body that they thought would be the most suitable for post-war operations, bearing in mind the PCO's desire to have cabs that more closely resembled private cars. Although still coach-built, the landaulet hood had gone and the lines were much simpler, but certain dimensions did not comply with the Conditions of Fitness, so it did not achieve approval from the PCO. (Jamie Borwick)

Griffin, got the cab type-approved by the PCO in late 1946. The cab would have a completely new, composite body, of pressed steel panels over an ash frame with a fixed head. The first new cab to be offered in peacetime, it was put into production in 1947, with some made at Drews Lane, Birmingham until 1949, after which most were made at the

Morris-Commercial plant at Adderley Park, Birmingham.

The engine was the prototype's 1803cc dry-sump unit, with a four-speed manual gearbox and the Rubery Owen channel section chassis had semi-elliptical spring suspension all round. With William Watson's retirement and his withdrawal from the cab

The prototype of the production Nuffield Oxford, photographed at Ward End. The wheels are 16in, although still of the steel artillery type. Note the 'for hire' sign, different from that on the production models, and the small ventilator on the side of the scuttle. (Norman Painting)

The first production Oxford, with a different 'For hire' sign, Geecen taximeter and a mounting above the back bumper for the licence plate. (Norman Painting)

trade, the way was open for Beardmore to step in and take over the dealership. Further, Beardmore had secured steel allocations, which were difficult to come by in the post-war years. The government had issued the decree that Britain must 'export or die', and the biggest exporters would receive the biggest amounts of steel, although taxis, by virtue of the nature of the product, would be exempt from this ruling. The deal was that Nuffield would receive enough of Beardmore's steel allocation to build the Oxford, in exchange for Beardmore's selling and servicing the cab. Additionally Beardmore would recondition as many of their own 1930s models as they could get hold of and sell them on to cab drivers desperate to get at what little work there was in the austere post-war years.

The war had caused great inflation, but, in addition, purchase tax at 33.33 per cent was levied on new cabs. The new Oxford would cost close to £1,000, more than double the price of the Morris-Commercial G2SW. The cab trade could not afford to buy enough Oxfords to replace the cabs lost during the war. Petrol too was more expensive and there was little money in people's pockets to spend on cab fares. The trade would struggle for a good few years, driving repaired pre-war models, some built as far back as 1930.

The FX3

With the 12/4 chassis out of production, Mann & Overton had no new cabs to sell. They had managed to buy in a number of pre-war cabs in almost new condition that had been requisitioned by the AFS, but they would not meet the expected demand. Thankfully, Leonard Lord, the head of Austin, had assured

---

Nuffield Oxford: Technical Specification

Engine

Type	Nuffield 4-cylinder in-line petrol, water-cooled, cast iron cylinder block, cast iron cylinder head with overhead valves, three-bearing crankshaft, dry sump lubrication
Cubic capacity	1802.5cc
Bore and stroke	75mm × 102mm (2.95in × 4in)
Treasury rating	13.9HP

Transmission

Type	manual, four-speed, synchromesh on 2nd, 3rd and 4th gears plus reverse, central gear change
Clutch	8in single dry plate

Dimensions

Wheelbase	8ft 11 1/2in (2.73m)
Length overall	14ft 5 1/2in (4.25m)
Width	5ft 6in (1.67m)
Track, front	4ft 8 5/16in (1.43m)
Track, rear	4ft 8in (1.42m)

Running Gear

Steering	cam and peg type
Ratio	18:1
Brakes	Girling mechanical all four wheels, twin leading shoe on front, 11in (28cm) drums all round mechanical pull up handbrake on rear wheels
Wheels and tyres	18in artillery-type wheels with 5.50 x 18 Dunlop Super Taxi tyres (steel disc on Series II and III)
Front suspension	I-section axle beam with longitudinal leaf springs and double-acting lever-arm hydraulic shock absorbers
Rear suspension	longitudinal, semi-elliptical springs and double-acting lever-arm hydraulic shock absorbers

Electrical System

Type	12v positive earth, two 6v batteries, 75amp/hr

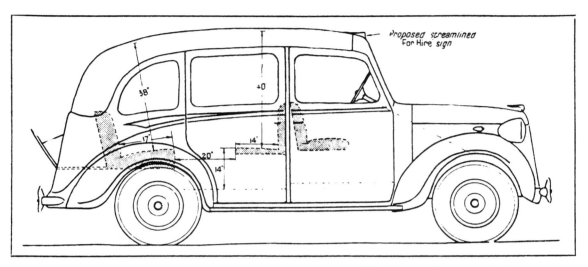

How The Steering Wheel *of 12 January 1946 announced the new Austin 14, 'The Cab you will operate in the Future'. Although more modern than the FL of 1938, it was still traditional in appearance. (Author's Collection)*

The Austin 14 Type FX chassis as delivered to Mann & Overton in December 1945. This was the first cab since the Citroëns and the Yellow Cabs of the 1920s to have disc wheels. Like the Oxford's, they were 16in. Just visible under the wheel arch is the cylinder of the hydraulic Jackall system , which enabled the cab to be jacked up without the use of a separate jack. (Derek Pearce Collection)

Robert Overton that Austin was committed to the London cab trade. Lord had registered the name 'Taxicar' with the Society of Motor Manufacturers and Traders. Thankfully, he decided not to use it, but of more practical use was the new cab chassis that Austin produced in late 1945. This was coded, in line with Austin's system, as the FX. It had a 14hp, 1.8-litre side-valve engine, an over-bored version of the current 12hp unit. Mann & Overton fitted the chassis with a pre-war body and put it on test, but it was not up to the job. By the end of 1946 Austin had designed a new chassis that, according to Austin's J.W.R. Penrose, 'caused some considerable amount of work for our drawing office over and above new models the Company is introducing at the moment'.

The new chassis was designated FX2, and with semi-elliptical springs, a beam front axle and rod-operated brakes, there were no big technical surprises. What was an innovation for Austin was the overhead valve engine, which was a 1.8-litre, 4-cylinder version of the 6-cylinder, K-Series 3.5-litre lorry engine. The chassis was submitted to the PCO for type approval on 9 March 1947.

Then there was the matter of the body: a traditional, coach-built body was out of the question. Even if the labour could be found, it would be far too expensive and repairs would be costly. An all-steel body was what was wanted, but Austin would be struggling for manufacturing capacity for their steel passenger car bodies. They certainly had no room to build around fifteen FX3 bodies a week. Luckily, Joe Edwards of Austin knew just the people who could help. During the war, Austin needed some expertise in making aircraft fuselage panels. The Ministry of Supply introduced them to Carbodies, a company on the west side of Coventry who had supplied MG with bodies and gone on to provide special coachwork for the Rootes Group and Rover. Under the Lend-Lease scheme,

Carbodies had been supplied with a material called Kirksite, an alloy with a low melting point, from which tools for body pressing could be made quite cheaply. Edwards invited Robert Overton to a meeting at the Ministry of Supply where he met Carbodies' managing director Ernest Jones and works manager John Orr. With Kirksite tools, Carbodies could build the body at a realistic price and a deal was struck to develop the cab. Austin would supply the chassis to Carbodies, who would build the body, mount it, paint and trim it and deliver the complete cab to Mann & Overton in London. They would provide 50 per cent of the money, with Carbodies and Austin supplying 25 each of the balance. This gave Mann & Overton the major share in the cab as well as the exclusive right to London sales.

Carbodies produced a coach-built prototype body on the FX2 chassis, and on 20 May Robert Overton and Herbert Nicholls of Mann & Overton and vehicle inspectors from the PCO went to Carbodies to look at it. They were generally pleased with the light and airy appearance of it in comparison to the pre-war landaulets, but the privacy valued by certain passengers at night had not been completely abandoned. Darkened glass was to be used in the small back window, and no interior driving mirror would be allowed.

The FX2 received type approval in June 1947, but the following October Austin announced that they would not be making the 14 and the 18hp cars they had first planned, but an interim 16hp model. This had a 2.2-litre engine, which would be supplied for the new cab. In October 1948 a second prototype was built with a pressed steel body and was given a new model code FX3. Mann & Overton announced it to the cab trade on 11 June 1948 and both prototypes went out for trials. The FX2, registered as JXN 842, went to Central Autos of Chelsea and the steel-bodied cab, JXN 841 went to W.H. Cook of west London. The FX3 had its formal introduction at the 1948 Commercial Motor Transport Exhibition at Earls Court that November alongside its four-door FL1 hire car version. It was offered in standard black cellulose for £936, including purchase tax at 33.33 per cent, with alternative colours

at extra cost. Now the London cab trade had the choice of two cabs.

Eight more FX3s went into fleet service in London between December 1948 and January 1949. Sales were slow. London, along with the rest of the country, was still struggling to

Enclosed Drive

When the FX3 went on general sale in 1949 it was advertised as the 'Enclosed-Drive Taxi-Cab'. It may seem odd to describe it as such when there was no nearside front door, but it was the first London cab to be presented for passing with full weather protection for the driver. In all earlier models the nearside was exposed to the elements, even driver's door windows were forbidden until 1937. Patents for two designs of partition were applied for in 1948 in the joint names of Carbodies and John Hewitt Orr, the company's works manager. One of the partitions had two panes

that slid back and forth, and the other a single pane that slid up and down. Both patents were granted in June 1949, but the PCO approved only the side-ways-sliding window. The rising partition fouled the meter drive and its bulk was thought to take up too much luggage space. Besides this, it was considered to be too difficult to remove in an emergency if the cab were to be rolled on to its offside in an accident. Now the cab driver was beginning to enjoy some degree of comfort, albeit some way behind that offered on luxury cars.

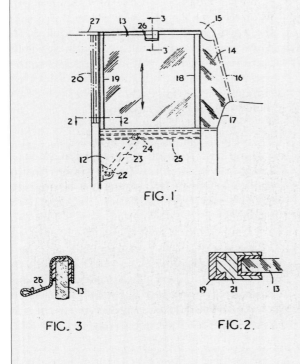

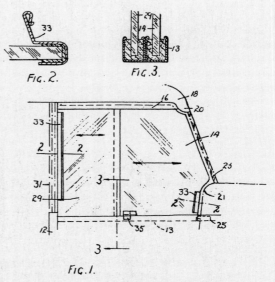

The two types of partition designed by John Orr of Carbodies for the FX3. On the left is the rise-and-fall type, rejected by the PCO as unsafe if the cab were to turn over. On the right is the forward-sliding type that was approved and later adopted by Nuffield for the Oxford and by Beardmore for the MkVII. (Author's collection)

recover from six years of war and greatly increased living costs. Fuel costs had almost doubled since the late 1930s and fares would not be increased from pre-war levels until 1951. To add to the misery, the Austin's big engine returned 18mpg (15.7ltr/100km)

compared with a 12/4's 25mpg (11.3ltr/100km). An attempt to improve fuel consumption was made by fitting a higher ratio back axle and a smaller, 1 1/2in carburettor, but its effect was minimal.

The FX2, photographed in Carbodies' canteen. This vehicle had a coach-built body clad in aluminium. It remained in service until the 1970s in York. Holding the white screen behind the cab is John Orr, Carbodies' works manager. (Jamie Borwick)

An Early FX3, passed after the PCO had allowed wheel trims. Previously they were forbidden so that, when Carriage Officers made inspections at cab ranks, they could see whether all the cab's wheel nuts were in place. Other early improvements included plastic headlining, a rubber mat to replace the original coconut mat and trafficators. (Jamie Borwick)

Diesel Power and a Better Deal for Buyers

In 1950 the price of petrol rose to 3s.3³/₄d. (16.5p) per gallon. The FX3's thirst particularly hit fleet proprietors who were paying for the fuel, which was inclusive in the drivers' cab rental. On top of this, a cab drivers' strike succeeded in raising their share of the meter from 25 per cent to 37.5. The proprietors needed something drastic to help them with this double blow.

Diesel road fuel, derv (from *d*iesel *e*ngined *r*oad *v*ehicle), was cheaper than petrol. At the end of the war the Standard Motor Company had signed an agreement with Harry Ferguson to design and make a new tractor, using the new 2.1-litre Standard Vanguard petrol engine. This tractor would become famous as the 'Little Grey Fergie'. Farm or 'red' diesel was tax-free and farmers preferred a diesel tractor so Standard engaged the research engineers Freeman Sanders to develop a diesel version of the Vanguard engine for the new tractor. As soon as the

diesel tractor was announced in 1951, John Birch, a bus, cab and coach operator of Kentish Town, north London, approached Standard. A 'Fergie' diesel, as the engine became known, was fitted into FX3 number KGT 109. Because the engine's power output of 29bhp was so low, Freeman Sanders modified it to produce a much more useful 40bhp. This, the very first diesel-powered London cab, was approved in August 1952. Trials were successful: from 1952 Birch converted all his thirty FX3s to diesel power and also offered a conversion to other proprietors for £255. Diesel power had arrived in the London cab trade.

Both the Hackney Transport and Engineering Company and Dives of Stockwell adapted the 1.8-litre Borgward Hansa engine to fit the FX3 in 1953 and Perkins offered their big 3-litre P4C diesel in both the FX3 and Oxford for £280. The London General had experimented with diesel engines, particularly the Mercedes-Benz 170 and the Borgward, but both were underpowered. The 'Fergie' proved to be the best, and the General converted

The Standard diesel engine installed in the FX3. (Graham Hill)

their entire fleet. Soon their FX3s were lining up at the forecourt diesel pumps, with filler caps painted yellow to ensure that they were filled with the right fuel. The General's fleet manager Geoff Trotter, described the conversion as 'an economic necessity'.

The Birch Cab

Like many people in the trade, John Birch knew how outdated the FX3 was and so he approached Standard in 1953 with a plan to build something new. A letter for Birch to Standard, written some time after the cab's introduction to resolve a dispute with the Treasury over whether purchase tax should be paid on the vehicle, clearly outlines what happened. It suggests that there was a serious intent to put the vehicle into production.

As a result of our conversations in 1953 it was agreed that Standard's should produce a prototype chassis meeting the constructional features demanded by the Commissioner of Police for licensing a London taxicab and the chassis was delivered to us in 1954.

The arrangement was that Standard's should provide the chassis on loan, that we should provide the body and that we should run the vehicle in London to obtain operational experience with it to be passed back to Standard's from time to time. The vehicle was completed in late 1955 and went into operation in early 1956 since when it has been used exclusively as a taxicab.

The Vanguard's wheelbase, at 94in (2.39m), was too short to carry a cab body, but, in their South African factory, Standard made a 101in (2.57m) wheelbase utility version of the chassis. One example, chassis number X541, was set aside and modified with its steering adapted to meet the turning circle. The engine was a standard diesel, number DEC 479E, mated to the Vanguard's three-speed gearbox. The Birch carried the Vanguard's independent coil spring and wishbone front suspension and hydraulic brakes.

The Birch's fully enclosed body was built by Park Royal Bodies Ltd. Park Royal's chief designer Alfred Hill drew up the plans to what was probably Birch's design. It had a unique arrangement of the four passenger seats and

The Birch cab. The designer Alfred Hill took the cab's front end styling from the contemporary Standard Ten. The severe lines of the body reveal that it was designed by a bus and caravan builder. It was nicknamed 'the ice-cream van'. (Jamie Borwick)

93

The luggage compartment of the Birch. Visible through the nearside front window is the back of the rear-facing, fourth passenger seat. Note the absence of a nearside front door. (Derek Pearce Collection)

the luggage compartment, where three passengers sat on the back seat and the fourth in a rearward-facing, fixed seat alongside the driver, separated from him by a partition. A survey made just before the Birch cab was designed showed that only one in ten cab journeys was made by more than one person, thus Birch decided that the fourth person could put up with a less comfortable ride. The luggage compartment was behind the rear seat, access to it was by a single door.

The cab was licensed by PCO on 21 December 1955, and it was put on a six-

month test at the beginning of 1956 with the plan to send it back to Standard from time to time. *Motor Transport* road tested it and liked it. Compared with the Fergie-powered FX3, it was smooth, thanks to its improved engine mountings and it was pleasant to drive. Acceleration was modest, but far more important was its fuel consumption of 37mpg (7.6ltr/100km).

However, its future was in doubt. The Standard Motor Company were planning a new model, the Phase III Vanguard, which did not use a separate chassis. Standard's fortunes were then waning and, in the light of this, their new managing director Alick Dick would hardly have thought that to tool up for a steel body for a purpose-built cab would be a profitable venture. In any case, Standard, like Austin, had problems finding adequate body-making capacity. Thus the likelihood of its going into production was virtually nil. The impending introduction of a replacement for the FX3 put the final nail into the coffin of the Birch cab. Nevertheless, it ran for several years before being used as an inspection vehicle for the Birch Brothers' coach fleet, based at Henlow Camp in Bedfordshire, to where the company ran a service from London. It was from there that it was most likely scrapped.

The End of the Oxford

In 1952 a new organization, the British Motor Corporation (BMC), was formed by the merger of Austin and the Nuffield Organization. Lord Nuffield subsequently retired and this gave Leonard Lord the opportunity to make Austin the dominant partner. The Oxford cab, production of which had been moved to Ward End to make room at Adderley Park for tractors and transmissions, was one of the first casualties of Lord's restructuring. Around 1,926 Oxfords had been made by the time production ended in 1953.

The Beardmore MkVII

Beardmore learned in a telephone call from BMC that they were about to lose the Oxford. They would have a year's grace before it finally ceased production, but were not given the opportunity to buy the rights to the cab and continue to build it themselves. Beardmore were left with the options of either servicing the existing Oxfords until spares ran out and then cease trading, or

---

Birch MkI: Technical Specification

Engine		**Dimensions**	
Type	Standard 4-cylinder in-line diesel, water-cooled, cast iron cylinder block, cast iron cylinder head with Freeman Sanders spherical combustion chambers, overhead valves, three-bearing crankshaft	Wheelbase	8ft 5in (2.56m)
		Running Gear	
		Steering	cam and roller
		Brakes	hydraulic all four wheels, drums all round, mechanical pull up handbrake on rear wheels
Cubic capacity	2092cc	Rear axle	semi-floating hypoid drive
Bore and stroke	80.96mm × 101.6mm (3.18in × 4.0in)	Wheels and tyres	16in pressed steel disc wheels with 5.75 × 16 Dunlop Taxicord tyres
Compression ratio	17:1		
Power	45bhp @ 3,000rpm	Front suspension	independent with wishbones and coil springs, telescopic shock absorbers
Torque	92lb/ft @ 2,000rpm		
Transmission		Rear suspension	longitudinal, semi-elliptical springs and telescopic hydraulic shock absorbers
Type	manual, three-speed plus reverse, synchromesh on 2nd and 3rd gears, column gear change		
Clutch	Borg and Beck 9in single dry plate, hydraulically operated	**Electrical System**	
		Type	12v positive earth

designing and making a cab of their own. They chose the latter.

Although Beardmore could not have the entire Oxford, its chassis was made by Rubery Owen and it was available to them. Throughout 1953 Beardmore's works manager J.A.M. Bates designed a new cab around it and planned modern running gear. Ford had introduced two new ohv engines, a 2262cc, 6-cylinder for the Zephyr and a 1508cc, 4-cylinder for the Consul. One pre-production chassis was fitted with the Consul and another with the Zephyr engine. The 6-cylinder chassis was fast, but heavy on fuel compared with the Consul chassis, and so Beardmore, conscious of fuel consumption, chose the Consul. The rear axle was of the ENV type used on the MkVII Jaguar saloon and the brakes were Lockheed hydraulic, also of the type supplied to Jaguar.

The chassis of the MkVII Beardmore. (Author's collection)

By contrast, the front beam axle came from a milk float. The Burman worm and nut steering box was a specially built variant, with a longer worm to cope with the turning circle. There were also telescopic dampers, which were coming into use on motor cars but not yet used on London cabs. The Oxford's engine had a dry sump, but the Ford engine had the well of its sump at the front. Rather than having an expensive new sump designed, Bates relocated the Beardmore's front axle 3 1/2in (8.9cm) further back on the springs to accommodate the well of the Ford engine's sump.

Although the Conditions of Fitness did not forbid improvements, PCO approval was needed for what Beardmore wanted, despite the fact that all these features were commonplace in contemporary cars. The PCO's vehicle inspecting officers were serving policemen who had been trained for the job and it was still their way to err far too much on the side of caution, with the result that London's cabs lagged behind what the rest of the motor industry considered to be normal. In October 1953 Luther and Bates met Mr Gould, the PCO Superintendent, and outlined the specifications they planned for the new cab. He expressed concern that the linkage of steering column gear change might jam in the new cab as it had begun to do in Ford cars, but he was not opposed in principle to these 'innovations', and work began on a prototype.

Next, a body was needed. Like the FX3, the design would be of pre-war appearance rather than modern. The board's claim was that the new MkVII would be the lightest, most economical, purpose-built London cab yet made. They also said that they were single-minded in that it would be hand-built by craftsmen from the finest materials to ensure long life and be a first-class investment. It has been said that Luther was very much a traditionalist and wanted an old style cab, but, in truth, Beardmore had little choice other than a

1906 Renault

This 1906 Renault AG is believed to be the oldest surviving London taxi. The Renault came into service in late 1906, but it was approved by the PCO before the Conditions of Fitness came into operation, which meant that it had neither a 10in ground clearance nor a 25ft turning circle. The body on this model was designed for two passengers, but extra tip-up seats were added shortly after it was built.

1929 Morris-Commercial 'G' Type 'International'

This is the only surviving example out of 1700 made between 1929 and 1932, and it was last licensed to work in 1939. The three-quarter landaulet body was the only type available. The 2.5-litre sv engine produced phenomenal torque.

1932 Beardmore Hyper

The MkII 'Hyper' Beardmore was the first cab to comply with the relaxed Conditions of Fitness of 1928. This is one of only two that survive. The full windscreen was a later addition. (Photos: Peter Kimberley)

1930 Austin 12/4 HL

Austin gave their first 12/4 cab the model code HL. Because it stood so tall the cab trade nicknamed it the 'High Lot'. This example carries a full landaulet body by Vincents of Reading and is understood to be one of the oldest surviving Austin 12/4 cabs.

1951 Nuffield Oxford

The MkIII Nuffield Oxford was the last model to be built. It featured the additional rear side window that was introduced on the MkII, but the pressed steel Easiclean wheels were new.

1949 Austin FX3

Understood to be the oldest Austin FX3 in existence, this petrol-engined example (below) carries Royal Maroon side panels, painted on to commemorate the coronation of Queen Elizabeth II in 1953. The FX3 had its own distinct bonnet mascot (left).

Beardmore MkVII

The survival rate of Beardmore MkVIIs is in quite a high proportion to the numbers built. The first examples carried three-door bodies by Windover, identified by the almost vertical boot. The all-black vehicle is a 1956 model. It has an opening windscreen, a feature that was insisted upon by the PCO to enable cabmen to see better in fog. The maroon-over-black cab is a 1966 four-door MkVII, one of the last to be built. Note the distinct sloping boot of its Weymann body.

Winchester Mk3

The Mk3 Winchester used Ford running gear on the original chassis and its body was built by Wincanton Engineering. The bumpers and grille are glass fibre mouldings. The mating of the Winchester's full-width body to a chassis designed for a pre-war coachbuilt body necessitated the use of an internal step (left) instead of a running board. As a result, the Winchester became known in the trade as the 'pick 'em up and pull 'em out' cab, because the passengers who were unaware of the step would fall flat on their faces as they got in!

Austin FX4

The FX4 remained in production for a remarkable thirty-nine years. This 1971 example is one of the first to have a 2.5-litre engine and to be built entirely by Carbodies. To this day, the fuel filler caps on London cabs must not be covered by a flap, to ensure that Carriage Officers may see that they are in place.

traditional, coach-built body. They could not afford the considerable tooling costs for an all-steel body and did not have access to any such facilities as existed at Carbodies; nor was there the space at Hendon for a high enough production run. Beardmore's north London neighbour Windover made them a traditional, coach-built body. But, although Windover had been making bodies for luxury cars for half a century, they had abandoned this type of work after the war since there were few makers left that needed the services of coach-builders and there were few customers to buy what were built. Now they were concentrating on bus bodies and had no design pattern for a modern, full-width car body. However, Windover did at least have the Oxford body as a pattern, which complied with the dimensions specified in the Conditions of Fitness and, of course, fitted the chassis. The cab's body would be clad in aluminium, which, although more expensive than steel, was at the time far more readily available and lighter. This would reduce the cab's total weight and thus

help its fuel consumption. In mid 1954 the new cab was submitted for type approval. The PCO found eighteen detail faults on the cab, but there was nothing that Bates could not remedy, and type approval was given to chassis number BM/7/1 on 10 November 1954.

Sadness marked 1954 with the death of Francis Luther, who was in his early seventies. To replace him, the board invited Francis Allsworth, the son of the George Allsworth, to return from the USA to take over as managing director. The younger Allsworth had been managing director of the Coupé Company before going to America to study production methods. Despite wanting an up-to-date body, he had to accept that it was too late to make major changes to the MkVII and it was introduced at the 1954 Commercial Motor Exhibition. The first production model, chassis number, BM/7/2, was delivered on 4 February the following year.

Beardmore began to make changes to the body almost immediately. The aluminium roof was difficult and expensive to form. By the

The first MkVII Beardmore, with its distinctive flat back. The first five examples were built to this design. Subsequent models had a notched back. (Author's collection)

time the first MkVII had been delivered a plastic roof had been given type approval. In June 1955 a modified body on chassis BM/7/6 was submitted to the PCO. As well as having the new roof, it had a different back end, with a defined 'notch-back' boot, and a shallower windscreen. Type approval for this style of body was given shortly after on chassis BM/7/7. Only chassis numbers 1 to 3 had the original body style. From chassis no.4 onwards all production MkVIIs would have the new back, but the new roof would not be seen on production MkVIIs for three more years.

Once again, what looked like bad fortune struck. In 1956, exactly a century after Windover was founded, they were purchased by Henlys, the big chain of motor dealers. The new owners announced that they would put an end to body making operations and turn Windover into an extension of their retail business. This they did, but honoured the existing orders for Beardmore, and the last Windover-bodied MkVII was delivered in December 1957. Beardmore had a few months to find a new body supplier and signed up with the Weymann division of Metro-Cammell-Weymann. For Beardmore,

the changeover to a new body maker went with no interruption to supply; in fact, there was an overlap, with the first Weymann-bodied MkVII being delivered almost a month before the last from Windover.

To keep the MkVII's price competitive with the FX3, Beardmore's profit amounted to a pitiful £50 per cab. At a production average of two per week that did not cover the wage bill. The company secretary Ken Jaeger tried in vain to make them understand that the cab was not generating any profit for future investment and the ultimate survival of the company. All Beardmore's board could see was the excess of the assets set against the liabilities on the balance sheet. Unfortunately, those assets were fixed and could not produce cash. When cash was needed, some hire-purchase agreements were sold to an outside finance house, which gave them the purchase price of the cab immediately.

Double Purchase Tax

In 1950 Britain was committing troops to fight in Korea, was attempting to put down a political insurgence in Malaya and was rearming to face the threat from the Warsaw Pact on the other side of the 'Iron Curtain'. The then Labour Chancellor of the Exchequer Hugh Gaitskell used the budget of April 1950 to raise some £830 million to pay for military expenditure. One of his measures was to levy double purchase tax on cars, including cabs. This put the price of an FX3 up to £1,210.3s.4d. Unsurprisingly, this resulted in

The mechanical taximeter lasted into the 1950s. This Metropolitan meter is geared to record the tariff set in 1951. When the flag was in the raised position, the cab was for hire. Swinging a quarter-turn to a horizontal position set the meter in operation. Turning it a further quarter turn stopped it. Note the circular lead seals, put in place by the National Physical Laboratory when the meter was assembled or reassembled after a tariff increase and by the PCO each time the cab was licensed. (Author)

*A preserved 1955
Beardmore Mk VII
with a Windover
body. (Author)*

Beardmore MkVII: Technical Specification

Engine

Type (petrol) — Ford Consul 4-cylinder in-line petrol, water-cooled, cast iron cylinder block, cast iron cylinder head with overhead valves, three-bearing crankshaft

Cubic capacity — 1508cc

Bore and stroke — 79.37mm × 76.2mm (3.13in × 3.0in)

Compression ratio — 6.8:1

Power — 47bhp @ 4,400rpm

Torque — 74lb/ft @ 2,400rpm

Type (diesel) — Perkins P99 4-cylinder in-line diesel, water-cooled, cast iron cylinder block, cast iron cylinder head with overhead valves

Cubic capacity — 1628cc

Bore and stroke — 76.2mm × 88.9mm (3in × 3.5in)

Compression ratio — 20:1

Power — 48bhp @ 4,000rpm

Torque — 73lb/ft @ 2,250rpm

Transmission

Type — manual, three-speed plus reverse, synchromesh on 2nd and 3rd gears, column gear change

Clutch — single dry plate, hydraulically operated

Dimensions

Wheelbase — 8ft 8in (2.64m)

Height overall — 5ft 10 3/4in (1.80m)

Length overall — 13ft 10 1/2in (4.23m)

Width — 5ft 6in (1.67m)

Track, front — 4ft 8 3/4in (1.43m)

Track, rear — 4ft 8in (1.42m)

Running Gear

Steering — Burman worm and nut

Brakes — Lockheed hydraulic all four wheels, drums all round, mechanical pull up handbrake on rear wheels

Front axle — I-section axle beam

Rear axle — overhead worm drive

Wheels and tyres — 16in pressed steel disc wheels with 5.75 x 16 Dunlop Taxicord tyres

Front and rear suspension — longitudinal leaf springs and telescopic hydraulic shock absorbers

Electrical System

Type — 12v positive earth

a significant drop in the sales of new cabs. One small ray of hope was a 33 per cent fare increase, with the flagfall raised to 1s.3d. (6.25p). The benefit of this was cancelled out in January 1952 when the price of the FX3 increased further to £1309, a restriction of the hire purchase period to 18 months and a rise in the price of petrol to 4s.3d. (21.25p) a gallon. To try to ease the burden on the trade,

Robert Overton and representatives from the LMCPA and the TGWU lobbied extensively for the removal of purchase tax on cabs. In the April 1953 budget, the new Conservative Chancellor R.A. Butler not only abolished it but also laid down legislation that banned the imposition of such a tax on cabs approved by the PCO. The effect of this was that the sales of new cabs increased and, at last, the pre-war

---

Austin FX3 Petrol and Diesel: Technical Specification

Engine

Type (petrol)	Austin, 4-cylinder in-line petrol, water-cooled, cast iron cylinder block, cast iron cylinder head with overhead valves, three-bearing crankshaft
Cubic capacity	2199cc
Bore and stroke	79.4mm × 111.1mm (3.125in × 4.375in)
Compression ratio	6.8:1
Power	62bhp @ 3,800rpm
Torque	102lb/ft @ 1,600rpm
Type (diesel)	Austin, 4 cylinder, in-line diesel, water-cooled, cast iron cylinder block, cast iron cylinder head with overhead valves, three-bearing crankshaft
Cubic capacity	2178cc
Bore and stroke	82.6mm × 101.6mm (3.25in × 4.0in)
Compression ratio	20:1
Power	55bhp @ 3,500rpm
Torque	89lb/ft @ 2,800rpm
Injector pump	C.A.V. rotary

Transmission

Type	manual, four-speed, synchromesh on 2nd, 3rd and 4th gears plus reverse
Clutch	Borg and Beck 9in single dry plate

Dimensions

Wheelbase	9ft 2 5/8in (2.81m)
Height overall	5ft 10 3/4in (1.80m)
Length overall	14ft 5 1/4in (4.40m)
Width	5ft 7 1/2in (1.71m)
Track, front	4ft 8in (1.42m)
Track, rear	4ft 8in (1.42m)

Running Gear

Steering	cam and peg type
Ratio	20:1
Brakes	Girling mechanical all four wheels, twin leading shoe on front, 11in (28cm) drums all round, mechanical pull up handbrake on rear wheels
Rear axle, pre-1955	worm drive
Rear axle, 1955 onwards	hypoid bevel drive
Differential ratio, pre-1950	5.2:1
Differential ratio, post-1950	4.8:1
Wheels and tyres	16in pressed steel disc wheels with 5.7 x 516 Dunlop Taxicord tyres
Front suspension	I-section axle beam with longitudinal leaf springs and double-acting lever-arm hydraulic shock absorbers
Rear suspension	longitudinal, semi-elliptical springs and double-acting lever-arm hydraulic shock absorbers

Electrical System

Type	12v positive earth, two 6v batteries

cabs still surviving were soon withdrawn from service. Some of these were sold to students, who often took them on tours of the British mainland, Europe and sometimes much further afield.

A New Austin Diesel Engine

Some large fleet proprietors wanted the benefits of diesel power, but were not happy with the 'Fergie' engine. They pressed Robert Overton to ask Austin to build a diesel engine of their own. Overton spoke to George Harriman of BMC and, in December 1953, Austin announced that they were going to develop such a diesel engine from the 2.2-litre petrol engine. By mid 1954 the new engine, also of 2.2 litres but with a different bore and stroke, was fitted in a small number of FX3s. The conversion received type approval and

went on trial for a period of six months. It returned 30mpg (9.4ltr/100km), more than halving the operational fuel costs of the petrol engine. The production diesel version, the FX3D, was announced at the 1954 Commercial Motor Exhibition. However, there were teething troubles, the blocks tended to split and, if the injector timing went out, it would fire before the top of the stroke and send the engine into reverse, pumping out clouds of smoke. Austin soon had the pump modified and the diesel FX3 became by far the most popular option. Mushes as well as fleet owners had Austin diesel engines fitted to their FX3s, including some that previously had Ferguson or Perkins conversions. The fuel rationing that was an outcome of the 1956 Suez crisis was confirmation that diesel power was here to stay and that Austin had made the right decision in making the new engine.

The Oxford received two upgrades in its life: the Series 2 had Easiclean steel wheels; the Series 3, pictured here, had additional windows, which improved its appearance and made its interior lighter. (Jamie Borwick)

Beardmore Diesel

Beardmore were not far behind with a diesel option. In 1955 they offered Perkins's new small diesel engine, the 4-cylinder 4.99, in a MkVII. This 1.6-litre engine (its capacity in cubic inches was 99, hence its type number) had been tested for some months in chassis number BM/7/4, with the specially sought registration, RYT 99 (RYT for 'right' and 99 for the engine). But, reliable as it was, the Perkins was noisy and not quite powerful enough for the job. Besides, it made the cab heavier by a full hundredweight (50kg), which further handicapped performance. Not surprisingly, the take-up was low, with fewer than one in ten diesels sold, compared to the reverse with the FX3.

The ten years following the end of the war were indeed difficult. The next would be even more so, but it would not be hardship that would be the main problem: a total outsider would threaten the cab trade's very existence.

Automatic Transmissions

Borg-Warner DG150M
It was a habit of older cabmen, used to crash boxes, to slip the clutch rather than change down. This meant that cab masters were constantly changing clutches. The automatic gearbox had begun to appear on luxury cars and some cab proprietors considered it to be an economic alternative to clutch replacement. Austin adapted an FX3 chassis to take the Borg-Warner DG150M unit, and in March 1957 type approval was given for twenty FX3s to be adapted.

Reports of its performance were favourable for the eighteen that were actually built. The FX3 never went into production with an automatic transmission but it provided Austin with some valuable information.

Hobbs Mecha-Matic
Hobbs Transmissions were an independent company that had been taken over by BSA in the early 1950s.

They designed and built an automatic transmission with a mechanical changing mechanism and no fluid flywheel which, it was claimed, cut down power loss. It was called the Mecha-Matic. To show its reliability, David Hobbs, the son of the company's founder, rallied a Jaguar XK120 and later raced a Lotus Elite, each fitted with the 'box. It had been tested by BSA in an FX3 (although not in London) as they had it in mind for the FX4 (Carbodies had not long been taken over BSA). Beardmore tested one in a MkVII, but it slowed the cab's performance to an unacceptable level. Ultimately this was a blessing in disguise. The single known Mecha-Matic gearbox still in existence is in the only surviving Lanchester Sprite, and the owner of this unit construction car of the mid 1950s attributes its survival to the Mecha-Matic's habit of occasionally dumping all its oil on to the underside of the car!

---

7   1956–66 Upheaval and Uncertainty

The 1950s saw Mann & Overton and Austin consolidated as the biggest names in the London cab trade. In the 1960s, when Britain began to enjoy an unprecedented period of prosperity, the trade would face the most difficult challenge in its existence, the minicab. This interloper would set off a chain of events that would last more than four decades.

Changes at Beardmore

When Ford brought out the Mk2 Consul in 1956, it came with a larger, 1703cc engine, but it was not until May 1958 that the new engine was fitted to the Beardmore. In October 1958 Beardmore's general sales manager Ted Vaughan wrote to the PCO, advising them that early on in the new year the assembling of cabs would be transferred from Hendon to the Weymann factory in Addlestone; Colindale was to be closed. Vaughan also wrote to all owners concerning the move to tell them that servicing in London would be carried out by an associate company of Beardmore, Graham Terrace Motors. It was an economic necessity to move body production down to Weymann's bus building factory in Addlestone, but Beardmore could not have guessed where this association would eventually lead.

The FX4

In 1954 Carbodies' owner Bobby Jones sold out to BSA and retired. Jack Hellberg moved from Nuffield to become Carbodies' com-

mercial manager and in March 1955 he was asked by Mann & Overton to collaborate with Austin to plan a new cab. To take account of the great increase in development costs, Austin's engineer Albert Moore and chief draughtsman Charles Benlow began with the existing FX3 chassis. They fitted it with the independent front suspension from larger, contemporary BMC cars and with the Austin Westminster rear axle. The engine would be the FX3's 2.2 diesel mated to a Borg-Warner DG150M automatic gearbox. There would be dual-circuit hydraulic brakes, using parallel master cylinders, mounted under the floor, with one master cylinder operating the front brakes and the other the rear. Neither a petrol engine nor a manual gearbox were to be offered – the cab masters' wishes had been granted.

Austin's design engineer Eric Bailey sketched out the body. The cab's original code was ADO6 (ADO standing for Austin Drawing Office) but this was changed to FX4, using Austin's pre-BMC numbering system. On 4 June 1956 Mann & Overton's David Southwell and the PCO's Mr Gould went to see the first mock-up that had been produced by Carbodies' works manager Percy McNally. Despite the modern mechanical specification, the cab's three-door body was an anachronism. Gould did not like its upward-opening 'crocodile' bonnet and he thought that the headrests fitted to the rear seat were unhygienic; he disliked the fixed windscreen, believing that an opening windscreen gave the

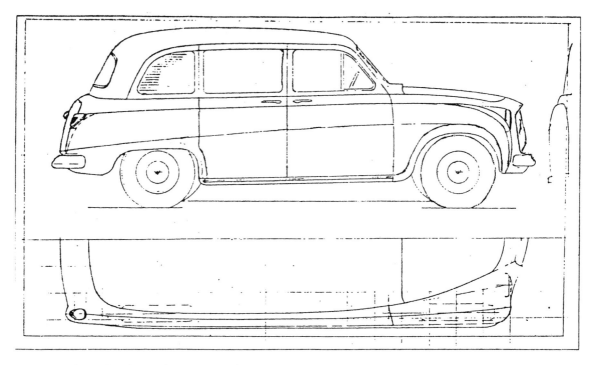

Eric Bailey's first outline drawing for the FX4. Bailey has been quoted as saying that he was aiming to produce a design that was not controversial, but he surely would not have imagined that he was developing what would become one of the world's most recognizable motor vehicles. (Author's collection)

driver better visibility in the pea-soup fogs then common in London before the passing of the clean air legislation. He was persuaded to approve a fixed one, but recommended the fitting of a fourth door.

Bailey then produced the shape of the FX4 that has become familiar the world over. At Carbodies the chief engineer Jake Donaldson developed the design for production. He hinged the one-piece bonnet and grille on the scuttle in one piece and designed the inner and the outer front wings and the lower body sills so that they could be unbolted for ease of replacement. For durability and ease of cleaning, the interior trim panels were one-piece plastic mouldings.

The need for a new cab was pressing: the number of cabs in London had dropped to

below 7,000. Application for type approval for the FX4 chassis was submitted to the PCO on 10 January 1958, and the first complete prototype, VLW 431, was presented on 27 June and passed on 14 July. When representatives from the cab trade had their first glimpse at Carbodies' factory they were disappointed. They disliked the way the doors were hinged at the back edge. Geoff Trotter, the managing director of the London General, called it 'a recipe for disaster' and described the bonnet as 'diabolical'. Barney Davis, the taciturn managing director of Felday Cabs, called it 'a bloody awful vehicle' and Robert Overton, dismayed with the cab's reception, wrote in his diary, 'What a headache this is going to be!'

VLW 431 was tested by York Way Motors of King's Cross and was used that year for pro-

VLW 431 was the first pre-production FX4. It went into service with York Way Motors during the summer of 1958 before the model was released for sale. It is pictured here outside one of the gates of South Park, Fulham, around the corner from Mann & Overton's premises. To preserve passenger privacy the much larger rear window was made of darkened glass, which reduced its effectiveness and the PCO would not allow an interior driving mirror. And there were some detail faults: door handles were too fragile and were replaced by much sturdier ones, and the circular hatch in the partition was soon replaced by a glass panel that slid up and down. (LVTA Archives)

A late FX3 and an early FX4 waiting for the traffic lights to change before crossing Westminster Bridge and heading, probably for Waterloo station. (Derek Pearce)

motional photographs and films. The FX4 was announced to the trade in September 1958, and shown at the Commercial Motor Show. The FL2 hire car version was exhibited at the Earls Court Motor Show. Type approval was granted on 25 November and the cab went on sale at £1,198. The press release projected London sales of fifty a week, which turned out to be very optimistic. Production difficul-

ties, due to the inadequate press tools, held up delivery and in June 1959 David Southwell of Mann & Overton wrote to the PCO to apologize for the delay. If a proprietor wanted to run a cab for longer than the proscribed ten years, he would have to apply for an extension. Because of the delay in the delivery of new FX4s, Gould had to extend the working life of a large number of FX3s in order to

---

1958 Austin FX4 Diesel: Technical Specification

Engine

Type	Austin 4 cylinder in-line diesel, water-cooled, Type 22E (automatic transmission) 22K (synchromesh transmission), cast iron cylinder block, cast iron cylinder head with overhead valves, three-bearing crankshaft
Cubic capacity	2178cc
Bore and stroke	82.6mm × 101.6mm (3.25in × 4.0in)
Compression ratio	18:1
Power	55bhp @ 3,500rpm
Torque	89lb/ft @ 2,800rpm
Injector pump	C.A.V. in-line

Transmission

Type	Borg Warner Type DG150M 3-speed with lock up on third gear

Dimensions

Wheelbase	9ft 2 5/8in (2.81m)
Height overall	5ft 8 11/16in (1.74m)
Length overall	14ft 11 7/16in (4.56m)
Width	5ft 8 5/8in (1.74m)

Running Gear

Steering	cam and peg type, ratio 20:1
Brakes	dual circuit hydraulic to all four wheels, parallel master cylinders, twin leading shoe on front, 11in drums all round, mechanical pull up handbrake on rear wheels
Rear axle	hypoid bevel drive
Differential ratio	4.8:1
Propeller shaft	open shaft with needle roller bearing universal joints
Wheels and tyres	16in pressed steel disc wheels with 5.75 × 16 Dunlop Taxicord tyres
Front suspension	independent coil spring with double-acting lever type shock absorbers
Rear suspension	longitudinal, semi-elliptical springs with double-acting lever type shock absorbers

Electrical System

Type	12v positive earth, two 6v batteries

---

maintain sufficient cabs on the streets. The press tools were designed by Percy McNally, who had a limited knowledge of the job. To sort out the problems, Carbodies brought back Bill Lucas, who had worked on the FX3 but had left when Carbodies sold out to BSA, to design new press tools for the roof, bonnet and boot.

But not all was well when those cabs were delivered. In the first couple of weeks the bonnet of a cab on its way to Heathrow airport flew open, causing an accident. Representatives of Borg-Warner showed members of the LMCPA some damaged components from returned gearboxes and blamed the damage on bad driving. They had some justification since older drivers had no expe-

rience of automatic gearboxes, but Borg-Warner discovered that the gearbox was a mismatch for the engine. A diesel engine's torsional vibration would be absorbed by a torque converter but the DG had a drive lock-up which transmitted the vibrations to the internal components of the gearbox, wearing them out prematurely.

In September 1961 type approval was given for the four-speed synchromesh gearbox from the Austin Gypsy to be fitted as an option to the automatic. In 1962, when the fittings for a manual gearbox were available on the chassis, the 2.2-litre petrol engine, which had been the original power plant of the FX3 was introduced as an option. Borg-Warner's new Model 35 automatic replaced the DG in

1964. No automatic gearbox was offered in the British market with the petrol engine, either for the FL2 or the FX4.

The Beardmore MkVIII

In 1957 Beardmore's managing director Francis Allsworth put in place the design of a MkVIII and a chassis was set aside for the prototype in February 1960. Its wheelbase was longer by 2in (5cm), but the beam front axle and the cart springs were kept. Outline plans were submitted to the PCO in February 1961 for a full width shape, and a prototype body in glass reinforced plastic (GRP) was built at Hampshire Car Bodies (HCB) of Totton, in Southampton.

On 19 March 1961 F.W. Perrett, the Chief Inspecting Officer of the PCO, visited HCB to look at the MkVIII. He saw that it complied with the Conditions of Fitness, but the restrictions of his job limited the way in which he could express his disappointment. He criticized the shape of the wheel arches as being too acute and the grille as being too flat. That the passenger doors were hinged on the central B post was noted, although not objected to. The roofline, which added

3in (7.5cm) over the MkVII's 76in (1.93m) height, was criticized for being too bulky. This report was a disappointment for Beardmore, but they pressed on.

To find development money for the MkVIII, Allsworth approached the London General Cab Company. His idea was to create a situation similar to that which existed with Austin, Carbodies and Mann & Overton. In the summer of 1961 The General's board went down to Weymann at Addlestone. The visitors were horrified as the factory doors were drawn back. Their opinion of the MkVIII was decisive: they hated it, it was not the compact cab they believed the trade needed. They had no option but to turn down Beardmore's invitation.

The Winchester

The lack of a viable alternative to the FX4 prompted the Owner Drivers' Society to enter the manufacturing field. For decades they had run the Westminster Insurance Society for owner-drivers. The consulted their membership and in 1960 put in hand the design of a new type of cab, called the Winchester. A company was formed to build

Francis Allsworth, Ted Vaughan and one other in conversation in the back of the Beardmore MkVIII in Beardmore's showroom at 167–9 Great Portland Street. Despite the picture's poor quality, one can see why both the PCO and the board of the London General disliked the cab. (Stanley Roth)

107

it, Winchester Automobiles (West End) Ltd, with Ken Drummond as managing director; he was a leading figure in the ODS and Westminster Insurance.

The Mk2 Birch

The same motive prompted John Birch in 1960 to try and design his own cab once more. This time it was based on the Standard Atlas van, which had been styled by Standard-Triumph's Giovanni Michelotti. Unfortunately, the Atlas was a disaster, it was underpowered and front-heavy, with a narrow front track that made it unstable. The engine and the front suspension were carried in a subframe that bolted on to a unit construction body, but the two parts were liable to part company. However, the Atlas had a 29ft (8.8m) turning circle, which could be reduced to meet the Conditions of Fitness. The regulations demanded a full chassis, so a new one

was fabricated, to which was the Atlas's front subframe was bolted. To power it, the Perkins 4.99 diesel was mated to the Standard four-speed gearbox.

Park Royal Vehicles modified an Atlas van body by reshaping the roofline with raked back rear window to create a large separate boot. Birch hoped that the cab would sell for between £200 and £300 less than the FX4's £1,198. But would the PCO approve of it? Birch would soon find out. In a letter to Sir Austin Strutt of the Home Office, the PCO passed its verdict on in May 1961. They said: 'Last Monday Mr John Birch produced his Standard Atlas motor chassis . . . for our inspection. We did not care for the design.' On inspection, the PCO felt that the Atlas's narrow front track would make it unstable and they did not like the fact that the kingpins were mounted direct to the transverse leaf spring, which, if it fractured, the PCO felt would leave the vehicle without steering. The chassis was not approved.

The chassis of the Mk2 Birch consisted of a Standard Atlas subframe bolted to a fabricated rear chassis assembly. The engine is a Perkins 4.99 diesel, mated to a Standard 4-speed manual gearbox. (National Archive)

The Minicab

When Prime Minister Harold Macmillan won the 1959 general election he had campaigned on the message 'You've never had it so good!' He was right: there was full employment and most people had more money to spend than they had ever had. Along with prosperity, came a growing demand for cabs, but cab numbers in London had slumped to 7,000. Carbodies could not build enough FX4s to make up the shortfall and the PCO could not put cab drivers through the Knowledge of London examination to drive them quickly enough if they could. Speaking in Parliament in November 1960, Rupert Spier, MP criticized the London cab trade for being outdated. He also called for a central telephone system to enable the public to book cabs and a smaller, cheaper type of cab. Dennis Vosper, MP, the minister responsible for cabs, answered by saying that smaller cabs would not be viable nor would they stand the accompanying wear and tear. There was, however, someone who disagreed with Vosper. He was Michael Gotla, a law graduate and the proprietor of the private hire firm, Welbeck Motors. In 1961, with financial backing from Isaac Wolfson of the Great Universal Stores Group, he put a fleet of red Renault Dauphine hire cars on the streets. He called them 'minicabs' and with them he planned to circumvent London's hackney carriage laws.

It is an offence for the driver of a private hire car, and that is what a minicab is, to accept a street or rank hiring in the same way as a taxi driver does. Private hire vehicles have to be pre-booked, but Gotla announced to the public that they could approach any of his drivers and pre-book the minicab with the office via a car's two-way radio. The drivers were under instruction not to take the passenger, but to make the booking and ask them to wait for a second minicab. The cab trade was in uproar, convinced that such a proce-

dure would not be followed, but that the driver would take the passenger without even making the radio call. The cab drivers were right and when they caught minicab drivers plying for hire, a violent situation often followed, as the minicab drivers, who were recruited from types who could 'look after themselves', retaliated.

Eventually, the courts ruled that the way that Gotla had instructed his drivers was illegal. Unsuccessful attempts were made by the cab section of the Transport and General Workers Union to outlaw minicabs altogether. To reform the laws governing plying for hire would have strengthened the police's hand in dealing with the minicab drivers' activities, but the Home Secretary R.A. Butler decided against it, feeling that the minicab was adequately controlled by existing law. Gotla's business failed not long after, but the die had been cast. The minicab trade boomed and eventually spread throughout the country, with minicabs outnumbering taxis many times over. But that was not the end of the matter, the call for cheaper cabs continued. Remembering the 'Jixi' fiasco, the trade were concerned about any changes to the Conditions of Fitness that might be made. Feeling that they would undermine the introduction of the new cabs that were under development, the LMCPA's secretary J.E.T. Welland wrote to Butler, suggesting that he set up an advisory body before making any decision. In response, Butler created the Hackney Carriage Advisory Committee, with Denis Vosper in the chair. The Committee's task was to review the Conditions of Fitness to see whether smaller, cheaper cabs were viable and could be produced in sufficient numbers or even replaced by saloon cars.

As a result, the MkVIII Beardmore, the Winchester and the Mk2 Birch, all designed to meet the existing regulations, were put on hold. Of these, only the Birch was a smaller, cheaper vehicle and, although the Home Office had a low opinion of it, the PCO were

A Genuine 'Minicab'?

The possibility that the Conditions of Fitness would be changed significantly or even scrapped had got Carbodies owner, BSA, seriously worried. BSA's most successful post-war chairman was John 'Jack' Sangster, a veteran of the Ariel Motorcycle Company. Serving between 1954 and 1961, Sangster was, at the end of his career, also chairman of Carbodies. When he retired he kept a close watch on the Coventry company, for which he had great affection.

Reading of the economic state of Welbeck Motors in the *Financial Times* in January 1961, Sangster realized that, if the Conditions of Fitness were altered to any considerable degree, Austin's and Mann & Overton's dominance of the market, and Carbodies' profit would be seriously affected. He decided that the best course of action was, 'if you can't beat 'em, join 'em'. BMC had recently introduced the Morris Mini-Minor and

Austin Seven, the world-famous 'Mini'. If the demand would be for small, economical vehicles, why not, Sangster reasoned, make a cab out of Britain's smallest proper car? Why not make a real 'Mini-Cab'?

A part of BSA that had been almost defunct since they had sold Daimler to Jaguar was Hooper, the coachbuilders. Sangster asked Hooper's chief designer Osmond Rivers to adapt an Austin Seven. He instructed Rivers to give the new vehicle as much headroom and legroom as he would the passengers in a Daimler limousine. Rivers did just that, adding sliding doors for easy access and well-upholstered seats. Eventually, the Hackney Carriage Advisory Committee recommended that the Conditions of Fitness should be retained and the 'Mini-Cab' was scrapped. As a footnote, Rivers's fee for designing the vehicle, £84, was paid by Carbodies.

Jack Sangster's 'Minicab'.
(Sir Henry Royce Memorial Fund)

placed in a quandary. In a letter written in May 1961, they said: '. . . failure to deal with and accept this vehicle (the Mk2 Birch) would cause immediate criticism.'

Beardmore were worried too. In July 1961 Allsworth wrote to the Commissioner of Police. saying,

We would appreciate any information you can give us as to this committee's progress and

when their findings, at least interim ones, can be expected. We already have in stock some £100,000 of specialist components as the basis for the first trial run of our new taxicab . . . With consistent and growing rumours that the new Assistant Commissioner will allow metropolitan taxicabs of substantially inferior specification that the present standard, we are reluctant to take on more liabilities . . . (and) much of the material might well have little more than scrap value. . .

A Renault Dauphine minicab of Welbeck Motors. Air France were early advertisers but withdrew when disputes between the cab trade and the minicab operators and drivers, both legal and personal, became headline news. (Stanley Roth)

In August, vested interests were invited to submit their case to the Committee. Allsworth's written submission supported the status quo, but he asked that manufacturers be allowed 'sufficient latitude to enable them to take rapid advantage of technological progress'. They also had the chance to offer their opinion verbally. Progress toward a conclusion was perilously slow, and, pressing the matter further, Allsworth wrote to Mr Perrett at the PCO in April 1962, saying, 'We are already committed to a new production programme of "conventional" taxicabs, and our financiers will not guarantee support for its implementation until they are assured that the existing regulations will, in general substance, continue in force.'

Eventually, the Advisory Committee decided to update the Conditions of Fitness but retain critical regulations such as the turning circle and the separation of driver and passengers. They did, however, remove the requirement for a separate chassis, citing that only luxury cars such as the Rolls-Royce and the Daimler used them. Certainly, the prominence of Mann & Overton and the FX4 played a crucial part in influencing the Advisory Committee's decision. Tellingly, the Committee said in an internal memorandum referring to the result if the regulations had been altered, 'We would be in danger of upsetting our major supplier, Austin.'

The Public Carriage Office

The first record of coaches plying for hire in London tells of one Capt Baily, a former sea captain, who placed four hackney coaches at the Maypole in the Strand. Many others copied him and soon the streets of London were clogged with hackney coaches, all fighting for trade. Laws governing hackney coaches were first passed in 1654 when, in the period that *Hansard* delightfully calls the 'Interregnum', England's Lord Protector Oliver Cromwell authorized the founding of the Fellowship of Master Hackney Coachmen. At the same time, he placed the licensing of hackney coaches and coachmen under the jurisdiction of the City of London. Most hackney coaches were cast-offs from nobility and were often badly maintained – 'hackney hell carts', they were sometimes called. An Act of 1662 laid down the minimum size of horse (in law, meaning a stallion), gelding or mare at 14 hands. Today, any equine under 14 hands 2in is considered to be a pony.

In 1679 the first Conditions of Fitness, designed to control the materials used in the design, manufacture and repair of hackney carriages were laid down. They were amended as new types of hackney coach were introduced, the most revolutionary being the French two-wheeled 'cabriolet'; the name cab is an abbreviation of this vehicle's name. In 1834 Joseph Aloysious Hansom designed a two-wheeled cab where the cabman sat high on the front of the roof, a most unsatisfactory position. John Chapman took this design and modified it in 1836 to produce the Hansom cab that we know – the 'gondolas of London' as the Prime Minister Benjamin Disraeli described them. Until the advent of the motor cab, the hansom and, from 1837, the four-wheeled 'growler' were familiar sights on London's streets.

In 1694, during the reign of William and Mary, the duty of licensing hackney coaches was passed to a part of the Treasury known as the Hackney Coach Office. This continued until 1831, when, for a brief period, control was placed in the hands of the Commissioner of Stamps. In 1838 the Office of Registrar of Public Carriages was created, but discontinued when an Act of 1843 gave authority to the Commissioner of the Metropolitan Police to control London's cab trade. Until the formation of the London County Council in 1889, London was governed by local vestries under the dubious auspices of the Metropolitan Board of Works. The Metropolitan Police Force, formed in 1829, was chosen because it was the only statutory body with jurisdiction over the entire metropolis. The absolute power the Commissioner had over the licensing London's cabs was diluted by an Act of 1869 when the Home Secretary was given overall authority. From 1838 the Commissioner also had control of driver licensing. In turn, the Commissioner devolved his authority to the Assistant Commissioner of Police (Traffic), who controlled the newly formed Public Carriage Office. In 1875 the Metropolitan Police took possession of new offices at Great Scotland Yard and in 1891 the Public Carriage and Lost Property Offices were transferred from Great Scotland Yard to a nearby new building, New Scotland Yard.

In the days of horse cabs, the PCO divided their 'patch' into ten districts and had twenty-four places where cabs could be inspected. Some of these were as rudimentary as a corner of the market yard in Bromley, Kent, where their activities were on view to every layabout and villain in the district. Upon the introduction of the motor cab, the huge numbers of vehicles involved created many logistical difficulties for the inspecting officers. However, in 1927 the PCO moved their headquarters to new a Metropolitan Police building in Lambeth Road, where modern facilities for inspecting cabs were provided. By then there were four districts with several passing stations in each. Located in police station yards, they were each open on specific days of the week, including Saturdays, and between 2 and 2 1/2 hours per day. District No.1 was served by Lewisham, Croydon and Lambeth, No.2 by Caledonian Road and Ilford, No.3 by Kilburn and Finchley and No.4 by North Fulham, Richmond, Kingston, Ealing and Sutton.

By the 1950s the PCO had just four passing stations, one in each district. With the exception of Lambeth Road, the stations were equipped with only basic equipment for the inspection of motor cabs. No.4 passing station was at Walham Green, Fulham, with two pits under cover. No.3 was on the site of Kilburn Police Station, which had been destroyed in the Blitz and had one roofed inspection bay. No.2 was on Caledonian Road and was said to be by far the worst. Equipped with neither pit nor ramp, the vehicle examiners had to examine the cabs' 'unders' by using a creeper. This was proving impossible with the FX4,

'The Yard' in the mid 1880s. Situated in Scotland Yard off Whitehall, this was the Metropolitan Police Public Carriage Office. The cabs awaiting inspection are, on the left, a hansom and on the right a growler. (Jamie Borwick)

which had a much lower ground clearance, without some form of axle stand or ramp. It was the busiest since the majority of cabs were garaged in north London and its vehicle examiners had to conduct their work amid the general business of the police station.

Lambeth Road was No.1 passing station. Here, the examiners inspected new types of cab and modifications of existing models for type approval. Other departments of the PCO based here dealt with driver licensing and conducted the Knowledge of London examinations. But the premises were crowded. The PCO had to work alongside the offices of the Receiver for the Metropolitan Police District, responsible for finance and administration, the Lost Property Office, the Receiver's Store and the Police Vehicles Main Garage, the Medical and Dental Branches and the offices for administering the licensing of London's bus drivers and conductors. The PCO shared the yard with the vehicles of the prison van, the children's bus and despatch van services and some of the Commissioner's and Receiver's fleets.

The Receiver's department wanted the Lambeth site for the construction of a new administration centre. In 1959 Sir Austin Strutt of the Home Office decided that some of the departments should be moved to other sites. He considered the housing of all the PCO departments in one building as a priority. The findings of a 1960 report by his department assessed the passing stations and how well they were used. Caledonian Road, although the worst equipped, was the most used and the decision was made to site the

new building somewhere near there. There was a site adjacent to it, vacant and available, but unsuitable for new premises. The most promising site was a disused former Territorial Army depot, once the headquarters of the Finsbury Rifles in Penton Street, Islington. The estimated cost for housing the PCO there in one building, £127,500, was acceptable. The alternative was to build two premises, one south of the river and a smaller north London facility at a cost of £150,919.

The LMCPA, the Transport and General Workers Union, the Owner-Drivers' Association and the Taxi Fleet Operators' Federation were all opposed to the centralization. They claimed that they would have to wait longer for their cabs to be inspected and this, plus the longer journey, would mean a loss of revenue and a deprivation of service to customers. They also claimed that the concentration of all vehicles at one place would cause traffic congestion. The objections were studied, but the Commissioner decided that a single building at Penton Street would be the best option. The building was opened in 1961 and has remained the home of the PCO to this day, housing the cab Passing Station, the offices of the Knowledge of London and the Lost Property Office. From 2000 it also became home to the PCO department that licenses private hire.

The Metropolitan Police retained control of the PCO until the formation in 2000 of the Greater London Authority. Then it and all of London's public transport, traffic management and main road network came under the umbrella of the GLA's transport body, Transport for London (TfL).

The End of the MkVIII Beardmore

Taking the comments of the PCO and the London General Cab Company about the MkVIII to heart, Beardmore convened a meeting at their London showroom in Great Portland Street and killed off the existing MkVIII. They commissioned a new design and a mock-up was constructed at Weymann in Addlestone. It was a full-bodied vehicle with all four doors hinged from the front, but underneath it was the basic MkVIII chassis, showing how the MkVIII debacle had drained Beardmore of what development money they had. They still needed a financial backer and so approached the London General, now a wholly owned subsidiary of Associated Newspapers, once more. In the summer of 1963 the General's board were invited to view the new cab, but again they said no. With this rebuff, Beardmore gave up the idea of developing a new taxi.

The Winchester Is Introduced

In October 1962, when the dust created by the review of the Conditions of Fitness had set-tled, the Winchester was finally introduced. Its price was £1,165, compared with the FX4's price then of £1,171. It was the first London cab to have a GRP body, which was built by James Whitson of West Drayton, Middlesex. The inclusion of an upright radiator grille was a deliberate nod to the FX4 so that the public would recognize the Winchester as a taxi right from its introduction.

The body was mounted on the Rubery Owen chassis inherited, via the MkVII Beardmore, from the Oxford and power was from a Perkins 4.99 diesel engine. The same Rubery Owen front axle and ENV rear axle as in the Beardmore were used, although the sump of the Perkins engine, which hung down at the rear, allowed for a slightly longer wheelbase. Unfortunately, the Winchester was a poor product, despite the best attempts of those involved. Much was made in publicity material of the internal 'running board' of the Winchester, which was revealed when the doors were opened, but in reality it was a necessity, the chassis was so high that the step had to be put in to enable passengers to get into the cab. The high chassis also made for an awful driving position – the driver found himself sitting almost on the floor, unable to raise the seat high enough without the steering wheel cutting into his legs, and operating

Beside one of the London General's early Austin FX4s, MCW's mock-up of the revised Beardmore MkVIII looks massive. Its rather bizarre interpretation of American styling influences is a sharp contrast to the traditional lines of the MkVII. (Vintage Taxi Spares)

The rear end of the revised Beardmore MkVIII mock-up is much tidier than the original version. (Vintage Taxi Spares)

the pendant pedals from such an awkward position as to cause serious backache.

Now there was a choice of three cabs, but in fact the picture was not so rosy. With a tiny production run of one vehicle a week, Winchester had no financial clout and could not buy in components is quantity. As such, the cab was almost a home-made product, with no two vehicles being completely identical. When a cab was ordered, the makers simply went to the local motor factors and bought components over the counter. Neither the Winchester nor the ageing Beardmore could match what the Austin could offer the cab masters in terms of availability or serviceability. For the same reasons, the Austin remained the preferred choice for mushers too.

Making the Most of the MkVII Beardmore

With the MkVIII scrapped, Beardmore's only option was to update the MkVII by fitting a fourth door across the luggage platform. Even that apparently simple change was delayed to

excess. In December 1963 a modified cab was presented, but the PCO did not like the handbrake, which was relocated to a position between the driver's seat and the door. This meant that it would be cable-operated, unlike the Austin cab's handbrake rods (the PCO referred to the cable as a 'wire rope'). It took two years before the PCO were satisfied with a handbrake cable and Beardmore sales suffered as a consequence.

In the meantime, new engines were tried, mostly in an effort to improve performance and fuel economy. A second Perkins diesel, the 4.107, was tested in 1962 in RYT 99. This engine was discontinued, but it would lead to the choice, in later MkVIIs, of the more powerful 4.108. In 1964 a 1.6-litre Hillman Minx petrol engine was tried since as the in-line Ford engine was due for replacement by a new V4. The Hillman engine never went into a production cab, but contacts were maintained with the Rootes Group.

With no new cab to develop and sales of the MkVII slowing, Beardmore were facing the end. In more modern times a ruthless

Winchester Automobiles (West End) Ltd chose Peterborough Road, Fulham as the location to photograph their new two-tone grey cab. The built-in roof sign says, 'Taxi for Hire'. (Author's collection)

board of management would have cut the losses, shut the company down and made everyone redundant, but this was not Beardmore's style. They were a small company with a strong loyalty to their workers and customers. The Beardmore company secretary Ken Jaeger would recall much later that Beardmore were like a happy family.

Winchester MkII

The Perkins 4.99 engine had made the Series I Winchester slow and very noisy and so for the 1965 Series II a 1600cc Ford Cortina engine and four-speed gearbox were fitted, with the option of a Perkins 4.108 diesel. The job of building the body, now finished in black, was transferred to Wincanton Engineering in Old Woking, Surrey.

Weymann's body for the MkVII Beardmore had slightly different lines from the Windover body. As may be seen on this restored 1966 four-door, the boot had a pronounced slope. (Author)

Wincanton Engineering Ltd took over the building of the body of the Winchester in 1964, hence the cab's registration. It was renumbered as the MkII and finished in black. (Author's collection)

Winchester: Technical Specification

Winchester Mk1

Engine

Type	Perkins P99 4-cylinder, in-line diesel, water-cooled, cast iron cylinder block, cast iron cylinder head with overhead valves
Cubic capacity	1628cc
Bore and stroke	76.2mm × 88.9mm (3in × 3.5in)
Compression ratio	20:1
Power	48bhp @ 4,000rpm
Torque	73lb/ft @ 2,250rpm

Transmission

Type	manual, three-speed plus reverse, synchromesh on 2nd and 3rd gears, column gear change

Dimensions

Wheelbase	8ft 10in (2.69m)

Running Gear

Steering	cam and roller
Brakes	hydraulic all four wheels, drums all round, mechanical pull up handbrake on rear wheels
Rear axle	semi-floating, hypoid drive
Propeller shaft	open shaft with needle roller bearing universal joints
Wheels and tyres	16in pressed steel disc wheels with 5.75 × 16 Dunlop Taxicord tyres
Front and rear suspension	longitudinal, semi-elliptical springs and telescopic hydraulic shock absorbers

Electrical System

Type	12v positive earth

Winchester MkII

As for MkI with the following changes:

Engine

Type (petrol)	Ford 4-cylinder in-line petrol, water-cooled, cast iron cylinder block, cast iron cylinder head with overhead valves
Cubic capacity	1599cc
Bore and stroke	80.98mm × 70.62mm (3.19in × 2.78in)
Power	71bhp @ 5,000rpm
Torque	91.5lb/ft @ 2,300rpm
Type (diesel)	Perkins 4.108 4-cylinder in-line diesel, water-cooled, cast iron cylinder head, three-bearing crankshaft
Cubic capacity	1760cc
Bore and stroke	79.5.mm × 88.9mm (3.13in × 3.5in)
Compression ratio	22:1
Power	52bhp @ 4,000rpm
Torque	78lb/ft @ 2,000rpm
Injector pump	distributor-type

Winchester MkIII

As for MkII but with the following changes:

Engine

Type (petrol)	Ford V4 petrol, water-cooled, cast iron cylinder block, cast iron cylinder head with overhead valves
Cubic capacity	1663cc
Bore and stroke	93.66mm × 60.35mm (3.69in × 2.37in)

Transmission

Type	Ford 4-speed synchromesh

Running Gear

Steering	recirculating ball, ratio 20.55:1
Brakes	hydraulic all four wheels, drums all round, mechanical pull up handbrake on rear wheels
Front axle	dropped beam
Rear axle	three-quarter floating, hypoid bevel drive
Differential ratio	4.44:1
Wheels and tyres	14in pressed steel wheels with 6.50 × 14 Dunlop Taxicord tubeless tyres

Electrical System

Type	12v positive earth

The Mk2 Birch Revived

The Mk2 Birch programme underwent a review. Standard had been taken over in 1961 by Leyland and the Atlas was upgraded to try and improve sales. Its final version was the Leyland 20 van, but its longer wheelbase pushed the turning circle up to 34ft (10.4m), which was too big to bring down to meet the Conditions of Fitness. And there was another problem: the van was being made at Standard-Triumph's new factory at Speke in Liverpool, but Standard needed space for other models. In 1964 the managing director George Turnbull negotiated with Carbodies to take over the building of the Leyland 20 body. Even if Turnbull had been prepared to ask his close friend, Carbodies' director and general manager Bill Lucas if he would be willing to make anything that could be converted into a rival for the FX4, Lucas's answer would certainly have been a resounding 'no'.

With the Leyland 20 body unavailable for the cab, Giovanni Michelotti was asked to design a new body. He produced a stylish clay model that was certainly an improvement on a converted van, but by now the Birch Mk2

was doomed. All that were left of the original Atlas components were the sub-frame and the front axle. The need to manufacture most of the components exclusively for the vehicle would greatly increase the development and the manufacturing costs. Standard-Triumph had become profitable under Leyland, but this was the result of being realistic as well as adventurous about their products. They certainly would not put money into the low-volume taxi (one cannot help but think that Turnbull had sounded out Lucas about the taxi market). Birch finally retired and sold off his transport operations. The single Mk2 prototype was used as a tender vehicle for Birch Brothers' coach fleet and was, most likely, eventually scrapped.

The Metro-Beardmore

In 1965 Beardmore's entire production was transferred to Metro-Cammell-Weymann's factory in Washwood Heath, Birmingham. All the cabs produced were fitted with four doors and a four-speed gearbox, with the option of the 1.7-litre Ford petrol or Perkins 4.108 diesel engine. Sales were very slow. Only loyal

When the body of Leyland 20, the last version Standard Atlas van, became too large for the Mk2 Birch, Standard-Triumph's stylist Giovanni Michelotti designed this modern, forward control body. The ineffectual chassis did not do justice to the style of the body. (BMIHT)

customers or those that would not deal with Mann & Overton at any price stuck with Beardmore.

In the same year, Metro-Cammell-Weymann's works manager D.D. Boote sent drawings of a new prototype, with simple, modern lines, and referred to as the 'Metro-Beardmore', to the PCO. It was intended that Roots Group running gear, including the 1.6-litre Minx petrol engine, would be used in the cab. Rootes were offering a Perkins 4.99 as a diesel option in the 15cwt Commer van but were experiencing trouble with supplies. To get around these problems, Rootes began developing a small diesel based on the 1.6-litre petrol engine, increasing the capacity to 1725cc. However, Rootes ended its development when Perkins brought out the 4.108 engine. If the Rootes diesel had been successfully developed, it may have powered the MkVIII or possibly the Metro-Beardmore, but this is only speculation. The reality was that the board of the London General Cab Company examined the Metro-Beardmore and considered it to be simply too big and heavy. Once more they rejected any offer of a deal.

A First Try at an FX5

The FX4 dominated the London market, but by 1965 the idea of a replacement came under consideration. Mann & Overton had consulted the trade, in particular Ronnie Samuels, who provided a list of the features he would most like to see in a cab; he wanted a smaller, cheaper-to-run vehicle, with simple servicing and a built-in taximeter and a separate chassis, and unexpected features such as sliding doors and forward control. It was assumed that the new cab would be numbered FX5 and the preparation of the general chassis drawings was begun.

The fact that Carbodies had not been profitable from the time of the BSA takeover until 1963 worried Mann & Overton. A quotation of £350,000 from Carbodies for an FX5 body prompted Mann & Overton to talk to other body manufacturers. The introduction of the Winchester opened the possibility of a glass fibre body and the sports car makers Jensen and Keeble were both consulted. However, Joe Edwards of BMC, who was a body specialist, recommended that

Hardly an attractive vehicle, MCW's first attempt at designing their own cab was the Metro-Beardmore. (Keith White)

The electromechanical meter was introduced in the 1960s and was a considerable improvement on the old mechanical meter, as it did not require to be wound up at regular intervals. Another advantage was the yellow illuminated 'for hire' sign, which was more visible at night than the raised flag. Below it is a blue strip light that lit when the cab was hired. This is a Geecen meter, available in two sizes; this is the earlier, smaller version. (Author's collection)

Mann & Overton should stay with pressed steel. He believed that GRP was still not developed enough for such heavy usage nor that Jensen had the management capability to fulfil the contract. In the event, the FX5 was shelved through lack of funds.

Winchester MkIII

The MkIII Winchester was introduced in September 1966. The rear axle and brakes, sourced from older Jaguars, would no longer be available, so Winchester fitted a new model, the MkIII, with Ford V4 Transit engine, four-speed gearbox, rear axle and brakes. Along with the axles and brakes, came 14in wheels, as a result of which the MkIII sat a little lower on the ground.

Mann & Overton Supreme Once More

For a third time, Mann & Overton found themselves with the right vehicle at the right time. The 12/16 Unic had been the only cab available at all in 1914, the Austin 12/4 the only cab in production in 1933 and now, in 1965, the FX4, despite its faults, was the only real option for the trade. Beardmore had failed to mount a challenge and the Winchester never would. Despite a valiant attempt at the end of the 1960s, no serious challenger would come forward for another decade.

The Ford running gear, and in particular the 14in, wheels set MkIII Winchester slightly lower on the ground. Note the black grille. This is a preserved 1967 model. (Keith White)

8   1967–80 The FX4 – Monopoly by Default

The review of the Conditions of Fitness in 1961 had a distinct effect on the rest of the decade. The trade would see the end of the Beardmore and the valiant but ultimately ineffective Winchester, as well as the first manifestation of the Metrocab. The 1970s would be the decade in which the FX4 would become the only cab available. This led both ordinary members of the trade and active trade union officials to believe that there was collusion between Mann & Overton and the PCO to maintain the former's monopoly. Major restructuring in the motor industry in the late 1960s, widespread industrial disputes, runaway inflation and the three-day week of the 1970s cast a dark shadow over the nation as a whole, making life in the cab trade very difficult.

The End of Beardmore

The last Beardmore MkVII was delivered in January 1967. The company continued to maintain the existing cabs from the Threeway Garage in St John's Wood, but, as the end drew near, regular customers were invited to go to Threeway and, for £100 a head, the foreman filled their cabs up with as many spares as were wanted. Once genuine Beardmore spares ran out, problems began to occur. The PCO would not allow repairers to use pattern parts for fear that they would be sub-standard. Owners had no option but to sell their cabs out of service and drive Austins. Beardmore ceased trading in 1969, but, since there were no creditors, the company was not liquidated

and still existed on record at Companies House until the late 1990s.

Winchester MkIV

When Beardmore announced that they were ceasing cab production, Rubery Owen stopped making the chassis. This put Winchester in a challenging situation. The old body had been a bad installation on the original chassis so, to resolve it, they took the opportunity to completely rework the GRP body into a more modern design and commission a new chassis. Built once more by Wincanton Engineering, the body was indeed a contemporary design. The back window was an FX4 item while the tail lights were from the Hillman Hunter estate. Inside, the finish was austere in the extreme, in plain grey with a double skin inside the roof instead of a fabric headlining. The new chassis, of rectangular steel tube, was designed and built by Keewest Engineering in Southampton, who were also responsible for making the chassis of the Gordon-Keeble high performance GT car. It was a crude job compared with Rubery Owen's well engineered item, but there was not the money for anything more sophisticated. Ford Transit front and rear axles were carried over, as was the 1.7-litre Transit V4 petrol engine and Perkins 4.108 diesel. The engine options gave the cab reasonable performance and fuel economy, but, in truth, the cab came too late to make an impact.

Perkins's publicity photograph of the Winchester Mk4. Note the Perkins logo on the grille. (Vintage Taxi Spares)

Gas Power for Cabs

The big issue as regards fuel in the 1950s was its price, but, in the late 1960s, concerns over exhaust emissions began to arise. The fleet owners W.H. Cook and Sons of London had invested in a fleet of petrol FX4s that they converted to run on liquid petroleum gas (LPG). Although the petrol FX4 returned about 18mpg (15.7ltr/100km), there was no fuel duty on LPG, and so the running costs of a gas cab were about two-thirds those of a diesel cab. A pressurized gas container was fitted into the boot floor and the spare wheel was bolted to the partition in the luggage compartment. At first, the project went well, despite some early problems with exhaust valves burning out due to the higher combustion chamber temperatures, but the benefits for Cook were lost early in 1971 when the government announced that it would put duty on LPG. The managing director Vernon Cook wrote to Parliament, saying, 'We regret that any excessive excise duty would kill off

the project and with it the end of hopes for a cleaner city.'

FX4 Facelift

The idea behind the formation of British Leyland in 1968 was to produce a more efficient industry and better cars that were more competitive in export markets. History shows that the reverse happened. It was an amalgamation of Leyland Motors, who owned Standard-Triumph, Rover and Alvis, and British Motor Holdings, the result of a merger of BMC and Jaguar. During the negotiations that preceded the formation of British Leyland and immediately following them, the latent financial troubles of BMC began to manifest themselves. The 1965 plans for an FX5 had been scrapped and now the cab trade expected, with some justification, a replacement for the FX4. Instead, they got a 'MkII' version of the FX4. This treatment was being administered to all BMC models and so it was no surprise.

The new version earned itself the nickname of the 'new shape' in the trade and the makers did at least address some of the complaints made about the cab. The hated roof-mounted limpet indicators were replaced by the tail lights from the MkII BMC 1100 and indicators and repeaters on the front wings. The batteries were moved to a position over each wheel arch. Previously, rainwater had collected under them and in the space of three or four years would rot through the metal and pour on to the driver's right foot.

Under-bonnet soundproofing was fitted, making driving less tiring and, in conjunction with a new partition sourced from the FL2 hire car, made communication with the passengers easier. The water pipes that fed the original passenger compartment heater ran under the cab. In winter the heater was useless. The heater radiator was relocated to behind the driver's seat and discharged from a grille between the cricket seats. The FX4's original driver's compartment was designed for an older generation and younger cabmen, noticeably taller, found it cramped. The whole partition was angled back, allowing the seat to be reclined to make more legroom. It also gave taller drivers chronic backache.

Westminster Bridge was a favourite location for photographers of London cabs. This is one of the first of the 'new shape' FX4 models, introduced in 1968. At last, the rear window was made of clear glass and an interior rear-view mirror was allowed. (Vintage Taxi Spares)

Jery Craig's cartoon in Taxi *on the subject of W.H. Cook and Sons' gas-powered cabs. (*Taxi *newspaper and Jery Craig)*

Enter the Metrocab

Although Beardmore had given up the idea of making a new cab, Metro-Cammell-Weymann's managing director Tony Sansome, one of the most forceful and dynamic people in British industry at the time, had an incentive to become a taxi maker. MCW's Metrobus had failed to make inroads into the London market and Sansome wanted to keep his production lines going by making a taxi. In September 1968 MCW sent the PCO drawings of 'Project HO 10180', named the Metrocab. Two weeks later the PCO accepted it, criticizing only the absence of the wheel size and an excessively humped floor.

A scale model was made for MCW by Specialist Mouldings of Huntingdon. As they had been involved with Beardmore, the board of the London General Cab Company were invited to Washwood Heath to look at a full-sized mock-up. Sansome asked the General

whether they would buy it if he put it into production. They said no, saying that it was a 'box on wheels' and much too big. However, they accepted MCW's invitation to act as consultants and possible purchasers of a revised model.

The London General's board then viewed another new model built by Haring Conti Associates of Sandy, Bedfordshire. The following 17 October MCW's Len Whomersley and G. Gupwell went to the General's Brixton premises to discuss the project with Geoff Trotter, Joe de Ciantis and the General's chairman Sir Neil Cooper-Keys. The General's board felt that the new cab would end up too much like the over-large FX4 and wanted MCW to investigate one of three options: a front engine with front wheel drive, a rear-mounted engine with rear wheel drive or a monocoque construction. They felt that unless MCW followed a more modern approach, they would '. . . not counsel Metro-Cammell

---

Metrocab Prototype: Technical Specifications

Engine

Type	Perkins 4.108 4-cylinder in-line diesel, water-cooled, cast iron cylinder head, three-bearing crankshaft
Cubic capacity	1760cc
Bore and stroke	79.5.mm × 88.9mm (3.13in × 3.5in)
Compression ratio	22:1
Power	52bhp @ 4,000rpm
Torque	78lb/ft @ 2,000rpm
Injector pump	distributor-type

Transmission

Type	Ford four-speed manual with synchromesh on all forward speeds
Clutch	diaphragm spring type, single 8.5in (216mm) plate, hydraulically operated

Running Gear

Steering	circulating ball, ratio 20.55:1, collapsible steering column
Brakes	dual circuit hydraulic to all four wheels, parallel master cylinders, twin leading shoe on front, 11in drums all round, mechanical pull up handbrake on rear wheels
Front axle	dropped beam
Rear axle	three-quarter floating, hypoid bevel drive
Differential ratio	4.44:1
Wheels and tyres	14in pressed steel wheels with 6.50 x 14 Dunlop Taxicord tubeless tyres

Electrical System

Type	12v, negative earth with alternator

to proceed any further along such a conventional and similar design as defined by the FX4 . . . a revolutionary design would reduce weight, improve performance and make the Metrocab marginally different'. On the other hand, MCW felt that the General's ideas were 'impracticable, too expensive and time consuming'. Eventually, they reached a compromise whereby MCW would develop a conventional prototype that was smaller than the FX4. Along with Trotter and de Ciantis, the PCO's Chief Inspecting Officer Mr Collins went to see an interior mock-up of it on 9 January 1969. Collins was reasonably satisfied with what he saw, and the General agreed that MCW should produce a running prototype.

At Metro-Cammell's railway engineering department, the engineering team under their director Frank Bonneres produced three designs of a simple, box-section frame, all X-braced for strength and rigidity. They were submitted to the Motor Industry Research Association for strength testing, and the best was selected for the prototype. Into it they fitted a 1.75-litre Perkins 4.108 diesel engine and a 30cwt Ford Transit all-synchromesh gearbox, back axle, steering box and narrowed beam front axle. The GRP body was a contemporary design by Haring Conti Associates and built by Henlycraft in Southampton. Although the driving position was a little cramped for tall drivers, the visibility through the big, curved windscreen was excellent. It was 15in (38cm) shorter than the FX4 and some 56lb (25kg) lighter. Many of the features on the cab, including a crash link in the steering, telescopic shock absorbers all round, an alternator and full servo brakes, highlighted just how far behind the times the FX4 was.

The Metrocab prototype, photographed before its introduction. It was some 15in (38cm) shorter than the FX4. (Jamie Borwick)

One crucial point that the PCO rejected was the type of steering ball joint. The Conditions of Fitness demanded that the ball joints should be non-pendant, that is, fitted with the bolt going downwards into the steering arm to which they are attached. The PCO maintained that the tight turning circle put excessive loading on pendant ball joints, causing them to wear quickly. MCW were determined to have pendant ball joints, arguing that they were used with safety on buses and lorries. The argument delayed progress until the Tansport Road Research Laboratory convinced the PCO to change their mind.

The first example, finished in blue to match the General's pre-war livery, was submitted to the PCO in December 1969. MCW made the mistaken assumption that the PCO would accept the same sort of rough and ready finish that motor manufacturers considered normal for early prototypes, but they soon found out that near production standard was what was wanted if type approval were to be granted. The PCO found no fewer than fifty-eight faults, the most serious being an outright condemnation of the front axle. In order to get

A fascinating comparison: on the left is a MkIV Winchester, centre is a 1970 FX4 and on the right is MCW's prototype. Clearly seen on the FX4 are the 'new shape' tail lights, borrowed from the BMC 1100/1300 range. Note also the 'Leyland' symbol on the front wing. This led some motoring historians to believe that Carbodies had been taken over by Leyland, when, in fact, they were bought in 1973 by Manganese Bronze Holdings. In the 1970s the London General Cab Co. merged with Overstrand Motors of Vauxhall to form the London Cab Company, hence the name on the building. (Jamie Borwick)

the track arrow enough to fit (although not, of course, intending this for production) MCW had cut the Transit front axle into two shortened halves and butt-welded them together. The PCO Chief Inspecting Officer Jack Everitt was not going to accept this at all and was backed up by a decisive statement from Ford. He wrote to MCW stating his disappointment over the condition of the Metrocab. He concluded by saying, 'You can be assured of our continued co-operation but I feel that in the past some advice has gone unheeded.'

In February 1970 the Metrocab was introduced to the trade at the London General's filling station at Southwark Street. However, type approval was not given until 31 July, after three more attempts by MCW. Even then it was on the understanding that it was 'to be regarded as a prototype for experimental purposes, and that further modification would have to be made before the cab goes into production'.

The Metrocab immediately went into service with the General. There was some uncertainty from the public about whether it was a taxi and, because of this, the General's drivers were offered a lower rental as an inducement to drive it. In nearly three years'

service and 100,000 miles (160,000km) the engine was trouble-free, delivering excellent fuel consumption. Despite some signs of localized starring in the gel coat, the GRP body stood up to the job very well. Certainly it was encouraging to the makers to see that it, as a prototype, could do the job at least as competently as an FX4. In some ways it did the job better: the brakes were much better and the body was draught-proof, leak-proof and rust-proof.

Now Tony Sansome wanted to know whether the General would place a significant order for it. He wanted it as a standby line in the bus body factory, but the unions at MCW were making some uncooperative noises, demanding that the cab be a full-time production vehicle. For the General's board the task of appraisal was agonizing, because they had been, in Trotter's words, 'surrogate fathers' to the cab from Beardmore's first approach to them. It at least followed their ideal of a cab that was lighter and cheaper to run; but it was an unknown commodity in a market that was already in the firm grip of Mann & Overton's FX4. And in order to service both types the General would have to carry two completely different sets of spares and employ craftsmen to repair the GRP body. By now, a further

Austin FX4 1961–71: Technical Specification

As for 1958 specification but with the following changes:

Engine
Optional until January 1972

Type	Austin 4-cylinder petrol, water-cooled, cast iron cylinder block, cast iron cylinder head with overhead valves
Cubic capacity	2199cc
Bore and stroke	79.4mm × 111.1mm (3.13in × 4.38in)

Compression ratio	6.8:1
Power	52bhp @ 3,800rpm
Torque	102lb/ft @ 1,600rpm

Transmission

Automatic	Borg Warner Type 35, three-speed with torque converter (available with diesel engine only)
Manual	Austin 4-speed, synchromesh on 2nd, 3rd and 4th gears

improved FX4 was available (see below) and the fleet drivers agreed that they would rather have it than the Metrocab.

Sansome did the only thing he could do and pulled the plug on Metrocab. There was a second prototype built. It was a much better finished cab, and, if it had gone into service, it might have affected the General's decision, but it was not to be. The Metrocab seemed doomed to the same fate as the Beardmore, the Birch and the Winchester – the history book.

The British Leyland LM11

The 'new shape' FX4 was intended to be a stop-gap. At British Leyland, Alec Issigonis, the man who had created BMC's Mini, and David Bache, who had styled the Rover 3-litre and the 2000, began designing a new cab based on the proposed replacement of the Austin-Morris JU250 15cwt van. The project, coded LM11, seemed sound in theory. The JU250's beam axle allowed the 25ft (7.6m) turning circle to be easily achieved, and the development costs would be relatively low, an asset considering that Austin-Morris was losing a great amount of money. However, as talented as Bache and Issigonis were in their own fields, the cab they produced was a disaster and so Carbodies designed a new mock-up. Issigonis and Bache had to admit that it was an improvement and they gave it the go-ahead. However, Mann & Overton saw no reason to invest in a vehicle that they thought to be unnecessary, especially as it was not an improvement on the FX4, and thus they abandoned the LM11.

A New Engine for the FX4

At the end of 1971 Austin-Morris introduced the AE250 1-ton van, to replace the ageing Morris LD. The 2.2-litre diesel that powered the LD was the same as the FX4's but the new van would have a more powerful 2.52-litre 25V engine. This was fitted in the FX4 and gave the cab much better acceleration and, with a higher ratio differential, a top speed of over 70mph (113km/h). Along with the engine came an alternator and a negative earth electrical system with a single 12v battery.

Carbodies Become the Sole Manufacturers of the FX4

The Austin-Morris division of British Leyland was losing money at a serious rate and Standard-Triumph's managing director George Turnbull was transferred to Austin-Morris to try and make it viable. Part of his task was to close or rationalize uneconomical factories, and one of these was the plant at Adderley Park, where Morris-Commercial cabs were once mixed in with lorries and buses, but now built only FX4 chassis. Turnbull offered the assembly plant to Carbodies and their director and general manager Bill Lucas accepted, provided that he could transfer the entire, albeit small, workforce to Coventry and not have to make anyone redundant. The tracks, jigs, overhead cranes and all the other equipment were moved in their entirety, with virtually no upset to taxi production. Now Carbodies would become the sole manufacturers of the FX4.

A New Owner for Carbodies

BSA was a huge concern, it encompassed the bulk of the British motorcycle industry, owning such names as BSA, Triumph, Ariel and Sunbeam. It had also owned since 1954 Carbodies, but when its most effective and influential chairman Jack Sangster retired, his successors failed to meet the challenge of the Japanese motorcycle industry and the combine went into free fall.

Mann & Overton's Robert Overton (second from right) and David Southwell (centre left) talk to Leyland's George Turnbull (right) and Carbodies' Bill Lucas at the 1970 Commercial Motor Show at Earls Court. Later at this event, Turnbull offered the FX4's chassis manufacturing plant to Carbodies. (Jamie Borwick)

Worried that the British industry would collapse, the government eventually asked Dennis Poore, chairman of Manganese Bronze Holdings, which owned Norton Villiers, to help. Poore was at first reluctant, but the government threatened to nationalize the remnants of BSA. Poore did not want to have a government-owned competitor and in 1973 Manganese Bronze bought what remained of BSA. Along with it came Carbodies Ltd.

The news of BSA's impending demise caused a great deal of worry at Carbodies and Mann & Overton. Would the new owners close Carbodies down? By now the FX4 was the only cab available and, if the new owners discontinued it, the Conditions of Fitness might have to be abandoned, the whole industry thrown into a downward spiral and the unique London cab would be a thing of the past. They need not have worried; Manganese Bronze's head office was in the City of London and Poore was great user of cabs. He was delighted to be the head of the company that made London taxis and the FX4 continued in production.

The chassis assembly shop at Carbodies' factory in Coventry. (Jamie Borwick)

A BSA swansong. Carbodies was part of the mighty BSA empire until 1973. So was Daimler, until it was sold to Jaguar in 1961. With no more Daimler limousines to call on, BSA felt that that they needed a distinctive vehicle when meeting VIPs at Birmingham station and so, in 1971, they commissioned a special FL2 limousine, painted gold with the BSA 'piled arms' symbol on the door. The director and general manager Bill Lucas, centre, and the engineering director Jake Donaldson, right, show the vehicle to BSA's company secretary H.R. Niven. (Jamie Borwick)

European Vehicle Regulations

In 1973, when Britain joined the European Common Market, it was not only exhaust emission rules that were to come into force the following year. New safety rules demanded the fitting of protective steering and anti-burst door locks and the requirement that all vehicles, either new or of an existing design, had to be crash tested. These regulations would have an effect on the two makes of cab on the market; one would be improved and the other lost for good.

Crash testing consists of loading a vehicle with dummy passengers, running it into a concrete wall at 30mph (48km/h) and filming it to assess whether real passengers would survive. Despite being deeply in the red, Austin-Morris were obliged to engineer the FX4 chassis changes required to enable it to

pass the test. This included incorporating a crash link into the steering column and fitting a new steering wheel with a rubberized centre. After a long search, Carbodies sourced a new type of door lock from Germany and adapted it, along with a push-button handle to suit and moved the interior handles to the centre of the door to accommodate the mechanism. They also reprofiled the rear seat cushion and fitted a new instrument panel.

Mann & Overton supplied a cab for the Motor Industry Research Association to test. Thanks to the robust chassis, it passed. The staff at MIRA said that it was one of the best results they had ever seen. One of the new models marked a milestone in FX4 production: on 28 March 1974 the 25,000th vehicle rolled off the production line.

The 2.2-litre Austin petrol engine that had been available in the FX4 and the FL2 since

The Lucas electric taxi was developed in the 1970s, primarily as a testbed for its vehicle powerplant. The taxi, designed by Tom Karen of Ogle Design, was fully compliant with the Conditions of Fitness but never received type approval. (Vintage Taxi Spares)

1961 would not meet the European legislation without modification. These models were now the only vehicles using this engine and, rather than spend money that it did not have, in modifying it to meet the regulations, BLMC scrapped it.

The End of the Winchester

The casualty of the European safety regulations was the Winchester, which was withdrawn from sale without being tested. Plainly it would not have passed: the doors would have had to be completely redesigned to accommodate more sophisticated door locks and it was not likely that the chassis and the fibreglass body would pass the crash test. Only fifty-five MkIVs were sold by the time production ended in 1972.

The FX4 Brake Servo Fiasco

The FX4's drum brakes had remained unchanged since 1958 and needed uprating to

match the increase in performance that the 2.5-litre engine gave. The options were either to fit disc brakes or improve the old ones. MGB disc brakes would fit the suspension uprights, but they would restrict the turning circle and there was not the money available to re-engineer the front suspension.

The Carbodies' engineer Peter James produced a design for full servo braking with pendant pedals that would mate to the drum brakes. But Austin could not, and Mann & Overton would not pay for it and so it was shelved. To compromise, Mann & Overton decided to have a servo working on the front brakes only, which was a design that most motor engineers considered unsound. Cabs with the new brakes went on sale in 1976 and performed in an unpredictable and dangerous fashion. Below 10mph (16km/h) the brakes would grab and the cab would lurch to a stop. One must ask why the PCO approved them, but, with the FX4 being the only cab on the market, they would be wary of interrupting supply or upsetting Mann & Overton. Front

131

The finishing shop at Carbodies in the mid 1970s. On the far left of the picture, finished bodies are taken to the mounting shop where they are fitted on to the chassis. The assembled cabs return to the finishing shop, where the final detail parts, such as windscreen wipers and bumpers, are fitted. Compare the door handles of the cabs with the FX4 pictured on page 126. Those fitted here are the push-button type, which complied with European safety regulations. (Jamie Borwick)

brake drums were wearing out in 5,000 miles (8,000km) and front brake linings were lasting a mere 2,000 miles (3,200km). Despite great pressure from the cab trade press and independent reports on the poor safety of the system, Mann & Overton stood firm. They maintained that drivers had to learn to drive the FX4 with the new system. Faced with the inevitability of the situation, the trade made the best of a bad job.

Problems between Carbodies and Mann & Overton

Tension had existed between Mann & Overton and Carbodies since the early 1960s when Carbodies needed cash to replace the original poor quality body pressings of the FX4. Bill Lucas, Carbodies' director and general manager, was for a long time unaware of many of the complaints, such as the vehicle's

1977 was Queen Elizabeth II's Silver Jubilee year and the London General's seventieth birthday. The General's managing director Geoff Trotter invited the Prince of Wales to visit Brixton. The Prince responded by inviting the cab trade to Buckingham Palace. To commemorate the occasion and the Jubilee, Carbodies prepared a special Silver Jubilee FX4, seen here with HRH at the wheel. As well as personnel from the General, the Prince met senior management form Carbodies, Mann & Overton and Austin. (Vintage Taxi Spares)

propensity to leak rainwater, its lack of draught proofing and the fact that it rusted so badly within five years that cab proprietors made to Mann & Overton. There were other irritating points too: because of the way the 2.52-litre engine was mounted in the AE250 van, it had its oil filler at the rear of the rocker cover; no attempt was made to make a special rocker cover for the cab, with the oil filler at the front. The result was that topping up the oil was a tricky business. On the other hand, money had been spent on fitting a fresh air vent in the first 2.52-litre cabs, which, because it was directed at the driver's right knee, proved useless. The rust problems and the some of the leaks had been cured with the 'new shape' but still customers were not satisfied.

Lucas liaised with the PCO to discover the most significant problems with the FX4. Mann & Overton, in their position as suppliers of the only vehicle on the London market, had little to worry about so far as complaints were concerned. They had a waiting list of two years for the cab and they could ask the

133

top price that the market could stand. Until the mid 1970s it was not a prime concern how many Carbodies needed to make, so long as the orders were met. However, matters at Carbodies were changing. Until 1977 the FX3 and the FX4 were always just one of their many jobs. Their last private car contract was making the Triumph 2000 Estate, production of which at its peak was more than twice that of the FX4. When this came to an end and the cab became the only vehicle they produced this would, in time, have a profound effect on the cab's and Carbodies' future.

The FX5

Tired of having to chase Mann & Overton for money for improvements, Bill Lucas went to Dennis Poore and said he wanted to develop a cab independently of them. Poore's board gave their initial agreement, and Lucas instructed the chief engineer Jake Donaldson to design what was to become the FX5. Designing a new vehicle from scratch had become enormously expensive, so it made sense to see whether an existing vehicle could be adapted. Donaldson thought that the roof

panel of a Range Rover would be ideal for a cab and over three years undertook a feasibility study. However, the conclusion was that the body shell was too bulky and wrongly proportioned for a taxi and thus it was rejected.

Next, Carbodies began work on a completely new body design. Donaldson and his assistant Peter James produced an extruded steel tube chassis, and mounted the McPherson strut front suspension and coil-spring rear suspension from the Rover 3500, which had been introduced in 1976. A quarter-scale model was made up from Donaldson's own design and shown to Poore, who immediately gave it the go-ahead.

Cab trade representatives were invited to see a full-size mock-up. Mann & Overton were included in the party; Carbodies had no reason to abandon them as dealers, only as major financiers. They liked the new cab, numbered, of course, FX5. However, where Carbodies once had the skills to design their own press tools, many of their skilled men had gone and the job of tool making would have to be put out for tender. Another factor was that the Triumph motorcycle factory at Meriden, owned by Manganese

Carbodies' FX5. The cab would have used the running gear from the Rover SD1 and a Peugeot 2.5 diesel engine. It got no further than a full-size mock-up. (Peter James)

Bronze Holdings, had been the subject of a prolonged and acrimonious industrial dispute. Production there was negligible and Meriden was draining Manganese Bronze of funds that might have gone into the FX5.

Mann & Overton Are Taken Over

The enormous leap in inflation in the 1970s that had pushed cab prices sky-high also increased Mann & Overton's annual profits from a steady £500,000 to £950,000 in 1976. This figure was relative of course, but the government had placed a restriction on dividends and the company had to comply with the law. The increase in profits attracted a number of interested investors, some of whom Mann & Overton were not keen to be involved with. Carbodies and Lucas tried to persuade Dennis Poore, the chairman of Manganese Bronze, to buy Mann & Overton, but he, still faced with the problems at Meriden, declined.

Mann & Overton were particularly interested to talk to Lloyds and Scottish Plc. They were financing Austin cabs in Glasgow and Mann & Overton knew that they would have the money to fund an FX4 replacement. In 1977 Lloyds and Scottish took over Mann & Overton, and Andrew Overton was appointed deputy managing director under David Southwell. Southwell left and Robert Overton retired in 1979 and Bill Reynoldson, Mann & Overton's new chairman and managing director of Lloyds and Scottish industrial and commercial division, appointed Andrew Overton as managing director.

New Engine Trials for the FX4

In 1974 the Labour Prime Minister Harold Wilson commissioned the Ryder Report on British Leyland. It called for the resignation of the chairman Donald Stokes and that the entire company and its model range should undergo a thorough shake-up. The alternative to this £1.5 billion plan was the end of British Leyland. Wilson resigned in 1975, to be replaced by James Callaghan. He decided not to implement Ryder, but instead, in 1977, appointed Michael Edwardes as chairman and managing director. Edwardes would cut out waste across the board and eventually bring the company back into profit. One immediate casualty was the Courthouse

---

Austin FX4 Diesel, 1971–82: Technical Specification

As for 1958 specification but with the following changes:

Engine

Type	Austin 4-cylinder in-line diesel, water-cooled, Type 25V, cast iron cylinder block, cast iron cylinder head with overhead valves
Cubic capacity	2520cc
Bore and stroke	82.6mm × 101.6mm (3.25in × 4.0in)
Compression ratio	20.5:1
Power	55bhp @ 3,500rpm
Torque	89lb/ft @ 2,800rpm

Transmission

Type (from 1979)	Borg Warner Type 65 three-speed with torque converter

Running Gear

Brakes (from 1976)	vacuum servo acting on front wheels only
Differential ratio	4.8:1

Electrical System

Type	12v negative earth, single battery

Green engine plant in Coventry, where the 2.52-litre diesel was made. Unlike the chassis plant, however, Carbodies were not offered the engine plant. It had been sold to Kalaskai Diesel of India. The managing director of Kalaskai was Kartic Narianan, and his son was a student at Rover-Triumph in Canley.

Austin-Morris did not offer a replacement engine, but gave Carbodies three years' notice to find one. The 2.25-litre Land Rover diesel was considered but Standard-Triumph's chief engineer Harry Webster advised that its power characteristics were wrong for the cab. Perkins' 4.108 diesel was too small and Perkins could not give Carbodies an assurance that their new 3-litre would last five years. Ford's 2.3-litre was an underpowered unit and the company would guarantee it only for 45,000 miles (72,000km), the sort of distance a London cab would do in a year. Through a contact at Rootes, Lucas got in touch with Peugeot, who were delighted to be involved with the London cab trade and had a new 2.5-litre diesel under development. The Birmingham fleet operator Horace Faulkner tested the cab for 22 hours a day, experiencing trouble only with a damaged cylinder head, which Peugeot's engineers fixed in a one-day flying visit.

A Monopoly or Not?

The trade was angry that, since the demise of the Metrocab and the Winchester, they could not foresee any replacement, either from Austin or any other source. Comparisons with modern saloon cars such as the Ford Zodiac, which was much better equipped and sold for about the same price, were made in the trade press. To make matters worse, the price of the ageing FX4 rose steeply as a result of the inflation of the 1970s. A 1971 FX4 cost around £1,200. It could be sold after three years at a profit, while a 1974 FX4 cost £2,000. By 1980 an FX4 cost £7,000.

Stories about collusion between Mann & Overton and the PCO, of how they were supposed to have contrived to keep the market sewn up and the customer pinned down became rife. Pressure from trade bodies instigated investigations by the Monopolies Commission, but Mann & Overton were not found to be engaged in any illegal or improper activities. The market was open to anyone who could build a cab that met the Conditions of Fitness. The trouble was that no one else wanted to know: MCW had dropped out, British Leyland had no money and now little interest, Rootes were failing and neither Ford nor Vauxhall showed interest. For the PCO, preserving the status quo was the safest option. To alter the Conditions of Fitness and allow cabs based on other production vehicles might in theory give the trade more choice, but to do it when there were no viable alternatives in the offing would be irresponsible. The damage caused in 1961 was warning enough.

In writing and enforcing such strict rules, the PCO brings upon itself a responsibility to the trade to ensure that there are vehicles available. If there were no supplier then the PCO would have to reconsider the regulations, but there if is just one supplier, then the PCO would say that the regulations can be met and need not be altered. However, there were not only no vehicles other than the FX4 that complied but there were no contenders that came close, despite the plans of many European and American makers for purpose-built or adapted vehicles that appeared in the cab trade press. For fifteen years the FX4 would be the only cab made anywhere in the world that would satisfy the Conditions of Fitness.

A New Managing Director for Carbodies

In 1979 Bill Lucas took early retirement from Carbodies. His replacement was Grant

'Passing a Cab' – the Annual Vehicle Licensing Procedure

London's taxicabs are subject to annual licensing. Before a cab goes to the passing station at Penton Street, Islington for its licence, it has to be thoroughly overhauled and scrupulously cleaned. At the passing station, the cab's mechanical and bodily condition are rigorously checked before the white plate that denotes that the cab is fit for work may be screwed to the back of the cab. If a fault is found that is considered dangerous or in contravention of the Conditions of Fitness or a Road Traffic Act, the inspecting officer (known colloquially as a 'CO') will issue a Reject Notice to the proprietor. The cab must be taken back to the garage, the fault rectified and the cab re-presented.

As well as undertaking the job of inspecting cabs for the annual licensing, COs go out on to the streets to make spot checks on cabs. If a fault is found with any cab, then the dreaded Reject Notice or 'Stop Note' will be issued and the cab's owner must fix the fault and present it at the Carriage Office before the cab may return to work. A quarterly inspection notice may also be sent to a cab proprietor, and the cab must then be presented, clean and in sound condition for inspection. This control has ensured that London's cabs are recognized as the safest in the world.

*The PCO's vehicle inspection department has seven ramps to enable the vehicle examiners to inspect the cabs in clean, comfortable surroundings. (*Taxi *Newspaper)*

Lockhart, previously a plant director with BL at Cowley. Major British cities such as Manchester and Glasgow already used London-type cabs, so to increase the market, Carbodies needed to tap the smaller conurbations and the export market. To make it more appealing to these markets that had the choice of modern saloon cars, Lockhart knew that he had to make improvements to the specification as best he could. But he faced strong resistance from Mann & Overton, who were loath to pay for any improvement or to cut the waiting list for new cabs in London. Their attitude was in total contrast to that in which Lockhart had worked, where the customer, not the dealer nor the manufacturer, controls the market.

However, Lockhart had some luck on his side. The financial regulations had been changed and a new option, lease-purchase, was available to the potential owner-driver. For the cost of one month's payment he (the London cab driver was still almost exclusively male at this time) could have a brand new cab. There would no longer be – if the cabbie could afford the payments – the steady build-up from owning an elderly cab to buying a new one in stages. The demand enabled Lockhart to increase production and, despite Mann & Overton's irritation, bring down the waiting list. This had an adverse effect on big fleets such as that of the London Cab Company, who found that their drivers no longer rented but sought finance from Hertz, Taxi Leasing Services or Mann & Overton, to buy a new cab of their own.

There was more: additional profit could be made in the form of 'optional extras'. A limited range of additional colours, such as cardinal red or white had long been available at extra cost, but there were few takers, cab masters preferred a standard colour and mushers preferred the anonymity of black. Alternative colours such as grass green, blackcurrant, brown and aconite (a bright mauve) had been offered in the mid 1970s, but were not popular. Now Carbodies offered additional colours, including midnight blue and a shade of tan. Vinyl roofs were offered as an option, as was a sunshine roof that hinged on the leading edge. The PCO's new Principal Bryan Philips was more approachable and wanted to bring the institution up to date without compromising its standards. One option that was finally approved, after several years of trying, was the fitting of a personal radio in a cab. Despite the practice being once forbidden by the PCO, who had always insisted that passengers' privacy was paramount, some younger cabmen began strapping portable radios to the dashboards of their cabs. The number of complaints received by the PCO was minimal and personal radios were finally allowed in cabs, provided that their volume was kept low and the driver turned the radio off at the passenger's request. Mann & Overton approved: they were making extra profit with little or no capital investment.

The musher, now spending quite a few hours in the driving seat, preferred to choose an automatic gearbox. The Borg Warner 35 'box had been available since the early 1960s, but it was designed more for a smaller engine than the 2.5-litre Austin diesel and, in consequence, its life was not as great as it might have been. For 1980 a tougher automatic gearbox, the Model 65, replaced the 35, ensuring the reliability needed by the trade.

9 1981–87 A New Challenger

The 1980s, the 'Thatcher years', were the age of the yuppie, of rapidly growing house ownership and the 'Poll Tax'. After horrendous inflation and sky-high interest charges, Britain began to enjoy more stable and more prosperous times. After years of waiting, the cab trade was promised a new cab. It got one: not a successor to the FX4, but, at long last, a competitor.

The CR6

Manganese Bronze's chairman Dennis Poore began to have doubts about whether Carbodies should build the FX5. Carbodies' new managing director Grant Lockhart had none. He scrapped it and revived the plan to build a cab based on the Range Rover body. First, it was vital to persuade Land Rover to sell Range Rover bodies at an economical price. The artwork and a scale model of the pro-

posed cab were presented to Land Rover's managing director Mike Hodgkinson, who liked the concept, but his attention was drawn to the cab's four doors. The Range Rover was then available only with two doors: Rover wanted a four-door model but could not afford to tool up for it. Lockhart offered to design and build the four-door conversion for the Range Rover as part of a deal that included Range Rover's supplying body panels to Carbodies for the new cab at a beneficial rate. It was then settled: Carbodies would build a new cab using a modified Range Rover body on the FX5 chassis. It was given the name: CR6; CR for City (not 'Carbodies' as is often thought) Rover and 6 simply because it followed the FX5.

Sadly, Jake Donaldson, whose health had been failing, died within months of the start of the CR6 project. He had been with Carbodies since the 1940s and had made a

Carbodies' scale model of the CR6 that was shown to Rover's board. (Peter James)

major contribution to the company and especially to the FX4.

The FX5 chassis was adapted to take a 2.25-litre Land Rover diesel engine and a three-speed Borg Warner automatic. Fitted too was the running gear from the Rover SD1, with a choice of Borg Warner automatic or Rover five-speed manual gearbox. The front end of the Range Rover was redesigned to take Morris Ital headlight and indicator units to make the cab distinguishable from a Range Rover. A quarter-scale model was released in June 1980 to the trade at a dinner in Manchester and development began.

Wheelchair Accessibility for the CR6

A seminar held by the Department of Transport in 1980, the International Year of the Disabled, asked wheelchair-bound delegates how the Department could meet their needs. The universal response was, 'start with taxis; pavements are so bad that, even if we could get on trains and buses, we can't get to the stations and bus stops'.

The organizer of the seminar Ann Frye asked Andrew Overton whether a taxi could accommodate a wheelchair. Carbodies had modified an older FX4 to accept one, and this they showed to representatives from the DoT. They also saw the CR6, and asked for it, suitably adapted, to be presented at their London headquarters by December. A second prototype was built and fitted with a split partition so that its luggage platform side could be slid forward to accommodate the wheelchair-bound passenger. Viewing the CR6 at the presentation, cab trade representatives liked its huge windscreen, its modern looks and up-to-date running gear. Representatives of disabled people's groups were delighted with it.

The Department of Transport provided funds to enable the CR6 to be made wheelchair-accessible and the Transport Road Research Laboratory at Crowthorne, Berkshire set up a road transport study group at Newcastle University and purchased both prototypes. From July 1982 they put them on test, not as a taxi, but as a wheelchair-carrying vehicle in Peterborough and Newcastle-under-Lyme, out of sight of the London trade.

Pictured at the wheel of the second CR6 prototype (the first was finished in black) is Geoff Chater, who had joined Carbodies from British Leyland in 1979. He later left to join MCW. (Peter James)

Carbodies Acquire the Intellectual Rights to the FX4

By 1981 Austin-Morris were supplying the engine, the manual gearbox and the Austin name to the FX4. National Type Approval and other European-inspired regulations were looming and, with far too many problems of their own, they were not prepared to get the FX4 ready to meet them. If nothing were done, the cab would be doomed. To ensure the survival of both the FX4 and themselves, Carbodies acquired the intellectual rights to the vehicle from BL and obtained national type approval for it in their own name. Now the cab would be badged as the Carbodies FX4.

Finding a New Engine for the FX4

Despite three years' notice, the impending loss of the Austin engine was causing Carbodies some serious problems. The 2.5-litre Peugeot engine still needed considerable development and the idea of using it had to be abandoned. The new Perkins 3-litre was considered to be too big physically and too powerful, and Ford would not give a release date for their new direct 2.5-litre injection engine. The Land Rover diesel was the only acceptable option, especially as strong links had been forged with Rover over the CR6. An example was fitted into an FX4 and in fleet tests with Horace Faulkner in Birmingham no major faults were found with the installation. Fortunately for Carbodies, this coincided with the CR6's test period at Newcastle-under-Lyme and Peterborough, but with time running out, Carbodies gave themselves three months to make the changes ready for production. The new engineering director Barry Widdowson restructured the company's engineering team in order to streamline the design process, but three months of 13hr days would prove to be insufficient.

There was also the choice of transmissions to be decided. Carbodies had plans to sell a greater number of FX4Rs to provincial markets. They preferred manual transmissions and so the five-speed from the Rover SD1 gearbox was adopted. The automatic option was the Borg Warner 65, with a floor-mounted change replacing the steering column gear selector. Now that the Land Rover engine had been settled on, the cab was renamed the FX4R.

Power steering was to be offered as an option, the first for a London cab. Because they were required to part-fund the installation, Mann & Overton were hostile to the idea, but the original steering box would not be in production for much longer and they had to acquiesce. The full-servo brakes developed in the mid 1970s were at last to be fitted, moving the master cylinders from under the floor to under the bonnet. Disc brakes had to be ruled out – there was neither the money nor the time to do the job. A petrol engine could be offered once more, since Land Rover petrol and diesel engines were built on the same cylinder block.

The FX4R was announced in late 1982, priced at between £8,869 for a manual FL without power-assisted steering and £10,071 for an automatic HLS with it. The FX4R could top 80mph (130km/h) with ease and the trade welcomed its quietness. The power steering would not be immediately available because early examples could not be prevented from leaking and the PCO would not pass them until the problem was cured. When it was available, it and the brakes received a qualified welcome: both very light in operation, with little feel. An interim version of the meter drive from the manual gearbox had to be engineered until a better version was developed, and early owners had to have the later version retrofitted.

But it was not long before the real problems started. Carbodies, who were body engineers

141

Apart from the badges and two bulges in the front of the bonnet to accommodate the power steering box, the FX4R was indistinguishable from the FX4. From 1984 the PCO allowed advertising on the front doors of cabs. The radio circuits were quick to respond to this idea. This FX4R, photographed when it belonged to the author, carries the logo of Computer Cab. (Author)

not mechanical engineers, had been recommended the wrong first motion shaft bearing for installing five-speed manual gearbox. In use, it would collapse, wrecking the gearbox. Engine vibration caused the mount of the stamped steel clutch actuating arm to wear a hole in the arm. The clutch pipe, borrowed from a Triumph TR7, had a plastic pipe heatshrunk over the steel unions; the heat of the exhaust perished the pipe, causing it to blow off under pressure. The radiator was inadequate, causing the cab to overheat in traffic in warm weather. This was a complaint that Mann & Overton claimed could not happen, despite the type-approval by the PCO and regular fitting of ancillary electric radiator fans.

But the most damning criticism was reserved for the engine. The combustion chambers were of an inefficient design, resulting in excessive black smoke and poor fuel consumption. The engine's maximum torque was lower than the Austin engine's was and so, although the cab was fast, it had poor acceleration. The rockers were pivoted off-centre, placing a great load on the valve lifters, which

wore excessively. The gear that transmitted the injector pump drive was pressed on the shaft and after a while it slipped, putting the injector timing out. The timing chain was weak and, in time, it stretched, worsening the injector timing. The power steering took a high percentage of the engine's power, lowering the cab's already poor performance.

Mann & Overton were swamped by complaints from irate owners, demanding that the engines be properly tuned to give them better fuel consumption. Mann & Overton fitted an automatic cab with a 1gal (4.5ltr) fuel tank and ran it for 25 miles (40km), the same as might be expected from an FX4, but the trade was unimpressed. Andrew Overton invited the London Cab Company's engineering director Roger Ward to visit the Land Rover factory. What Ward, an ex-marine engineer specializing in diesels discovered, shocked him. Where one in one hundred Austin engines was tested, every Land Rover engine received a 2hr test and a 120-point computer check. When an engine did not pass the test it was removed and retuned. The engineers at Land Rover were bitterly disappointed at how their engine

142

Austin FX4R Petrol and Diesel: Technical Specification

As for FX4, 1971–1982 specification but with the following changes:

Engine: Diesel

Type	Land Rover, 4-cylinder, in-line diesel, water-cooled, cast iron cylinder block, cast iron cylinder head with overhead valves, five-bearing crankshaft
Cubic capacity	2286cc
Bore and stroke	90.47mm × 88.9mm (3.56in × 3.5in)
Compression ratio	23:1
Power	62bhp @ 4,000rpm
Torque	103lb/ft @ 1,800rpm
Injector pump	distributor-type

Transmission

Automatic	Borg Warner Type 65, 3-speed

Dimensions

Length overall	15ft 1/2in (4.58m)
Width	5ft 8 5/8in (1.74m)

Running Gear

Rear axle	hypoid drive
Ratio	3.909:1
Steering	cam and peg type, 24:1 ratio, power assisted, optional at first, standard from early 1983
Brakes	dual circuit hydraulic to all four wheels, tandem master cylinder with full servo-assist, twin leading shoe on front, 11in drums all round, mechanical pull up handbrake on rear wheels
Wheels and tyres	16in × 5J pressed steel wheels with 175 R16 radial ply tyres

was behaving. The cab trade ceased to buy FX4Rs. During the high inflation of the early 1980s a 1979 or 1980 FX4 changed hands at more than the £7,000 it had cost when new, while FX4Rs at £11,000 or more remained in the showroom.

Cab drivers and proprietors were justified in aiming criticism at Carbodies. But Carbodies, as we have noted, were not mechanical engineers, who had taken outside advice that proved to be wrong. Considering this and the almost impossible time scale, it is remarkable that the cab materialized at all. Some FX4Rs ran well, others very badly, but the cab was a step towards modernity, albeit a faltering one.

The FX4Q

It is unusual for a company to introduce something that competes direct with its main product. But that is exactly what Carbodies did with the FX4Q. When sales of the FX4R

slumped, Lockhart developed the 'Q' cab. This model was based on an old cab chassis which was completely rebuilt. This enabled Carbodies to use the Austin diesel engine, which they re-imported from India. Carbodies were allowed to do this as the cab from which they had acquired the identity had been approved with that engine before the emission regulations that outlawed it were introduced. Carbodies fitted the chassis with a completely new body and running gear, FX4R brakes and a Borg Warner automatic gearbox. No manual gearbox option or power steering was offered. However, Department of Transport legislation demanded that all examples were given the non-year-related index number suffix 'Q'.

Carbodies' subsidiary Carbodies Sales and Service sold it through the London dealers Rebuilt Taxis Ltd, a subsidiary of the London Fleet proprietor E.A. Crouch in Westgate Street, Hackney. It was around £1,500 cheaper than the FX4R automatic and it greatly upset Mann & Overton. Angry owners who had bought FX4Rs were claiming that the Q was an admission by Carbodies that the R was a failure. The Q was far from perfect, however. There were some warranty problems due to the use of reconditioned components and the poorer build quality of the engine. The Q never posed serious threat to the sales of new cabs.

The Metrocab

In 1983 the editor of *Cab Driver* Ernie Keats learned from John Paton, the dealer for Austin, and later Carbodies', cabs in Scotland, that Metro-Cammell-Laird were planning to build a new cab. Keats published the details of the new project, called the Metrocab, in his issue of 16 December 1983 issue. The cab was, Paton said, to be built in partnership with Taggarts, the biggest distributors of BL cars in Scotland and the north of England. Like its predecessor, the new Metrocab would have a GRP shell with completely detachable aluminium front

The production Metrocab was to have a 2.5-litre Land Rover diesel and a Borg Warner automatic transmission. (Geoff Chater)

wings. The diesel engines that were under consideration were a 2.5-litre Land Rover or a 2.3-litre Peugeot. It would have a choice of a four-speed manual gearbox or a four-speed ZF automatic and come with all the features and accessories found on a modern car.

The story was, in essence, true, but the project opened out in a very different way from what Paton had been told, and some

This artwork rendition of the Metrocab was first published in The Steering Wheel *in 1983. (London Cab Company)*

time later than projected. The plan of the MCW chairman Tony Sansome was for MCW to have a presence in every type of public land transport, and he knew where he could find someone with experience in building cabs: Carbodies. In 1984 he recruited Geoff Chater, an ex-Jaguar man who had joined Carbodies in 1979 as a production manager. For the job of chief design engineer he found, in the Talbot, ex-Rootes plant at Ryton, Coventry, Bob Parsons. Although MCW's main drawing office was at Washwood Heath, Chater and Parsons were allocated space for development at MCW's plant at Oldbury, to the west of Birmingham, to keep them away from prying eyes. When Chater asked what his budget was he was told there was none; when he asked who the rest of his team was, he was told, 'just you two'. With these 'resources', a sketch on rough piece of paper by Sansome, a directive to produce results in an impossibly short time and their collective skills of automotive design and practical experience of working with the PCO, they set to work.

Throughout this story we have seen proof that a small production run does not afford cab makers the luxury of exclusive parts.

Every company's 'parts bin' is likely to be raided for suitable components. The best engine available at this time was the new 2.5-litre Land Rover diesel, which Carbodies had already had mated to the Borg Warner 65 automatic and five-speed Rover manual gearboxes. Parsons designed a fabricated box-section chassis, galvanized as proof against rust; to this he bolted the complete front suspension from the FX4. Rights to it belonged still to BL, not Carbodies, so it would not be a problem for Carbodies to use it. However, the Metrocab's longer wheelbase required some adjustment of the steering geometry to satisfy the PCO. Parsons fitted a left-hand drive version of the FX4's power steering box, although, of course, on the right of the vehicle. The rear axle was a proprietary GKN unit that could be adapted to fit either an independent set-up or a rigid axle. A rigid set-up was chosen, hung on semi-elliptical, steel, multi-leaf springs. Brakes from the FX4 were fitted; they were readily available and their commonality would be advantageous to the Metrocab's serviceability.

Seeing the bad press that the first FX4S models were receiving (see page 150), with timing belts breaking, Chater decided to

The first mock-up of the 1980s Metrocab, based on the original artwork Geoff Chater described it as 'Rommel's half-track'. (Geoff Chater)

abandon this engine in favour of Ford's new FSD direct injection diesel, fitted in the new generation of Transit van. It had pushrod operation for its overhead valves, with the camshaft driven by a toothed belt. Although the engine came with Ford's own five-speed manual transmission, it had to be matched to the Borg Warner 65 automatic for the Metrocab.

As they were starting with a blank sheet of paper, Chater and Parsons could build a cab with modern styling and set about creating a mock-up similar to the artwork that had been published in *Cab Driver*. On seeing it, Sansome was disgusted; it was hideous and he told its creators to destroy it. Chater and Parsons then produced a much more stylish mock-up. Again, it had modern styling, much

cleaner lines and neat proportions. The windscreen was the largest seen on a post-war cab and the doors would hinge forward, on the B-post. It would seat five people and, most importantly, it would have wheelchair accessibility built in from the start. The wheelchair occupant would travel facing rearwards, on the nearside front of the passenger compartment. This was established as the safest way for a disabled occupant to travel by the Motor Industry Research Association.

The body would be made of glass fibre, bonded to a steel cage. MCW had no facilities for making a GRP body and so the job was contracted out to Reliant, the company that had probably the most experience in handling the material. The first prototype, finished in white, was made and road-tested. Now

The second Metrocab mock-up was far better looking and very close to the final version. (Geoff Chater)

The pre-production Metrocab was finished in white. The grille was actually made of wood. (Geoff Chater)

came the difficult part – getting a prototype type approved by the PCO. They did not like the cable-operated handbrake, insisting at first that rods should be used. Parsons persisted and eventually persuaded the PCO to accept what had been normal industry practice for decades. It was not as though the PCO had not previously encountered cable handbrakes – Beardmore had fought hard to persuade them to accept the four-door MkVII with one as early as 1963. In 1986, a mere year and half after work began on it, the Metrocab was given type approval.

The most notable difference between it and the FX4 was the amount of space inside the cab, both front and back. The driver at last had a decent-sized windscreen to look through and more than adequate headroom. The dashboard carried the instrument panel from an Austin Montego and the switches were large, push-button items, mounted in the centre of the dash. Electric windows were standard on the front doors, an important point since the wider body meant that the driver would have to struggle to close the platform window if it were of the FX4 constant-balance type. Because of its squarer shape, the Metrocab's interior was more spacious, particularly in the back, giving it a very airy, light feel, despite the

black vinyl trim. The windows in the rear doors were of a sliding type, using channels and catches from the BMC Mini.

Manganese Bronze Plc were not at all pleased with the announcement of a competitor. Grant Lockhart, by this time the managing director of Carbodies Sales and Service, claimed that, 'the UK market is not sufficient to support one manufacturer, let alone rivals'.

A London Dealership for Metrocab

Taxi Leasing Services were a finance company set up in the late 1970s in Southwark, south London by David Day and John Lewis, offering lease finance to cab drivers following a change in the financial regulations. In 1982 TLS acquired the America Street Garage in Southwark, and began offering Perkins Phaser 3-litre engine conversions for FX4Rs. TLS were advertising in the *Cab Driver*, formerly *The Steering Wheel*, and had established a good relationship with its editor Ernie Keats and his assistant Stephen Tillyer. They all knew that the time was right for a new cab, if one could be found, and news of the Metrocab spurred them into action. A partnership was formed between Day, Lewis, Tillyer and Keats, with the intention of acquiring the Metrocab distributorship for the south of England. Against competition from the London Cab Company, they were awarded it. Premises were found in Southwark Street, close to London Bridge, and the new company Metro Sales and Services eagerly awaited the Metrocab.

The RG7

In September 1982, following the announcement of the Metrocab, *Cab Driver* carried a story of another proposed new cab. This was the RG7, named after the company that was to build it, Ross Graham Ltd. They had acquired premises in South Wales, a part of the UK that the government were keen to see redeveloped after the collapse of the coal industry. The story unfolded in two parts. The first claimed that the cab would resemble the MkIV Winchester, suggesting that Ross Graham had acquired the body moulds; the second said that the cab would use either a Ford Transit or a Leyland Sherpa chassis. There was no third part to the story: the project disappeared without a trace.

Mann & Overton Move

Mann & Overton's Wandsworth Bridge Road premises were becoming cramped and they could not offer the kind of service there that was consistent with modern standards. They decided that it was time for them to move and in November 1983 they erected new, purpose-built, riverside premises around the

*Andrew Overton, photographed at about the time he became managing director of Mann & Overton. (*Taxi *newspaper)*

corner in Carnwath Road, funded by their owners, Lloyds and Scottish. The facilities included a full body shop, a service area that could be viewed by the cabs' owners, a modern showroom and a spares shop, selling genuine parts and a wide range of accessories.

Another Attempt at an 'FX5'

The FX4R and the protracted development of the CR6, as well as other ill-starred, private car projects had stretched Carbodies' finances to the limit and Mann & Overton feared that the Coventry company might go bankrupt. Clearly they had to protect their interests by investigating whether a cab might be made by another maker. With Lloyds and Scottish money, Andrew Overton authorized the design of a new cab, once more tagged the FX5. They engaged Robert Jankel, the man behind Panther cars, to design a new chassis. Powered by a 2.3-litre Ford diesel, the chassis was built, but work was halted as the situation at Carbodies had improved with the appointment of Barry Widdowson as managing director.

The Formation of London Taxis International

In 1984 Mann & Overton's owners, Lloyds and Scottish Plc, were taken over by Lloyds Bowmaker and they decided to sell off Mann & Overton. Carbodies' managing director Grant Lockhart persuaded Manganese Bronze's chairman Dennis Poore to buy the company. From this purchase, London Taxis International was created, with three divisions: a manufacturer, LTI Carbodies; a dealer, LTI Mann & Overton; and LTF, London Taxi Finance. Overton moved to Holyhead Road to become sales and marketing director and Peter Wildgoose, Mann & Overton's sales director, was appointed managing director.

'The Knowledge'

Visitors to London are amazed at the London cab driver's ability to find his or her way around. This is thanks to 'the Knowledge', a strict, rigorous, topographical test that every aspiring cab driver has to undergo. The Knowledge of London has its origins in 1851, the year of the Great Exhibition. But before candidates tackle the topographical tests, they have to have a medical examination and undergo a criminal record check. Any heath problems or the discovery of a major misdemeanour will most likely preclude any applicant from going further. The candidates are given a small book, the 'Blue Book', which contains lists of over 200 'runs', specific routes from known points all within a 6-mile (about 10km) radius of Charing Cross. The candidates must go out on a moped or even on foot, to complete the first five pages and then take a written test. After that, it is back on the road to complete the rest of the runs. At regular intervals, however, candidates are called back to the PCO for a series of one-to-one oral examinations, called 'appearances'. When the candidate has satisfied the examiner, he must learn the routes from central London to the major suburbs. When the candidate has passed this part, he must take a driving test. It is not unknown for a candidate, after spending perhaps two or even three years on the 'Knowledge' to fail the driving test repeatedly and never be given the coveted 'green badge'.

Another type of driver's licence, the suburban 'yellow badge', may also be acquired. This is for one of seventeen sectors outside the 6-mile radius, including areas such as Romford, Wimbledon and Harrow. These were introduced in 1937 in order to relieve the unemployment that was then on the rise in Britain. Holders of a yellow badge may ply for hire only within their specified licensing area, but they may take a fare anywhere. Originally, a suburban area covered a 2 1/2-mile (4km) radius of a main point such as a railway station, but in 1984 the individual areas were grouped together into six large sectors. Candidates had to study a much larger geographical area and it was considered that this took too long to undergo. In 1991 the sectors were subdivided, creating seventeen smaller sectors. The Knowledge for any of these areas takes less time since there is less to learn, but it is no less thorough. However, the earnings for a suburban driver are generally lower than those of a green badge holder. Now many cab drivers opt to take a yellow badge first before going on to 'do the green'.

Knowledge boys in the 1950s ready to do some 'runs'. Most have mopeds, although one brave soul has a pedal cycle. This picture, from the collection in the Jewish Museum in Bethnal Green in London, tells a story of its own. Many Jews fleeing from Russia at the end of the nineteenth century settled in the East End and faced harsh anti-Semitism, which often manifested itself in the refusal of some Londoners to employ them. The Public Carriage Office, as a public body, gave a cab driver's licence to anyone capable of passing the Knowledge, regardless of race, creed or colour. Thus, given an opportunity to work, many Jews became cab drivers and some went further to build cab fleets of their own. (Jewish Museum, Bethnal Green)

The FX4S

The FX4R was a commercial failure: its power steering and brakes were welcomed but what was most needed to redeem it was a more powerful and reliable engine. Land Rover had enlarged their diesel engine to a 2.5-litre, but there was some doubt at LTI Carbodies about using it for the FX4. In 1984 Barry Widdowson engaged Ricardo Engineering, a long-established engine design and research establishment in Sussex, to find a better engine. They chose the Japanese Nissan TC series. What Carbodies also needed was dedicated transmissions to avoid the problems encountered with the 'R'. No automatic gearbox was available with the TC range, which itself would soon be obsolete, and it was decided to wait for the replacement TD

range. In the meantime, Carbodies decide to fit the 2.5-litre Land Rover engine. It at least would mate to the same transmissions, but the 2.5 engine's installation was not straightforward because the new fuel pump was mounted very low on the front of the block. This necessitated raising the engine at the front and tilting it the left. New engine mountings sourced from the Metalastik catalogue, which proved to be inadequate, causing vibration problems at tick-over.

Internal plastic draught excluders were designed for the door sills and insulation was added under the dashboard. Rocker-type switches, necessary because Lucas no longer made the old toggle switches, and, at last, electric screen washers were fitted, giving the FX4 the sort of standard equipment that private car owners had enjoyed for many

A pre-production FX4S. New rolled steel bumpers were produced when Wilmot Breeden's tools for the original chrome bumper blades wore out and LTI were unwilling to pay for new ones. Note the fuel shut-off tap on the front wing, just behind the wheel. Production vehicles had a switch under the bonnet to turn off the electric fuel pump in case of an emergency. The 'S' was the first FX4 to have silver-painted wheels. (Peter James)

years. To the chagrin of the trade, the old radiator remained. There was also a new gearbox. Borg Warner closed their Letchworth plant in Hertfordshire, where the gearbox was being built. No more in-line boxes were to be made in Europe, so Carbodies were supplied with the Australian-made Model 40 transmission.

The new model, the FX4S, was introduced on 4 November 1985 at Carnwath Road. It was identified by badges carrying LTI logo – the first cab to do so – and black steel bumpers. It was priced at £11,239 for the basic manual model, which was marginally more expensive than the FX4R. With much more torque from the engine, the performance of the 'S' was much better than that of the 'R', although it was a little noisier and it sold in far better numbers than the FX4R. LTI also offered the new engine as a replacement for the FX4R's 2.2 at a cost of £2,400.

The FX4S was not fault-free, despite LTI's new approach to building the cab. There

was a short-term, although serious problem caused by a faulty batch of engine timing belts. When they broke they caused major internal damage. The radiator, still the same type that was fitted to the FX4R, was just as inadequate for the 'S'. Electric fan makers sold a few more fans to cab proprietors.

The Department of Transport Take Over Control of Taxis

On 1 April 1984, after 115 years under the Home Office, responsibility for taxis and private hire in England and Wales was transferred to the Department of Transport. As far as London was concerned, the Minister of State would be responsible for licensing, the cost of taxi and driver licensing fees and the level of fares. Enforcement would remain the duty of the Metropolitan Police, who were still under the jurisdiction of the Home Office.

LTI FX4S: Technical Specification

Engine
As for FX4R but with the following changes:

Type	Land Rover, 4-cylinder in-line diesel, water-cooled, cast iron cylinder block, cast iron cylinder head with overhead valves, five-bearing crankshaft
Cubic capacity	2495cc (153.45 cu in)
Bore and stroke	90.47mm × 97.00mm (3.56in × 3.19in)
Compression ratio	21:1
Power	69.8bhp @ 4,000rpm
Torque	115lb/ft @ 1,800rpm
Injector pump	C.A.V. type D.P.S. with self-bleed injectors

Transmission

Automatic	Borg Warner Type 40 3-speed with floor-mounted gear change and built-in oil cooler

Dimensions

Length overall	15ft 1/2in (4.58mm)
Width	5ft 8 7/8in (1.75m)

LTI FX4S-Plus
As for the FX4S but with the following changes:

Running Gear

Rear suspension	longitudinal composite leaf springs and telescopic hydraulic shock absorbers
Colours	midnight blue, rattan beige, royal burgundy, ermine white, carmine red, city grey

Wheelchair Accessibility for the FX4

Towards the end of 1985, LTI Carbodies' subsidiary, Carbodies Sales and Service Ltd had produced a wheelchair-accessible version of an FX4Q, much against the wishes of LTI. The body engineer Roger Ponticelli turned the doors around to hinge on the B-posts and made the partition slide back and forth to accommodate the extra room needed by the bulk of the wheelchair. The conversion was offered from April 1986, with the doors hinged on the rear pillar, for £1,700 plus VAT, on both used and new cabs. This was a relatively economical interim method of providing transport for wheelchair users.

The CR6 – Problems Mount

The wheelchair trials of the CR6 were a qualified success, but a 1983 report by Newcastle University recommended a higher roof and wider doors, requirements that would increase the total cost of the cab programme by £2 million, as well as its size. The Department of Trade and Industry and the Department of Transport would continue to fund the CR6, but there would be a shortfall of £0.7 million. The Greater London Council's Labour administration was exercising a policy of equal opportunities for disabled people. This would include improving public transport, and the GLC were willing to give a grant to make up the shortfall.

A third CR6 prototype was built, with a longer wheelbase and a higher roof. It made the bulky cab even bigger. But black clouds were on the horizon. Thanks to the slump in FX4R sales, Carbodies' income was drastically reduced and high inflation hampered matters even further.

Mann & Overton had paid nearly £1.93 million towards the CR6. They were due to pay a further £1.92 million to a project that was now estimated to cost £4.5million, as well as another £1.4million needed to extend

*The FX4W wheelchair conversion made by Carbodies Sales and Services Ltd had its doors hinged on the B-post. (*Taxi *newspaper)*

the factory. In January 1984 Carbodies post-poned the CR6's release date to 1985.

Changes at Land Rover also threatened the CR6's future. Land Rover's body plant demanded, and got, the manufacturing rights for the four-door conversion but they re-engineered the front doors to accept the two-door model's external hinges. The CR6 doors were now exclusive to the cab, which almost doubled their cost. Now no Range Rover panels were used on the CR6, a complete reversal of the original plan. And the image of the Range Rover had moved on, no longer was it a comfortable utility but a luxury acces-sory and to Rover's marketing people the use of a taxi based on the Range Rover was anathema.

Dennis Poore was becoming uncomfort-able about the whole project. In January 1986 LTI announced that the CR6 was to be axed. A press release claimed that the tradi-tional appearance of the FX4 was what the market now wanted and resources would be directed into the further development of the existing cab.

The Launch of the Metrocab

On 10 December 1986, amid a cloud of stage smoke and to the sound of 'Fanfare for the Common Man', the Metrocab was launched at the Wembley Conference Centre. MCW's managing director Peter Steadman told his audience that £5 million had been earmarked for investment in the cab, and not a penny of it was coming from the govern-ment. This was a sideswipe at the CR6, which had swallowed a considerable amount of taxpayers' and London ratepayers' money in its aborted development. The Transport Minister David Mitchell, who was also present, no doubt appreciated this fact. Referring to the wheelchair facility, Mitchell said, 'The Metrocab would transform the lives of dis-abled people.'

The Metrocab's huge windscreen and excellent headroom impressed everyone who sat in the cab, but, if the market was ready for the Metrocab, the Metrocab was not ready for the market. The prototypes had been fitted with a Borg Warner Model 65 three-speed

Following the trials in Peterborough and Newcastle-under-Lyme, the second CR6 prototype was fitted with a higher roof. (Peter James)

153

Amid a cloud of stage smoke, the Metrocab was launched at the Wembley Conference Centre. (Stephen Tillyer)

automatic gearbox, but Borg-Warner's board would not offer to MCW the Australian-made Model 40 box that was being used in the S-Plus. Ford had a four-speed, automatic transmission, but the only diesel engine to which it had been fitted was in a low-speed airport service vehicle and this adaptation was being readied for the Metrocab. After three months testing in the Birmingham area, it seemed to work. MCW honestly believed that they had got it, if not exactly right, then as good as they possibly could. They launched the cab, and it was almost their undoing.

Metro Sales and Service had 200 orders within two or three months of the launch, but the delay due to the testing of the gearbox

caused many of those customers to cancel. However, delivery began in early May 1987 and soon the Metrocab was selling steadily to a still sceptical cab trade. The first model was delivered to a suburban cab driver Mrs Sheila Anker, the wife of Robert Anker, a London Vintage Taxi Association member. Steve Tillyer took the cab to the PCO for passing. It was the first ever five-seater to be presented to the PCO. With a great sense of occasion, they dug into their store cupboard and found an old plate with the number 1. Subsequent plates issued to Metrocabs and all subsequent five-seater cabs carried the prefix 'E'.

There was some hesitancy in the trade to buy an unknown vehicle, even though they had wanted something new for years.

Although the trade had criticized Mann & Overton and latterly LTI over the FX4, at least they were they devil they knew. MCW, despite their size, were an unknown quantity. The other concern was the Metrocab's shape. After the CR6 was scrapped, LTI had begun to convince the trade and the public that the 'traditional' appearance of the FX4 was desirable from the point of view of recognition, moving away from what had been proposed in the CR6 and was a reality in the MkIV Winchester. Now here was a cab that copied the styling of the recent Mk2 Ford Granada Estate. Would the public accept it? There had been ample publicity over its introduction and the first wet Friday night put most passengers' doubts to rest very quickly.

A pre-production Metrocab, pictured in the heart of London's West End. The meter is mounted on the dashboard, with its 'for hire' light on its front. The PCO would not allow this, insisting that the sign should be mounted on the door pillar. The man on the pavement on the right of the picture is Geoff Chater. (Stephen Tillyer)

Mixed Fortunes for Metrocab

Trouble with the Metrocab's gearbox materialized very quickly. Cabs were being brought in with damaged gearboxes. On one Monday morning Metro Sales and Service staff arrived for work to find seven cabs lined up outside, all with gearbox trouble. They had to replace the faulty boxes with identical ones, in the knowledge that they were likely to fail as quickly. All they could do was promise that MCW were working to correct the faults. Ford finally found the cause when the testing procedures they were using were altered to match the stop-start work pattern of the cab and they could see the damaged gearbox parts: the problem lay in the torque converter, which was flexing under load and wearing out the short input shaft to such a degree that its splines would eventually shear. The repaired cabs were back on the road within two to three days, but cab drivers are quick to tell their colleagues of their troubles and word soon got around. The stress that was on Metro Sales and Service was colossal. They sent the Metrocab's designer Bob Parsons a list of no

The first Metrocab sold by Metro Sales and Service was delivered to Mrs Sheila Anker and, as can be seen here, given plate number 1 by the PCO. Pictured from the left are Metro Sales and Service directors Ernie Keats, David Day, Stephen Tillyer and John Lewis. (Stephen Tillyer)

fewer than ninety-one faults, ranging from broken air cleaner intakes to faulty brakes. Parsons worked hard to rectify what he could, but there was little money from MCW, they were in deep financial trouble and their parent company Laird were making moves to sell it off.

The FX4S Plus

LTI had to meet forthcoming EEC vehicle regulations that would ban the use of doors that hinged on the rear pillar. The Alpha Project was begun to address the task and, in addition to rehanging the doors, included a plan to reshape the existing body shell and enlarge the windscreen. This plan was considered a waste of money when the real demand was one that LTI at the time could not meet – a completely new cab. In the meantime, they began a series of step-by-step improvements to the FX4. The first of these, described by the new engineering director Ed Osmond as 'bite-sized chunks', would be to bring about some major cosmetic and detail engineering changes to the FX4S.

Brought in to work on the Alpha Project was Jevon Thorpe, a young consultant who had spent his educational placement from Coventry University at Reliant under Ed Osmond. In 1986 Osmond asked Thorpe to redesign the FX4S's interior. Denis Poore was impressed by Thorpe's design for the new dashboard and smart, five-seat, grey interior and employed him to bring the new design into production. The new interior would be the major feature of a revised model, the FX4S-Plus. It was announced at the 1987 Taxi Driver of the Year Show, held in Battersea Park every September. The seats were offered with a vinyl or velour trim option, push-button switches mounted centrally on the dash, fresh air ventilation and optional electric front windows. It had taken since about 1960 for an FX4 to have all the equipment found

Metrocab Series I: Technical Specification

Engine

Type	Ford FSD 425 4-cylinder in-line direct injection diesel, water-cooled, cast iron cylinder block, cast iron cylinder head with overhead valves	Brakes	dual circuit hydraulic to all four wheels, tandem master cylinder, twin leading shoe on front, 11in drums all round, mechanical pull up handbrake on rear wheels
Cubic capacity	2496cc	Rear axle	hypoid bevel drive
Bore and stroke	93.7mm × 90.5mm (3.7in × 3.56in)	Differential ratio: manual	4.56:1
Compression ratio	20.6:1	Differential ratio: automatic	4.78:1
Power	56kW (75bhp) @ 4,000rpm		
Torque	168Nm (123.9lb/ft) @ 2,500rpm	Propeller shaft	2-piece with centre roller bearing

Transmission

Automatic	Ford A4LD 4-speed with Ford Cosworth torque converter, hydraulic lock-up and electronic kick-down	Wheels and tyres	16in × 5J pressed steel disc wheels with 175 R16 tyres
Manual	Ford MT75 5-speed synchro-mesh	Front suspension	independent coil spring with double-acting lever type shock absorbers
		Rear suspension	longitudinal, semi-elliptical springs with telescopic shock absorbers

Dimensions

Wheelbase	9ft 5in (2.9m)	**Options**	
Length overall	14ft 9in (4.51m)	Trim	cloth interior trim
		Colours	midnight blue, Metro blue, damson, diamond white, black

Running Gear

Steering	power-assisted box with idler

Apart from an extra badge on the grille that said 'Plus', the FX4S-Plus was indistinguishable externally from the FX4S. All the changes were internal or mechanical. (Author)

Jevon Thorpe, designer of the FX4S Plus's interior, went on to design the TX1 and in 1997 to become managing director of LTI Carbodies. (Taxi *newspaper*)

in a modern family car. The Plus's mechanical specification was almost unchanged, with the exception of laminated plastic rear springs and telescopic shock absorbers on the rear and a larger radiator, but still there were no disc brakes. As well as black, the range of colours on offer was midnight blue, rattan beige, royal burgundy, ermine white, carmine red and city grey. The vinyl roof and sun roof options were carried over and the personal radio was moved to the dashboard instead of its add-on position in a roof console. There was criticism in the trade press that there was no facility for a built-in, two-way radio. Each London radio circuit had to bolt its sets to the partition between the driving seat and the luggage platform. Surely, the press said, the dashboard could have been design to incorporate a two-

This wheelchair accessibility conversion with a sliding partition, shown here fited in an FX4S was offered on the FX4S-Plus. Note how the rear door folds back against the rear wing. While it fulfilled a need, to move the partition each time took time, creating problems when picking up a wheelchair-bound passenger in a busy street. The partition also rattled excessively. (LVTA Archive)

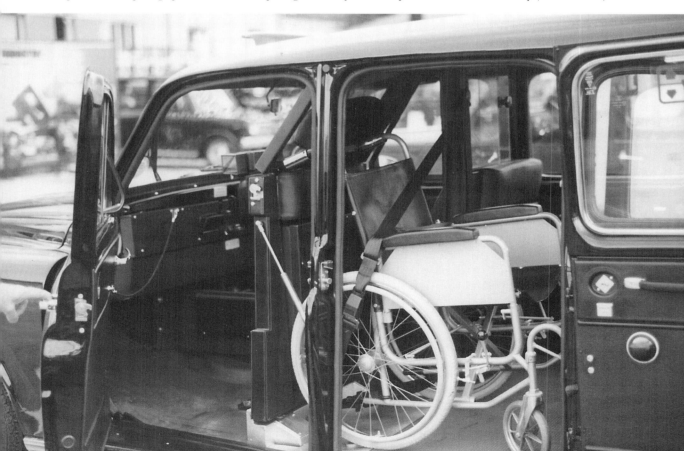

way radio? LTI's answer was that they had considered it, but, if they also counted the large number of sets available to the provincial trade, there were simply too many different types, shapes and sizes of radios for it to be practicable. The S Plus did not have built-in wheelchair accessibility, but an improved version of the original conversion, with a fixed partition and a nearside rear door that opened through 180 degrees, could be fitted for a further £998. As LTI had intended, the Plus soon outsold the Metrocab.

Changes at the Top for Carbodies

In 1986 Grant Lockhart left LTI and was replaced by Barry Widdowson, who had been brought in to organize production. Around the same time, LTI was shocked by the sudden death of Manganese Bronze's chairman Dennis Poore, who was well into his seventies. He was replaced by his son-in law Jamie Borwick.

10 1988–2005 Facing the Future

Although Britain ended the 1980s with her economy thriving, serious fiscal errors by the government plunged the country into recession, and in January 1991, when the Gulf War began, American tourists stopped visiting London, banned from flying by insurance companies scared of the consequences of a hijack. With the trade robbed of one of its main sources of income, the cabs were ranked up everywhere, day and night, and cabmen, burdened with rapidly rising interest rates on their mortgages, were suffering. However, Britain eventually began the climb back to a more stable economy, but the effects of the recession would linger in the trade's memory for a long time to come.

There would be the introduction of a third, niche market cab. But more significantly there would be a challenge to the Conditions of Fitness from some well-known, well-respected people in the car trade who were dedicated to the principle of purpose-built vehicles who felt that the turning circle prevented the introduction into London of cheaper alternative to those vehicles already available.

Trouble for Metrocab

The Metrocab had been selling well, gaining at one point during 1988 25 per cent of the market. Then the dream turned into a nightmare. In October the *Financial Times* carried an article saying that the Laird Group were to sell off MCW without first finding a buyer.

The 12 January 1989 edition of *Taxi*, the largest London cab trade journal, picked up the story, saying:

> Long-mounting losses on bus operations, coupled with a failed bid to take over Leyland Buses, has persuaded the Chairman of Laird to sell off the MCW bus, train and taxi manufacturing subsidiary . . . The taxi manufacturing section, which is profitable, with over 1,200 units worth £18 million already sold, may be sold separately. Although the decision to sell was made in July, Laird waited until December [1988] to make the announcement.

Then, MCW's board sacked Peter Steadman and, shortly afterwards, three other directors. Rumours ran like a virus through the cab trade. Metrocab, the troublemakers said, was dead. In an interview published in the 26 January issue of *Taxi*, Ernie Keats, of Metro Sales and Service stated, 'Metrocab production and sales are still continuing.' Two weeks previously, he had written to all Metrocab owners, telling them that some twelve major companies had approached Laird with a view to purchasing the transport interest. He wrote: 'The rumours, clearly designed to cause as much damage as possible, originate from sections of the trade who want to return to a monopoly to improve their own financial gains which have obviously suffered from Metrocab innovation and competition. In other words, a return to their "good old days".' Although Keats was careful not to name any names, he had, as editor of *Cab Driver*, recently lost advertising support from LTI.

By mid June 1989 Metrocab's new owner was revealed. It was Reliant, who had been building GRP-bodied cars since 1961 and were producing a range of composite plastic products as varied as high roofs for Ford Transits and spark-proof floors for oil platforms. They were also making the Metrocab's body for MCW. The Reliant Group's owners, Chris Johnson and Carl Turpin, had profited during the property boom of the 1980s and, knowing how that business can fluctuate, were looking for an industrial concern in which to place their money. They chose the Reliant Group.

They refurbished 24,000sq.ft (2,200sq.m) of the Reliant Kettlebrook factory in Tamworth, Staffordshire for use as a finishing shop and Metrocab production was moved there from Washwood Heath and many of the staff to Tamworth as well. The following year, Reliant brought Geoff Chater into the company. The fall of MCW dealt a bitter blow

to Metro Sales and Service. They were involved in litigation with MCW over warranty claims and believed that they had an understanding with Reliant that they would continue as London dealers. But it was not to be; Reliant awarded the dealership to Nelson Crouch in east London and Exclusive in west London.

The Fairway

Development of LTI's answer to the Metrocab, code-named 'Beta', was already under way. It would be an uprated FX4, not an entirely new cab, which would incorporate wheelchair accessibility and a better powertrain. The first, necessary to meet legislation due to come into force on 1 February 1989, was adapted from the aftermarket conversion already offered on the S Plus. New, swan-neck hinges were fitted to the nearside rear door, enabling it to be locked open in a 90-degree position. The rear seat could be cushion folded up to allow the wheelchair to be turned to

*Chris Johnson (left), Reliant Group's executive deputy chairman, and Carl Turpin, the Group's chief executive, with the product of their new acquisition. The rectangular badge on the grille, covering the original Ford oval, would carry Reliant's eagle logo. (*Taxi *newspaper/ Reliant Group)*

The Fairway was the first FX4 to have a name. It was an appropriate choice for two reasons: it had been a name used on two previous models of a private car made by Carbodies in the 1930s, and many London cabmen love their golf. All-over advertising, known as a livery, had only recently been approved by the PCO and it gave adverters the opportunity to make the most of their imagination, as can be seen with this Guinness cab. (Taximedia)

The Fairway inherited the FX4S-Plus's moulded dashboard. (Taxi *newspaper*)

LTI Fairway: Technical Specification

As for the LTI FX4S Plus with the following changes:

Engine

Type	Nissan TD27 4-cylinder in line, water-cooled, cast iron cylinder block, cast iron cylinder head with overhead valves
Cubic capacity	2664cc
Bore and stroke	96mm × 92mm (3.8in × 3.6in)

Compression ratio	21.8:1
Maximum power (DIN)	60.3kW (80.8bhp) at 4,300rpm
Maximum torque (DIN)	165Nm (121.3lb/ft) at 2,400rpm

Transmission

Automatic	Nissan, 4-speed with electronic overdrive
Manual	Nissan, 5-speed synchromesh

---

place the passenger in a rearward-facing position.

At last, the TD Series Nissan engine was available, and there were 2.3-, 2.5- and 2.7-litre versions. LTI chose the last, along with its dedicated five-speed manual and four-speed automatic transmissions. Excellent as the engine was, it troubled LTI to install a Japanese engine in such a thoroughly British vehicle. And it was expensive, but time would prove that it was the right powertrain.

The new model was released in February 1989. For the first time in the FX4's history, it was given a name: Fairway. It was offered with three trim options, bronze, a basic model, silver, with a vinyl roof, a sunroof, carpeting all around, and gold, with wood finish door cappings, headrests and heavy-duty carpet in the passenger compartment. Added to the Plus's colour range were city grey, Sherwood green, champagne beige and burgundy. The Fairway was hailed as the best FX4 ever, and sales reflected the trade's opinion of it.

Hooper Buy Metrocab

Reliant's tenure of Metrocab had all too short a date. In the recession of the early 1990s the property market collapsed, bringing down with it the fortunes of the Reliant Group.

Fortunately, Geoff Chater had managed to turn the substantial losses of the vehicle and plastics side of the business into a healthy profit, ensuring that the cab-making business was a viable concern. On 27 December 1990 the receivers KPMG Peat Marwick handed over the assets of it to Hooper & Co. (Coachbuilders) Ltd. Hooper is, and was, the most famous name in coachbuilding, but the company that bought Metrocab was owned by the American lawyer John Dick and had no direct connections with the old company that ended its days as part of the mighty BSA empire. On 7 January 1991, with a small force of twenty people, the Tamworth factory began work once again.

Metrocab Improvements

During 1991 Metrocab (UK) Ltd worked on improving the cab. The confidence that Hooper created in the brand was reflected by £700,000 worth of home orders and £800,000 worth of export sales, taken at the Taxi Driver of the Year Show in early September 1992. At a press day in late September, Paul Crowder, Hooper's chairman, launched the latest version. It had disc brakes, the first to be fitted as standard on a London cab. This project had started at Reliant, when Bob Parsons approached

Girling and asked them to find the most suitable type of calliper to fit the old BMC steering upright. They produced a solid disc that stood out further from the upright than the drums so Parsons selected a deep dish, six-stud wheel to accommodate it. New rear brakes had 25 per cent more drum area. A new range of colours was available, including a choice of metallic paint and leather trim was an extra-cost option. However, Crowder's big surprise was that, metallic paint and leather options aside, there would be no price increase.

At the beginning of 1992 Metrocab announced the fitting of a new, 'greener' version of the Ford engine, incorporating a new Bosch fuel-injection system, which would give a better fuel consumption, lower emissions and better acceleration. The cab's initial acceleration was further enhanced by the fitting of a new lower ratio differential and the latest Cosworth torque converter. The driver's compartment featured an improved dashboard, better storage space, a better quality carpet and an uprated heating and ventilation system.

The Fairway Driver

The Nissan engine had brought the FX4's performance up to that of modern traffic, but its front suspension was the same as on the 1958 model. LTI's engineering director Ed Osmond addressed these matters in the next

*Two new Hooper Metrocabs pictured before delivery on Lambeth Bridge. Redesigned wheel trims and black bumpers mark them out. These examples still have drum brakes. (*Taxi *newspaper)*

stage of the cab's development, code-name 'Gamma'. The components manufacturer GKN was engaged to design a new front suspension system with new wishbones with ball joints and coil springs with concentric telescopic dampers. The old back axle was replaced by a new GKN light commercial unit, hung on new steel two-leaf parabolic springs.

The new front suspension allowed for the long overdue disc brakes. The brake manufacturers AP Lockheed worked in conjunction with GKN to produce a twin pot calliper system with vented discs. Along with these, the wider drums and six-stud wheels that were introduced on the Metrocab were fitted. LTI had heard that Metrocab were about to introduce front discs and did not want to be at a disadvantage. Putney Bridge Engineering had developed an aftermarket disc brake conversion for the Fairway, and, as a stopgap, LTI arranged for this conversion to be available as a dealer installation by Mann & Overton on new or older Fairways.

The new model was named the Fairway Driver and was released in February 1993. A manual cost £19,912 and an automatic

The Fairway Driver was fitted with this new front suspension system, developed by GKN, and ventilated disc brakes by AP Lockheed. (LTI)

The Fairway Driver was distinguished from its predecessors by ts large domed wheel trims, which covered the deeply dished wheels. Another striking livery was that of the United Airlines, where the front of the cab was painted yellow like a New York Yellow Cab and the rear black like London cab. (LTI/Taxi newspaper)

LTI Fairway Driver

As for the Fairway but with the following changes:

Running Gear

Brakes	ventilated discs with 4 pot callipers at front, 10in drums with self-adjusters at rear with pull up handbrake
Front suspension	independent with double wishbones and coil springs, concentric telescopic shock absorbers
Colours (solid)	black, diamond white, cardinal red, midnight blue, Burgundy, Sherwood green, storm grey

The Disability Discrimination Act required all purpose-built taxis to provide facilities for disabled passengers. LTI worked closely with the Coventry branch of Arthritis Care to find the best type of equipment to fit to the Fairway Driver. This resulted in the development of a swivel seat and a separate low step. The young woman in the picture is the daughter of LTI's then sales and marketing director the late Peter Wildgoose; she was chosen for the picture because she really did have a broken ankle. (Taxi newspaper)

£21,312. At first, the cab was prone to steering shimmy, where the front wheels would vibrate dramatically at any speed from 30mph (48km/h) upwards. After a short period of denial by Mann & Overton that it happened at all, it was cured by the fitting of a steering damper.

Asquith

At their factory in Banbury, Oxfordshire, Asquith's business was building 1930s-style vans and minibuses on modern running gear. The owners of these vehicles could have all the visual appeal of a vintage commercial with modern-day running costs and reliability. Around 1990 a cab driver who was visiting the factory saw Asquith's 'Highland' van and commented to the marketing director Crispin Reed that all it needed were windows and it would be a vintage-style cab. Reed had also read a work published in 1924 called *Motor Bodywork – the Design and Construction of Private, Commercial and Passenger Types*, by Herbert J. Butler. This contained details of motor cab bodies. At this, Reed made the decision to build a retro-style cab. He also had an eye on the export market, and knew that if the cab complied with the Conditions of Fitness, then it, as a bona fide London taxi, would have a far greater sales potential.

The company built a mock-up and exhibited it at the London Motor Fair in 1991. They then set to work building the first prototype. The body was of GRP around a steel frame, with four full doors, five-seat capacity and wheelchair accessibility. Underneath was a separate chassis. When the first prototype was presented to PCO, they dismissed it out of hand, saying that the quality of the cab was totally unacceptable. Reed obviously had a lot to learn about the London cab trade and the PCO in particular.

After much work, a better prototype was built and tested in late 1992. Reed then found customers, whom he asked for a £500 deposit. The cab would have the option of a Ford Transit diesel, similar to that in the Metrocab but with a higher compression ratio, or a Ford petrol engine both coupled to an automatic transmission. The axles and steering were sourced from General Motors; the coil spring front suspension was from the Vauxhall Midi van and the rear axle was from the Vauxhall Frontera, hung on Dunlop air suspension. Disc brakes were fitted all round.

The cab was introduced by the transport minister Steve Norris at Marylebone Station in April 1994. Reed expected to sell twenty cabs a year in Britain, with a greater emphasis on the export market. The base price was £29,950, but high-specification interiors and air conditioning could be ordered at

extra cost. Although the cab's buyers loved the idea of the vehicle and were pleased with the reactions of their passengers, they were less than pleased with the problems that arose, particularly with the back axle, and the way that Asquith dealt with them. Asquith had failed to meet the need for an immediate supply of spare parts and a highly efficient warranty service that the cab trade demanded. They did not appoint a London dealer or service agent, but instead sent parts down to London to whomever the owners could find to handle the cab. And few cab garages would: there were many that would not work on Metrocabs for fear of finding problems that they could not fix in the short time demanded by the trade, or did not want to stock spare parts for several types

*Asquith's sales and marketing director Crispin Reed with the Asquith retro-look taxi. The company planned a private hire version with a landaulet body, a body style that had been banned by the PCO in the 1950s. (*Taxi *newspaper)*

Asquith: Technical Specification

Engine: Diesel		Transmission	
Type	Ford FGR direct injection 4-cylinder in line, water-cooled, cast iron cylinder block, cast iron cylinder head with overhead valves	Automatic	Ford 4-speed with electronic overdrive facility
		Manual	Ford 5-speed synchromesh
Cubic capacity	2496cc	**Dimensions**	
Bore and stroke	93.7mm × 90.5mm (3.7in × 3.5in)	Height	2,000mm (6ft 6in)
		Length	1,750mm (14ft 1in) 4293mm
Maximum power (DIN)	60.3kW (81bhp) at 4,300rpm	Width	1,750mm (5ft 9in)
Maximum torque (DIN)	168Nm (124lb/ft) at 2,500rpm	**Running Gear**	
		Steering	power-assisted steering box with steering idler
Engine: Petrol		Brakes	discs on all four wheels, dual circuit hydraulic, servo-assisted, pull up handbrake on rear wheels
Type	Ford 4-cylinder in line, water-cooled, double overhead camshafts	Front suspension	independent with double wishbones with coil springs and telescopic shock absorbers
Cubic capacity	1998cc	Rear suspension	Dunlop air suspension
Bore and stroke	86mm × 86mm (3.4in × 3.4in)	Rear axle	hypoid semi-floating
Maximum power (DIN)	88kW (118bhp) at 5,500rpm	Wheels and tyres	16in × 5J cast alloy artillery-type wheels with 175 R16 Michelin XC4S radial ply tyres
Maximum torque (DIN)	171Nm (126lb/ft) at 2,500rpm		

of vehicle. The fear was much worse with the Asquith.

Metrocab Six-Seater

In April 1994 Metrocab (UK) Ltd announced a new six-seater version of the Metrocab. Instead of a dogleg partition, a straight one was fitted, and a third tip-up seat accommodated the sixth passenger. The 60–40 split rear seat could be lifted to allow a wheelchair to be manoeuvred into place. A seven-seater version with a seat beside the driver was also available for the provincial market. The six- and the seven-seater model were sold alongside the original five-seater and within six months accounted for 30 per cent of all Metrocab sales.

Metrocab Series II

The most significant of Hooper's changes to the Metrocab were seen in late 1995 with the introduction of the Series II. It incorporated the new, more powerful and more economical 76PS version of the Ford engine, which had been introduced at the beginning of the year. The Series II had a much improved paint finish, a redesigned front end with new colour-coded grille and profiled bumpers, new light clusters, reshaped side glass and a redesigned interior. The boot floor, where the wheelchair ramps were stowed, was recessed to make more room for them. The cab was a considerable improvement on the original model, but it is significant that the basic chassis, engine and bodyshell remained the same, showing how sound the original design was.

168

Two Fairway Drivers, pictured at Oxford Circus. The cab on the left has an accessory grille, which LTI intended to offer on the Fairway when it first appeared. The cab on the right features 'supersides' advertisements, an innovation allowed very recently by the PCO. (Author)

The Fairway Driver 95 featured detail improvements, including electric front windows as standard, a Clarion radio/cassette player, a finger-operated lock on the driver's side of the sliding glass partition and red edging to the seats to aid partially sighted passengers. The price of the Driver 95 was £20,210 for the manual transmission and £21,618 for the automatic version. (Taxi newspaper/LTI)

*The Series II Metrocab received a front and rear re-style, with a more upright grille, new light clusters and moulded bumpers. The extra-deep wheel trims accommodated the deep wheels necessitated by the disc brakes. (*Taxi *newspaper)*

CETA: Metrocab's Global Taxi

The Disability Discrimination Act of 1995 would demand that all purpose-built taxis had to be wheelchair-accessible by 2000. Diptac (the Disabled Persons Transport Advisory Committee of the Department of Environment, Transport and the Regions) regulations were to specify the dimensions for wheelchair accessible cabs, but by the mid 1990s these still had not been written. Both LTI and Metrocab had to guess what the regulations might be. The Metrocab had been on the market for almost a decade and would need replacement sooner rather than later if Metrocab (UK) Ltd were to at least keep pace with LTI, if not

*Metrocab (UK)'s Global taxi, the CETA project, could carry two wheelchair passengers side-by-side. (*Taxi *newspaper)*

outsell them. An alternative to producing a new cab was to modify the Series II by making the roof much higher, which would be impossible to engineer successfully and Geoff Chater refused to consider it. The best alternative was to build a new model and, in 1998, John Dick gave approval for its development, code-named CETA. Styled by Roy Axe, former head of design at Chrysler UK and later of Austin-Rover, the vehicle was noticeably larger than the current model. The Ford FSD diesel would not meet the forthcoming Euro 3 exhaust regulations, so a new engine had to be found. Ford offered the new DuraTorq 2.4 turbo diesel but it would not fit into either the current model or the CETA. The project began to use a great deal of development money and, at the same time, there was still no sign of the Diptac regulations. Metrocab's board took the decision to scrap the CETA and in early 2003 it was transported to Dick's private auto museum in Germany.

A New Asquith

The announcement of an Asquith with a modern body reached the trade press in 1996. As happened with the retro model, a mock-up was displayed at the London Motor Fair. A new company, the New Asquith Motor Company, was formed to make it in Sri Lanka, to fulfil the company's intention to sell the cab for about £1,000 less than a Fairway or a Metrocab. The cab was to be fitted with the same air suspension system as was used on the retro-style model, allowing the back to be lowered to enable disabled passengers to enter more easily. Production was planned for late 1997, but nothing more was heard of it because the company was in financial trouble. In early 1997 the Asquith Motor Carriage Group was formed to acquire the assets of the original company, leaving, it was alleged, the liabilities with the customers who had invested in the cabs. Asquith Motor Carriage went into voluntary liquidation in December 1998.

The Series II Metrocab's bootlid, rear window and rear side windows were reshaped. The boot was also fitted with a slam lock. (Taxi newspaper)

171

*Asquith's modern-style cab was to be built on the retro-vehicle's chassis. It was designed by Dale Harrow, who taught transport design at the Royal College of Art. (*Taxi *newspaper)*

The TXI

However good the Fairway was, it was still based on a vehicle that was in its fourth decade of production. As part of their strategy to design and build a new cab, LTI looked at alternative vehicles, including the Renault Espace MPV. It was conceivable to adapt other makers' vehicles to meet the Conditions of Fitness, but the lesson of the CR6 was still remembered: not to depend on another man-ufacturer's donor vehicle. For this reason, LTI decided to stay with purpose-built vehicles. As we have noted, a crucial factor in the design of a new cab was the Disability Dis-crimination Act.

After carefully considering a redesign of the FX4, LTI opted to build a complete new cab. This was originally code-named Delta so as to be sequential with the previous models, but it was renamed Eta to avoid any obvious associ-ation with the Automotive Engineering

Centre's hybrid power cab. The export market, which LTI had finally begun to tap successfully, demanded that the new vehicle, would have to have a 'retro' look. Forthcoming M1 European passenger vehicle regulations demanded that all doors should hinge forward and regulations made under the Disability Discrimination Act demanded that those doors should have a minimum height of 1,350mm (53in); the FX4's were just under 1,200mm (47in). When the FX4 was designed, the Conditions of Fitness required that inspection panels should be built into the floor of a cab so that the top of the chassis could be examined for rust. This regulation had been scrapped, although the Fairway still had a removable plywood floor. Now LTI could incorporate a welded floor, increasing the bodyshell's rigidity. The wheelbase of the Fairway Driver's chassis was lengthened by 75mm (3in), the track widened by 60mm (2.4in) and the ball joints on the front

London Taxis International TXI: Technical Specification

Engine

Type — Nissan TD27 4-cylinder in line, diesel, water-cooled, cast iron cylinder block, cast iron cylinder head with overhead valves

Cubic capacity — 2664cc

Bore and stroke — 96mm × 92mm (3.78in × 3.62 in)

Compression ratio — 21.8:1

Maximum power — 60.3kW (81bhp) @ 4,300rpm

Maximum torque — 165Nm (121lb/ft) @ 2,400rpm

Transmission

Automatic — Nissan 4-speed, with overdrive lock

Manual — 5-speed synchromesh on all forward gears

Dimensions

Length — 4,580mm (15ft)

Width — 2,036mm (6.7ft)

Height — 1,834mm (5ft)

Wheelbase — 2,886mm (9.5ft)

Running Gear

Steering — power-assisted steering box with steering idler

Brakes — ventilated discs with 4 pot callipers at front, 10in drums with self-adjusters at rear with pull up handbrake

Front suspension — independent with double wishbones with coil springs and telescopic shock absorbers

Rear suspension — two-leaf, parabolic springs with telescopic shock absorber

Rear axle — hypoid semi-floating

Differential ratio: manual — 4.1:1

Wheels and tyres — 16in x 5J pressed steel wheels with 175 R16 radial ply tyres

Colours

Solid — black, burgundy, white, midnight blue, bottle green, targa red

Metallic — Maldives blue, storm grey, charcoal, Oxford blue, nightfire red, glacier green, British racing green platinum silver

Roy Axe of Design Research Ltd and Jim Randle the director of the Automotive Engineering Centre put forward the idea of a luxury car with a hybrid gas turbine electric power unit. LTI considered using this powerplant and this quarter scale clay model, christened Delta, was unveiled in November 1993 as part of the project. The technology was considered to be too complicated for use in a taxi, so the idea was dropped. (Taxi newspaper)

173

suspension and the steering box were uprated. The bombproof Nissan engine and transmissions were carried over.

The new cab took just twenty-eight months to design and put into production. It was launched at the London Motor Show in October 1997 by Glenda Jackson, MP. At the launch, LTI Carbodies' managing director Jeven Thorpe said: 'We have brought saloon car standards of comfort, safety and refinement to the driver's working environment. And, despite the large number of changes and improvements, the end result is still recognizable as a London taxi.'

The TXI went straight into production, although it was not until the spring of 1998 that delivery could be made in significant numbers.

Metrocab Series III

The Metrocab Series III, unveiled in November 1997 at the RAF Museum, Hendon, was Metrocab (UK)'s answer to the TXI. The managing director Mike Thurlow hoped that the new cab would increase Metrocab's share of the British taxi market to more than its then 25 per cent (in some parts of the

*The first TXI, left, alongside the last Fairway Driver: Manganese Bronze's chairman Jamie Borwick wanted to call the new cab the 'Fairmile', but the design team were not convinced. They wanted to revert to Austin's old numbering system. At a brainstorming session Jevon Thorpe wrote the word 'TAXI' on a flip chart; he crossed out A, leaving what would be the cab's new name – TXI. The last Fairway was built on 7 November 1997 just one year short of the FX4's fortieth birthday and was presented to the National Motor Museum, with the registration number R1 PFX (= RIP FX). (*Taxi *newspaper/LTI)*

Optional on higher-specification TXIs was this upholstery fabric, featuring cartoon taxis. The internal door handles and seat edges were yellow to aid partially sighted passengers. (Taxi *newspaper/LTI*)

Wheelchair Conversions for Older Cabs

The Disability Discrimination Act demanded that all purpose-built taxis should be wheelchair-accessible by 31 December 1998. Since 2000 new vehicles have had to be built with a wheelchair facility, and, if proprietors wanted to keep older vehicles, particularly the FX4S and S-Plus on the road from 1999 onwards, they would have to have them converted. One of the companies set up in late 1995 to convert older cabs to wheelchair accessibility was Taxi Access of Maida Vale. Taxi Access was run by Steve Hawes, a long-time member of the Licensed Taxi Drivers Association. The conversion included hinges that allowed the nearside rear door to open through 90 degrees, a stepped partition and a set of ramps. At £1,500, its cost enabled owners of older cabs in good condition to continue to run them for at least two more years.

West Midlands the market share was as high as 40 per cent). The Series III featured no fewer than sixty-one detailed improvements. Among them there was a more efficient Ford engine, quieter manual gearbox, an uprated starter motor and alternator and an improved silencer system. On the body, many of the parts were resin-injected to produce a better finish and electric windows were fitted in the rear doors. For the passenger compartment, there were optional radio speakers and a new partition with greater visibility. The driver's compartment had a new dashboard, an intercom as standard and a new heating and ventilating system. However, the timing of its introduction was not wise; Geoff Carter had not been able to convince Metrocab's board to wait. It would have taken LTI several months to get TXI production up to speed, and the

*The standard interior trim of the Series III Metrocab was velour. The extendable stay, part of the mechanism for the lifting rear seat cushion, can be seen below the seat. The new passenger door windows are electrically operated. (*Taxi *newspaper/LTI)*

Series II Metrocab would have had the market to itself. Instead, Metrocab themselves encountered production difficulties with the Series III and were unable to meet any demand.

Metrocab TTT

The Euro 3 exhaust emission regulations were due to come into force in January 2001 and Metrocab's Ford FSD engine would not comply with them. The new Ford DuraTorq turbo diesel, which was designed for the Transit and for medium-sized passenger cars, seemed a good choice, but it would not fit the Metrocab. To solve the problem, Metrocab negotiated with the Japanese manufacturer Toyota and chose their 2.4 turbo diesel and its dedicated four-speed automatic and five-speed manual. The new model, named the TTT (Triple-T), was announced in March 2000, almost a year before the Euro 3 deadline. The new engine was significantly quieter than the old Ford. The front suspension and ventilated front disc brakes from the LTI TXI were at last available to other customers and they were fitted, along with a new rear axle. The 'for hire' light featured an LED display for greater visibility in daylight. A factory-fitted 'Lux Pack' could be specified, which included, among other features, chrome effect wheel trims, rear carpet, rich velour trim, flat bed wheelchair ramp, step facility and lap seat belts for the rear-facing seats. A wide range of solid and metallic colours were also available. The Triple-T met with much praise; cab trade journalists and prominent trade personalities compared its performance to that of a car.

TXII

Like the Ford FSD engine in the Metrocab, the TXI's Nissan TD27 would not meet Euro 3 exhaust emission standards. LTI instead adopted the Ford DuraTorq turbocharged diesel. It seemed to be an ideal unit and the Ford Motor Company was particularly pleased to be associated with the London cab trade. The engine produced 9 per cent more bhp than the Nissan and greater torque, despite its smaller displacement. However, the Ford engine did not come with an automatic transmission so LTI invested £2 million to adapt the Nissan four-speed automatic 'box to fit it. Introduced in January 2002, the new model, called the TXII, featured additional improvements that included a passive anti-theft system, fully integrated into the engine management system. Externally,

Toyota were pleased to provide the engine for a London taxi. Pictured here with the Metrocab TTT are, from the left, Yoshihiro Kumagai, of Mitsui & Co. UK, Adrian Harrison, managing director of the Hooper Group, Mike Thurlow, executive director of the Hooper Group and Osamu Arakawa of the Toyota Motor Corporation. (Hooper/Taxi newspaper)

Metrocab TTT: Technical Specification

Engine

Type	Toyota 2LT 4-cylinder in line, turbo diesel, water-cooled, cast iron cylinder block, cast iron cylinder head with overhead valves
Cubic capacity	2446cc
Bore and stroke	92mm × 92mm (3.6in × 3.6in)
Compression ratio	22.2:1
Maximum power (DIN)	66kW (88.5bhp) at 3,500rpm
Maximum torque DIN	218Nm (160.3lb/ft) at 2,250rpm

Transmission

Automatic	Toyota hydraulic torque converter, 4-speed with hydraulic lock up and electronic kick-down
Manual	Toyota 5-speed synchromesh

Dimensions

Wheelbase	2,900mm (9ft 6in)
Height	1,755mm (5ft 9in)
Length	4,496mm (14ft 9in)
Width	1,778mm (5ft 10in)

Running Gear

Steering	power-assisted steering box
Brakes	ventilated discs with 4 pot callipers at front, 10in drums with self-adjusters at rear with pull up handbrake
Rear axle	hypoid bevel drive
Differential ratio: manual	4.56:1
Differential ratio: automatic	4.78:1
Wheels and tyres	16in × 5J pressed steel wheels with 175 R16 radial ply tyres
Colours: solid	black, white, Delage red, Jaguar racing green, Piemont cherry
Colours: metallic	panther black, triton grey, charcoal, regent blue, Windsor blue; in addition, any other single solid or metallic could be specified at extra cost

*The picture says it all: the first TXII off LTI's production lines. (*Taxi *newspaper/LTI)*

the TXII was almost identical to the TXI, with the exception of new badges and full-width glass in the rear doors, which had a restricted opening to reduce the possibility of bilkers escaping through the window. The cab was offered with the same three trim options, bronze, silver and gold, as its predecessors. Dealer-fitted options included CCTV for added driver security, an electric swivel seat and a plug-in occasional front seat.

In service, the 2.4-litre turbocharged engine was not as good as it promised to be. There were severe driveline vibration prob-lems and drumming at certain speeds, caused by the mounting of an engine designed for a transverse installation into an in-line configu-ration, and there were other, more serious problems. Electrical faults resulted in a small number of TXIIs catching fire. Sales slumped and Manganese Bronze's shares plummeted. Eventually, LTI began to resolve the problems and sales improved. However, there would be another problem that would slow sales of purpose-built cabs: a challenge to the Conditions of Fitness by makers of alternative taxis.

LTI TXII: Technical Specification

As for TXI but with the following changes:

Engine

Type — Ford DuraTorq 4-cylinder in-line, turbocharged diesel, water-cooled, cast iron cylinder block, cast iron cylinder head with overhead valves, 4 per cylinder

Cubic capacity	2402cc
Bore and stroke	96mm × 92mm (3.78in × 3.62 in)
Compression ratio	21.8:1
Maximum power	60.3kW (81bhp) @ 4,300rpm
Maximum torque	165Nm (121lb/ft) @ 2,400rpm

The TXI and TXII are now the most numerous models of cab on the streets of London. Pictured leaving Paddington Station, the front two cabs are TXIs whilst the light-coloured cab to the rear of the one on the right is a TXII. Radio Taxis and Comcab are London's largest radio taxi circuits. (Author)

Challengers to the Conditions of Fitness

When LTI sought to increase their market share by persuading provincial licensing authorities to adopt London-type cabs, they not only made some allies but generated some antagonism too. LTI's case was based on the London cab's wheelchair accessibility. The provincial operators' argument against the adoption of London-type cabs was that they were not willing to find the extra cash to buy a much more expensive, purpose-built cab to carry a very limited amount of wheelchair work, which, in most cases was not subsidized as it was in London with the Taxicard scheme. For years, provincial operators had bought saloon cars, either new or comparatively new, for much less than the cost of an FX4 of a similar age but ran them for a shorter time. LTI countered the cost argument by saying that the price of a purpose-built cab was equivalent to that of two saloon cars run consecutively. However, the local authorities that adopted London-type cabs stuck to their guns. The market was then ripe for a competitor to London-approved cabs that was cheaper and more modern, provided the licensing authorities were willing to relax the turning circle regulation.

The Jubilee Automotive Group (JAG) of Wednesbury, Staffordshire, produced a taxi conversion on a FIAT Scudo van that complied with the Conditions of Fitness in every respect but one: the turning circle. More than that, the vehicle, named the Eurocab, carried a base price of around £18,000 in comparison to the Fairway's £23,000-plus. JAG's Mike Holland managed to persuade an increasing number of provincial licensing authorities to adopt this type of vehicle as well as a conversion of the Mercedes Vito.

Holland and his associates then decided to try and tackle the London market. The people allied with him were dedicated to the purpose-built taxi market and included Geoff Chater, who had left Metrocab in January 1999, John Paton, who had begun selling Austin FX3s in Glasgow in 1957, and a former Metrocab dealer from Scotland Gerry Facenna. Holland presented the Eurocab to the PCO. First of all, the Eurocab had to meet European Whole Vehicle Type Approval (EWVTA) Class M1 as a passenger car, as had the Fairway, the TXI and the Metrocab. This was awarded in February 2001. They presented to the PCO, who were duty-bound to reject it, since its turning circle was too large. The next logical step was to challenge the Conditions of Fitness. On

Allied Vehicles' Peugeot E7 taxi has been a popular choice for provincial taxi operators. Time will tell whether it will be accepted by the PCO for London. (Taxi newspaper)

being faced with this challenge, the Mayor of London Ken Livingstone, as PCO supremo, commissioned a consultation exercise by the Transport Research Laboratory. A number of Eurocabs were tested briefly around London to see whether they could cope with the tight turns required to access some ranks and railway stations. The vehicles were not found to be at a disadvantage. However, on 4 June 2003 the PCO released Notice 10/03, which announced TfL's decision to retain the turning circle. The Notice said:

About half of London's annual 90 million taxi trips are hailed on the street, and this is where the turning circle is useful for both drivers and passengers.

Outside London, taxi pickups are predominantly from taxi ranks. Without the turning circle, many of London's ranks would have to be relocated or redesigned, as they would not be practical or safe if taxis had to do three point turns. Such vehicles [for instance, the Eurocab] would have difficulty accessing places such as Euston Station, East Croydon Station, Clapham Junction Station and the Savoy Hotel.

The Private Hire Trade Under Review

The blatant flouting of the law by minicab drivers had been a serious problem for the cab trade. Indeed, private hire drivers had touted openly in the West End of London during the Second World War and a significant element thought little about obeying the law throughout the 1960s, 1970s and 1980s, but during the recession that hit Britain in the early 1990s, touting grew to epidemic proportions. The main issue was one of public safety: minicab drivers working in London were not subject to the checks on health or criminal record as taxi drivers were and rogue drivers were committing serious sexual assaults on women. The largest trade body in the capital, the Licensed Taxi Drivers' Association, had been formed in the 1960s to combat the minicab. Due to apathy from successive governments and disunity in the trade, little was done in the capital apart from the banning of signs on the vehicles. The picture was different outside London, where the Local Government (Miscellaneous Provisions) Act 1976 gave local authorities the power to license private hire (that is, minicabs).

In the early 1990s the LTDA began a campaign for the introduction of a one-tier system of licensing for taxicab and minicab drivers in London that would, the Association maintained, ensure safety for the travelling public. The LTDA was a member of the London Taxi Board and the LTB took on board the principle of the one-tier system and lobbied the government to adopt the contents of its paper 'The Plan for the Unification of London's Taxi and Minicab Services'. This proposed that both taxi drivers and minicab drivers should be subject to the knowledge tests, medical and criminal record checks, which, the LTB maintained, would produce equitable conditions. Instead, the Minister of Transport for London Steve Norris, decided to review the taxi and private hire trades nationally. He published a Green Paper, which was welcomed by the London Taxi board but upset the provincial taxi trade, who felt that their operations were in the main satisfactory. Justifying his action, Norris stated, 'What is clear is that any changes that are made with regard to safety, however beneficial they may be, cannot be made without an impact on the industry as a whole.'

Eventually, the national trade was left largely as it was, but London's minicabs would at last be licensed. They would come under the jurisdiction of the PCO and the whole process would be undertaken in three stages. First, the companies would be licensed, then the vehicles and lastly the drivers.

Far from overwhelming taxis, the effect has been that private hire trade has had to use smarter vehicles, the vehicle owners are compelled to insure their vehicles and the companies have had difficulty in finding enough drivers who are prepared to submit to criminal record and health checks. Those that do are demanding higher fares and thus, with a reduced number of private hire vehicles available, companies have been obliged to charge higher rates. If the playing field is not exactly as level as the Taxi Board wanted, at least the gradient is nowhere near as steep.

The major risk of abolishing the turning circle requirement was that there would be a rapid reduction in vehicles with the facility in favour of those with cheaper upfront costs but without the manoeuvrability.

Over time it is very likely that there would be no vehicles with the tight turning circle with the consequential loss of customer benefits noted above. The greater choice sought by drivers would be short-lived with there ultimately being no more choice than now.

However, TfL, the body now overseeing the PCO did not give carte blanche to the existing manufacturers. The Notice went on to say:

> Retaining the turning circle has the effect of limiting the number of suppliers of London taxis in the short term (until other manufacturers produce vehicles which comply) to two, with one very dominant.
>
> It is proposed to exercise stronger oversight of these suppliers to ensure that their vehicles comply meet the needs of both passengers and drivers. It is also proposed to encourage the two manufacturers to work closely with driver and passenger representatives to improve comfort and ergonomics, and to remedy the shortcomings of existing designs. If they are deemed to be abusing their duopoly position, this will result in a further review of the Conditions of Fitness to confirm that the best interests of London are being served.

To the Notice, the Mayor added: 'I am already looking forward to the next generation of taxis which I expect to build on the current features to provide better comfort for both drivers and passengers including better suspension, better accessibility for wheelchair users and people who are disabled, and improved environmental performance.' The Notice ended by stating, 'It is now intended that another review of the Conditions of Fitness will be conducted not later than 2013.'

Other changes to the Conditions of Fitness to ensure that the vehicles complied with them were the requirements that cabs have a one-piece rear window and that sliding doors should be power-assisted. This would mean extra work for the builders of the Peugeot/FIAT vehicles, as they had unassisted sliding doors for the passengers and two side-opening rear doors. The result was not liked by the challengers. On 4 September 2003 Allied Vehicles, producers of the Peugeot E7 taxi, a similar vehicle to the Eurocab, instigated a judicial review in the High Court against TfL. A major point of the challenge was that, under European law, the Conditions of Fitness prevent major European manufacturers from selling vehicles in London, contrary to the law on the free movement of goods between EU member states. Allied Vehicles found support from the Licensed Taxi Drivers' Association, were campaigning hard for the Conditions of Fitness to be amended to allow a greater choice of vehicle for London. Their position was that they did not wish to see the end of LTI or Metrocab, but to see London's cab drivers offered the choice of a more expensive vehicle with a tight turning circle or a slightly cheaper vehicle with a wider turning circle. This was to reduce the chance of any company in a monopoly situation from abusing its position.

The crux of the matter for major vehicle producers is that the London taxi market is so small that it is uneconomical for them to produce a special vehicle for it, and that the almost universal adoption of front-wheel drive makes the engineering of a tighter turning circle wholly uneconomical. If the turning circle requirement were relaxed, then the vehicle platforms of a wider number of manufacturers might be used as a base for specialist converters such as Allied and JAG to make purpose-built cabs out existing or future models that would be acceptable in London. Added to this, the ever-increasing number of safety and environmental regulations demand greater and greater investment in research and development. This may go beyond the financial limits of small-scale, complete vehicle manufacturers such as LTI and Metrocab and these manufacturers might be forced to abandon manufacture. If this happened the PCO might well be forced to scrap the turning circle stipulation out of sheer necessity.

In Notice 19/04, the PCO announced that they were reconsidering three elements of the Conditions of Fitness review: the turning circle requirement, the requirement that sliding doors should be power-assisted and the requirement for a one-piece window. The results were promised for early 2005.

Clean Air for London

The air in the capital had become progressively cleaner since the passing of Clean Air Act of 1956, following from the Great Fog of 1952 that brought visibility down to a few feet and killed literally thousands of people. Ever tougher legislation to control exhaust emissions made the air cleaner still. Already, some London boroughs were running experimental electric or LPG-fuelled vehicles and many buses and refuse vehicles were claiming to be 'green', but the Greater London Authority had it in mind to clean up the capital's air even further.

No specific legislation other than the national laws existed to control the exhaust emissions of cabs. The Mayor Ken Livingstone sought to legislate to bring the levels of diesel emissions down gradually to a high degree of cleanliness. At first he instigated a framework to eliminate cabs older than twelve years gradually by 2007, but this was bitterly opposed by all trade bodies. Next, in 2003, he brought out proposals that would demand the installation of a form of exhaust fitting that would cut the particulate content of a cab's exhaust by injecting ammonia. Cabs built before September 1998 would have to have this equip-

ment fitted when presented for licensing after 1 January 2006 and Euro 2-compliant cabs would follow. The trade, spearheaded by the LTDA, fought this vehemently. They were not opposed to the idea of their members working in a clean environment, far from it, they welcomed the principle, but strongly objected to the fact that cab proprietors would have to pay at least £2,000 for the equipment, that the equipment was unproven and that there was only one type available. Above all, the statistics which cited older cabs as being significant contributors to the state of London's air were highly suspect. In March 2005, in the face of this opposition, Livingstone pushed the deadlines back to 1 July 2006 for LTI vehicles registered before 16 September 1998 and Metrocabs registered before 4 December 1997, and later cabs by a similar amount. Nevertheless, the equipment required still remained untested and the matter unresolved by the winter of 2005.

Metrocab Fall and Rise Once More

In December 2003 Metrocab went into administration, with the loss of a hundred jobs. Production had halved to ten per week. This was blamed in part in the trade press on the PCO's plan to introduce a 'quickie' Knowledge, which would increase the number of cab drivers in a short space of time. Drivers who remembered the slump of the early 1990s decided to hang on to their existing cabs, rather than risk buying a new model that they might not be able to afford. Metrocab had spent a substantial sum on the CETA project and could not afford to sustain the losses they had incurred. They had no option but to put the company into administration.

After six months of negotiation, Metrocab (UK) Ltd was bought by KamKorp Europe Ltd, a division of Kamkorp, a high-tech development specialist based in Singapore. In September 2004 Mark Morris, the acting

Exhaust Emissions

Diesel Emission Problems

When diesel engines were first introduced in London cabs, a PCO vehicle examiner would give the exhaust a perfunctory test by looking at the smoke while he revved the engine. This practice was discontinued some time in the 1970s, but cabs have been required to undergo exhaust smoke tests at MoT testing stations from 18 April 1995, and a certificate has to be presented with the cab when examined for relicensing.

While petrol engines produce noticeable levels of hydrocarbons and carbon monoxide, the levels of these compounds are negligible with a diesel engine. For some time it was considered that diesel engines were therefore more acceptable than petrol engines, until nitrous oxide and the level of carbon particulates present in the exhaust emissions of diesel engines were discovered to be harmful. At first, combustion chamber and injector design was thought to be an effective method of reducing these problems. However, these would be more effective on direct injection engines, such as the Ford FSD, rather than in an indirect injection engine such as the Nissan TD series.

LPG

One alternative fuel was liquid gas, either petroleum (LPG) or natural (LNG). LTI examined the use of an Iveco petrol engine adapted to run on LPG in the TXI, but it did not prove to be as clean as the standards demanded, nor did the economics work out favourably for the cab operator. LPG in Britain carries a much lower fuel duty, but a petrol engine returns only about two-thirds of the fuel consumption of a diesel engine. If the duty on LPG were increased significantly, it would obviate the financial advantage. Also, petrol engines return perhaps less than half the service life of a diesel, necessitating, in a vehicle designed to last ten years, a replacement engine sometime during its life. This would have an adverse effect on the whole-life cost of the cab, something that both LTI and Metrocab have always put as a significant sales point when trying to persuade provincial cab operators to switch to London-type cabs. Another disadvantage is that the authorities that run the Dartford and the Mersey Tunnels forbid the passage of gas-powered vehicles.

A gas conversion for the Fairway from the Ecological Engine Company was offered by the LTI dealers KPM (UK) Plc. Called the Ecocab, it consisted of the Eco 120 1.8-litre, 4-cylinder, spark-ignition engine, sourced from the MG TF and converted by Janspeed to run on LPG. An Energy Savings Trust grant was available to buyers, which brought the price of the conversion down to £2,950. With LPG at 38p/ltr, it appeared to be an economical option, but the engine was underpowered and owners reported serious overheating problems. On the other hand, the London Central Cab company offered the fitting of the 2.3 Ford DOHC petrol engine, adapted to run on gas in both LTI cabs and in particular the Metrocab. This engine appears to be running without trouble. London Central is run by David Day, who was one of the partners in Metro Sales and Service.

HEV Technology

Hybrid electric vehicles (HEVs) use petrol or diesel engines to drive a generator. The electricity produced is stored and used to run an electric propulsion motor and, for much of the time that the vehicle is running, it generates no exhaust gas. Typically, HEVs are about one-eighth as polluting as a petrol-powered vehicle of similar sized. Furthermore, the fuel (petrol of diesel) consumption is significantly better. Unlike a battery electric vehicle, the range of an HEV is not limited by its battery capacity, only by the fuel in its tank.

The Canadian firm of Azure Dynamics produce power units for HEVs. In April 2003 Manganese Bronze Plc signed an agreement with Azure Dynamics to develop a hybrid electric motive power system for use in a cab. Azure took delivery of a TXII in June 2003 and fitted it with their second generation with the G2r powertrain, designed for vehicles of between 5,000 and 8,500lb GVW (2,270 and 3,860kg). To establish whether HEV powerplants are the best option for the London cab of the future, the running costs must be weighed against the serviceability of older HEVs. Could they be maintained in the small garages that service most of London's older cabs? If not, the whole-life cost of a cab, one of LTI's main selling points for the TXII, could be severely compromised.

managing director of Metrocab (UK), announced that the company would begin trading again. He expected that new Metrocab TTTs would come off the production line by the end of the month and that the company would then have a clearer idea of when they could reach full production. He promised to supply existing Triple-T owners with spare parts, and announced a totally revised model for 2005. In April 2005 Metrocab announced that they had begun delivery of new cabs, with the first of its new production run, a manual model, going to the Birmingham Taxi Warehouse. Production would be built up gradually to four or five a week within ten weeks. By the end of November 2005, production remained at between one and four cabs per week, with the majority going to the provincial market. Theoretically, that gave the cab trade in London and the provinces the choice of another vehicle, but in practice it was hardly a choice at all. One must assume that Metrocab (UK) Ltd was maintaining a presence in the marketplace to assure the PCO that they were capable of producing cabs so that the Conditions of Fitness would remain favourable to Metrocab and LTI. If this were so, and the PCO announce 'no change', they would presumably step up production.

The Future

By the winter of 2005, the PCO had not announced its decision of the review of the Conditions of Fitness. As we saw with the 'Jixi' fiasco in the 1920s, prevarication can be as harmful as a wrong decision. The test of the alternative vehicles was brief and thus their true capability remains unknown. One option would be to put a small number of them on long-term test, but this idea has not even been formally proposed, let alone tried.

The PCO is expected to stand as firm on the issue of the turning circle as Bassom had done 99 years previously. But surely, time will overrun the Conditions of Fitness in their existing form. Relaxation of the turning circle rule may mean that the London taxi's manoeuvrability may be compromised, but it will surely ensure its survival.

There is too much at stake for the cab trade for the PCO to make the wrong decision. When the minicab arrived in 1961, no radical and viable alternative to the existing vehicles could be presented to the PCO. Thus for the PCO to throw out the established in favour of the unknown would have been irresponsible in the extreme. Now, makers of converted vehicles are saying 'here is that alternative'. Is the PCO wise, in these circumstances to resist change?

There remains the question of whether the London trade would want to drive what is effectively a converted van as opposed to a purpose-built vehicle akin to a limousine. But if they are allowed in, it may be a short-term option. The underlying truth is that allowing a larger turning circle will permit a wider choice of vehicle platforms and that may well lead to LTI or Metrocab building stylish cab bodywork on the floorpans of a wider number of manufacturers. A change may indeed encourage major manufacturers to build their own purpose-built cabs.

There are technical and financial advantages to this. The cost of developing a new motor vehicle far exceeds that which a small independent manufacturer aiming for a low production run might be able to justify. A ready-made platform has all the development costs, including compliance with exhaust emission and safety regulations built in, and at a far smaller unit cost than LTI or Metrocab might incur. Furthermore, modern engines are developed to produce compliant levels of emissions as part of a package with the vehicle. Put that engine in another maker's vehicle, such as a taxi with a different gross weight and different gearing, and the exhaust emissions will be different and possibly noncompliant, resulting in extra development work for the specialist manufacturer. Thus, it is a compelling argument that relaxing the turning circle rule will encourage a wider choice of vehicles and the possibility of lower vehicle prices and running costs: one of the very arguments that have been raging for almost a century.

The Public Carriage Office has an awesome responsibility. We must hope that its people make the right choice and ensure that the London taxi survives for, if not a further century, then for as long as there is an acceptable fuel for it to run on and a demand by the public for it, its drivers and the standards they have met for the past 100 years.

Glossary

The London cab trade, like any other, has its own terminology and its own slang. It is derived from many sources, including the old horse cab trade, traditional Cockney rhyming slang, the Yiddish dialect of London's Jewish community, the early French connections and, lately, minicab drivers who have 'become legit'.

Appearance a knowledge boy's periodic oral examination at the PCO

Bilker (strict legal term) a passenger who runs off without paying a cab fare

Bill cab driver's licence

Blue Book book containing all the runs that a knowledge boy must complete

Broom pass off an unwanted job

Brown Coat vehicle examiner at the PCO (now outdated)

Butterboy a newly passed-out cab driver (name derived from Turpin Engineering's Yellow Cabs; Turpin ran a knowledge school and the successful candidates were contracted to drive their cabs)

Cage the passenger compartment of a cab

CO PCO vehicle examiner ('carriage officer')

Cole Porter a cabman who works very long hours (from Cole Porter's song, 'Night and Day')

Doubling up sharing a cab with a partner, one driver working days, the other nights

Extras small additional charges set on the meter to cover extra passengers, luggage or bank holiday charges

Feeder a subsidiary rank supplying cabs to a main rank

Flounder cab (rhyming slang: flounder and dab)

Flyers Heathrow Airport

Four-hander four passengers

Full flat, half-flat a way of renting a cab, for a fixed price per week either singly or as a partnership

Green Badge badge worn by a cab driver licensed to ply for hire over the whole of Greater London; the name is also applied to the individual driver

Hickory taximeter (rhyming slang: 'hickory, dickory, dock' – clock)

In and out a return journey

Kipper season February to March (traditionally ending with the start of the Ideal Home Exhibition) the quietest part of the year for the cab trade

Knowledge of London the arduous test that anyone wishing to become a London cab driver must undergo

Knowledge Boy someone learning to become a cab driver (male or female)

Legal, to legal off to be paid the exact (legal) fare

Link man doorman at a hotel or night club

Little people, the taxi drivers' name for minicab drivers

Minicab colloquial expression for a private hire car, hired from local offices or by telephone performing, in the main, short journeys

Mush an owner driver; derived from the French *marche*, or march, referring to the owner driver's need to keep plodding on

On point the cab at the head of a cab rank

Overhaul the mechanical and bodywork repairs required before a cab is presented for its annual licensing

Passing submitting a cab for its annual inspection as part of the issuing of a licence

Pedicabs unlicensed, unregulated rickshaw-type bicycle 'cabs' that ply for hire in London's West End

Plate the licence plate affixed to the rear of a cab

Punter passenger

Rails, the main railway stations

Roader long job

Roasting spending a long time on a cab rank without taking a job

Set an accident

Stop note a 'reject notice' issued to a cab proprietor who has an unroadworthy cab

Shtumer (Yiddish) a false radio or telephone job, where a cabman is sent to an address where there is no requirement for a cab

Touts, scabs minicab drivers who ply for hire illegally

Trap to find a street hiring

Unders the mechanical parts of cab, which have to be steam-cleaned at the time of a cab's overhaul, before being presented at the PCO

Yard, the Public Carriage Office

Yellow Badge cab driver licensed to ply for hire in a specified suburban area

Wangle the manoeuvres that comprise a part of the PCO driving test

White coat senior vehicle examiner at the PCO (now outdated)

Wind-up minicab drivers' expression, brought into the licensed cab trade, *see* Shtumer

Index

Index